ACTOR-NETWORK THEORY

SAGE was founded in 1965 by Sara Miller McCune to support the dissemination of usable knowledge by publishing innovative and high-quality research and teaching content. Today, we publish over 900 journals, including those of more than 400 learned societies, more than 800 new books per year, and a growing range of library products including archives, data, case studies, reports, and video. SAGE remains majority-owned by our founder, and after Sara's lifetime will become owned by a charitable trust that secures our continued independence.

Los Angeles | London | New Delhi | Singapore | Washington DC | Melbourne

Mike Michael

ACTOR-NETWORK
THEORY

Trials, Trails and Translations

Los Angeles | London | New Delhi
Singapore | Washington DC | Melbourne

Los Angeles | London | New Delhi
Singapore | Washington DC | Melbourne

SAGE Publications Ltd
1 Oliver's Yard
55 City Road
London EC1Y 1SP

SAGE Publications Inc.
2455 Teller Road
Thousand Oaks, California 91320

SAGE Publications India Pvt Ltd
B 1/I 1 Mohan Cooperative Industrial Area
Mathura Road
New Delhi 110 044

SAGE Publications Asia-Pacific Pte Ltd
3 Church Street
#10-04 Samsung Hub
Singapore 049483

Editor: Natalie Aguilera
Editorial assistant: Delayna Spencer
Production editor: Katherine Haw
Copyeditor: Jane Fricker
Proofreader: Lynda Watson
Indexer: Bill Farrington
Marketing manager: Sally Ransom
Cover design: Shaun Mercier
Typeset by: C&M Digitals (P) Ltd, Chennai, India
Printed and bound by CPI Group (UK) Ltd,
    Croydon, CR0 4YY

Library of Congress Control Number: 2016944803

British Library Cataloguing in Publication data

A catalogue record for this book is available from
the British Library

ISBN 978-1-4462-9395-9
ISBN 978-1-4462-9396-6 (pbk)

CONTENTS

ABOUT THE AUTHOR

 Mike Michael is a sociologist of science and technology, and a Professor in the Department of Sociology and Social Policy at the University of Sydney. His research interests have touched on the relation of everyday life to technoscience, the role of culture in biomedicine, and the interplay of design and social scientific perspectives.

1

INTRODUCTION

So, How Does This Book Start, Then? How Should I be Reading it?

Not so long ago, I ran a postgraduate workshop on Actor-Network Theory (henceforth ANT). An introductory overview had been specifically requested by students, many of whom did not seem to have much of an overt interest in ANT. My sense, though, was that several people had a vague feeling that it was of potential relevance to their research: they felt somehow impelled to find out about it. It surprised me that ANT was something that these students felt they 'should' know about as neophyte researchers in sociology, working in such fields as the politics of migration in Southeast Asia, the role of romance narratives in gay relations, or the representation of intellectual disability. How has ANT come to attract this sort of slightly anxious attention?

In a quick and dirty Google Scholar search of ANT's presence in a number of (primarily) social scientific disciplines, I looked at the number of mentions of these disciplines across the citations for two 'classical' ANT texts. At the time of first writing (late 2013), Michel Callon's (1986) 'Some elements in a sociology of translation: domestication of the scallops and fishermen of St Brieuc Bay' had received about 4700 citations altogether. Around 4000 of these mentioned Sociology, 1100 Anthropology, 1000 Geography, 800 Management and Organization Studies, 1000 Science and Technology Studies (700 STS), 200 Cultural Studies, 200 Political Theory, 500 Political Science, 400 Social Psychology. Bruno Latour's (2005) volume, *Reassembling the Social: An Introduction to Actor-Network Theory*, has gathered around 6700 citations. Around 4200 of these referred to the term Sociology, 2000 Anthropology, 1800 Geography, 900 Management and Organizational Studies, 200 Science and Technology Studies (800 STS), 900 Cultural Studies, 300 Political Theory, 700 Political Science, 500 Social Psychology. The point of these all too crude figures is simply to hint at the reach of ANT – it has come to be an intellectual port of call for many disciplines and their subsidiaries (and that includes disciplines beyond the social sciences – e.g. design, history, philosophy). Whether as a positive resource or a source of irritation, ANT has become a conceptual framework (or, latterly, an analytic and methodological sensibility) that many writers feel obliged to reference. Why should that be so?

This piece of scene-setting – situating ANT as a focus of widespread interest – is also an exemplification of some of the processes that ANT has analysed in detail. Data have been gathered and arranged in order to establish the prominence of ANT across a variety of social science disciplines. The impression that is conveyed is one in which ANT is clearly an important perspective, one deserving of attention. This numerical accounting of ANT's pre-eminence aspires to a translation of interests: you want to be a respected researcher, ANT can transform you into a respected researcher, that means that you need to know about ANT (and fortunately, it also implies, by extension, that you really want to read this book). Analysis of the role of a 'technical' form of representation (immutable mobile) in forming associations (between a researcher and ANT in this case) is typical of 'classical' ANT analysis. However, there is also a hint of the latterday complexity of ANT – or post-ANT – in these opening sentences. Juxtaposed with the numerical accounting is a short autobiographical note of my experience of the popularity of ANT amongst postgraduate students. Here, students felt a certain concern that ANT might be useful, they wanted to find out something about what it can offer, they wanted to examine how it might potentially inform their research. In sum, there was a sort of appropriation of ANT that ideally would be fertile though need be neither faithful nor fine-grained. In the former case, one is being potentially 'enrolled' into – recruited to the cause of – ANT because of the persuasive potency of the evident 'factuality' of its prominence amongst a range of disciplines. In the latter case, students use my workshop as a means to explore the usefulness of ANT. And perhaps, somewhere down the line, they might develop a taste for it, gently import it into their projects, and put it into dialogue with other approaches with which they are more familiar.

So it would seem we are witness to two versions of ANT: one which is more 'agonistic', using particular forms of representation to persuade – *enrol* – people to ANT's cause; and one which is more 'collaborative', where ANT can be drawn on in various ways. In this light, ANT is not a singular framework, even at this basic level of how associations are drawn between social 'actors' (ANT and postgraduate students). Another way of putting this is that we have two ANT 'realities' (or ontologies) – let's call them for convenience's sake, a 'numerical-agonistic' one and an 'affective-collaborative' one. But, of course, these two versions of ANT are hardly distinct, they can play off and through each other.

The foregoing is simply a way of saying that ANT cannot be easily packaged. While it might once – in its very early days – have been reduced to an analytic recipe, this is certainly no longer the case. Indeed, some would dispute whether ANT was ever really a 'theory' at all. As Bruno Latour once quipped (to paraphrase): there are four things wrong with actor-network theory – actor, network, theory and the hyphen in between actor and network. Later he claimed, his tongue not too far from his cheek, that a better name for actor-network theory would be 'actant-rhizome ontology' (Latour, 2005a, p. 9). The upshot is that this book does not aspire to present ANT as a neatly demarcated approach that can be 'picked up' and applied across different empirical domains (e.g. media, sexuality, technology, environment, medicine, transport, markets, everyday life, etc., etc.). Rather, it is a complex, and oftentimes disparate, resource (closely aligned with a particular, evolving, set of sensibilities) that opens up a space for asking certain sorts of methodological, empirical, analytic and political questions about the processes of the (more-than-)social world.

Having said that, as we shall see, there are plenty of cases where ANT has been treated as just such a toolbox – a set of concepts or empirical orientations that can be disaggregated and dropped piecemeal into a particular research project or analytic exercise. What this appropriation of ANT does, however, is miss out on the sensibilities that underpin it. But, ironically, these ANT sensibilities are not always easy to get a handle on, not least when, as we have already seen, ANT turns out to be rather slippery. For John Law (2009), ANT is multiple, realized through various case studies rather than an abstracted body of theory (so, again, 'it' is not a theory). And for Annemarie Mol (2010), ANT entails a sensibility marked by adaptability: 'a set of sensibilities ... a rich array of explorative and experimental ways of attuning to the world' (p. 265).

The broader point is that there is both a set of sensibilities and practical orientations that comprise ANT, yet those sensibilities and practical orientations are adaptable, realized through concrete case studies, and multiple.

What Makes ANT so 'Special'? Why Does it Deserve my Attention?

This is not an easy question to answer. After all, 'special' is a pretty vague term – it can connote both attraction and revulsion. So let's use 'special' as proxy for a nexus of terms that might include 'intriguing', 'promising', 'insightful' and 'aggravating', 'simplistic', 'unhelpful'. These attributed qualities reflect a number of elements that go to make up ANT, not as a unitary entity, or a discrete tradition, or even a cast of academic characters, but as a fluid set of analytic and empirical practical orientations and sensibilities.

As indicated above, this set of practical orientations and sensibilities, while once quite tightly knit, has proliferated in a number of ways. For instance, the intellectual antecedents of ANT used to be found in the sociology of scientific knowledge, the social studies of science and technology, in ethnomethodology, in Greimas's semiotics, in the philosophical works of Michel Serres and Alfred North Whitehead. Recently we have seen a new a forebear emerge, namely Gabriel Tarde. This is, taken altogether, a contrarian lineage – one that cuts an alternative route through the history of social scientific thought. This might seem at once intriguing (what does such a lineage promise?) but also aggravating (where are Kant, Marx, Durkheim and Weber?).

Relatedly, let us consider how ANT has differentiated itself from more mainstream approaches to the social scientific study of the 'social'. For ANT,

the 'social' is not a given but a heterogeneous product laden with the nonhuman – technologies and natures are as much a part of society as humans.
Further, the 'social' is not structured in micro, meso and macro layers or spatially arranged into the local and the global (and sometimes the 'glocal'); rather,
according to versions of ANT, the social is 'flat', made up of a single layer of
associations amongst human and nonhuman entities, though the layer itself
can be 'topologically' contorted in all sorts of ways. Moreover, such standard
social scientific categories as class, or gender, or ethnicity have been largely
eschewed. In ANT accounts, instead, the conversation is more usually about
actors or actants, mediators and intermediaries, and, of course, these need not
be human. Indeed, sometimes the heterogeneity of these entities is emphasized:
as both human and nonhuman they are hybrids, or monsters. When it comes
to political processes, the focus is less on national parliaments, revolutions,
political parties, new social movements, non-governmental organizations and
the like; rather, the emphasis is on multinaturalism, cosmopolitics, political
ecology and hybrid forums. Finally, when it comes to the status that might be
ascribed to ANT's methodology and analytics, nowadays there seems to be a
concern with the ways in which method and analysis are complexly constitutive of their objects of study. Method 'performs' the social, and in the process
makes it in particular ways. This concern is captured in such terms as 'method
assemblage', 'othering', 'factishes' and the 'ecology of practices'.

Coming from a more traditional social scientific background, one is confronted with a whole new (and shifting) vocabulary that perhaps holds a
certain allure, but also can seem daunting and not a little obfuscating. Any
ambivalence toward ANT will only be reinforced as one becomes aware of the
sheer range of empirical topics, with which, in one way or another, it has
engaged. If, in ANT's very early days, work was concentrated on the processes
of scientific and technological 'innovation', it has subsequently been spun out
in various empirical directions. A short, but hopefully indicative, list might
include the following: the examination of the role of mundane technology in
ordering everyday life; the querying of the notion of modernity which is placed
in juxtaposition to that of 'amodernity'; analyses of the processes by which
divergent medical 'realities' are proliferated and managed; investigations of the
complex means by which markets are performed; a rethinking of what it means
to introduce the nonhuman into political processes of negotiation, notably in
relation to environmental issues. How has ANT made such empirical inroads?
Is such adaptability a sign of conceptual and theoretical dissipation or a peculiar strength of ANT (Mol, 2010)?

Again, we are challenged by the fact that ANT is not a static edifice – it has
been adapted, nuanced, expanded, and problematized by numerous scholars,
not least by its founders. But further, it has become blurred as it has been
deployed by scholars from different traditions, or has become embroiled in, and
drawn from, broader scholarly concerns, both conceptual and empirical. The
term 'network' is now entangled with the term assemblage; the concern with
everyday technological artefacts must speak to the anthropological tradition of

'material culture'; and the figure of the hybrid has long been in conversation with that of the cyborg. In other words, there are traces of ANT in other works whose relation (or even debt) to ANT is, not infrequently, highly complex and not always clear.

The upshot of all this is that what ANT 'is', or, indeed, what it is becoming, is not at all transparent. To reiterate, the aim of this book is not to demarcate and explicate what ANT definitively 'is'. Rather, it is to provide a set of possible relations through which one can engage productively with ANT. However, this is also to say that, as one enters into those relations, ANT does not necessarily remain the same – the 'use' of ANT in its specificity can mean that ANT 'itself' changes.

Having made this point, I nevertheless want to set out a number of general practical orientations and sensibilities that can be said to characterize ANT. By 'sensibilities and practical orientations' I mean a sort of comportment toward the study and analysis of the world which at once seeks out and is receptive to particular elements, processes and relations (though this might end up meaning that there are multiple worlds). What follows is a minimal list and it will be much expanded and nuanced as the book unfolds. At this stage, the aim is merely to introduce some of these 'practical orientations and sensibilities' as a way of setting the scene, and providing some markers, for later discussions.

- To study society, or some aspect of it, is to focus on relations – how these are produced and reproduced, ordered and disordered. Such relations are not simply social but heterogeneous – they necessarily entail the role of nonhumans as well as humans. These nonhumans include mundane objects, exotic technologies, texts of all sorts, nonhuman environments and animals.

- The relational processes of ordering and disordering entail circulation – circulations of people, texts, objects and artefacts, bits of natures and cultures.

- These relations and circulations need to be studied in their specificity as it is not always easy to tell what enters into them and what emerges from them. What sort of humans and nonhumans become embroiled within these relations and circulations? And what sort of humans and nonhumans, or combinations, are produced in the process?

- This entails both paying close empirical attention to these relations, circulations and entities, and resisting any temptation to make assumptions about them (such as assumptions about their character in terms of class or gender, for instance).

- These relations and circulations presuppose a certain 'flatness' to the world – what can enter into a relation are only those elements in their concreteness and specificity. More and more elements might be drawn into these relations, and these relations can take on different patterns and forms – but what is analytically resisted is recourse to 'broader' or 'higher' or 'deeper' social processes such as class or gender or market dynamics as a way of accounting for these relations. Rather, it is through the attention to specificity that we come to an understanding of class, gender or markets.

- To this end, a 'neutral' vocabulary is in order. Reference to abstracted terms such as actors and hybrids, association and enrolment, mediation and translation, networks and assemblages, is a means of shedding any sociological presuppositions about the constitution of the world.

- Yet ANT is itself a network made up of specific elements. In their empirical engagements, and in the process of accounting for their work, ANT scholars are themselves concerned with crafting relations. As such, care needs to be taken over the 'neutrality' of its terms which are of course engaged in mediating associations. These terms are not innocent.

- Relatedly, ANT is the outcome of such relations – relations through which certain terms have become part of ANT's terminology. Again, this suggests that there is nothing neutral about those concepts, they come with historical baggage.

No doubt the foregoing is dense, and many of the terms are not a little obscure. To make things a little easier, I have put together a short, selective glossary of key terms at the end of the book (key terms are indicated in bold italic on their first relevant appearance). This should be treated with the scepticism it deserves – it is there as a means of orientation rather than as a site of definition. After all, ANT has been subject to much problematization, not only by scholars hostile to ANT, but also by those ostensibly working under its auspices. Indeed, ANT long ago entered a post-ANT phase – a phase characterized by an elaboration and proliferation of the 'sensibilities and practicalities' listed above. This book will attempt to address both the early and later versions, and their continuities and discontinuities.

What is the Point of This Book? What Should I Expect to Get out of it?

If the foregoing conveys a sense of the unfolding multiplication of ANT, is this book primarily a chart of ANT's complex intellectual trajectory? Certainly, something along these lines is attempted. However, it will soon become apparent that a very particular line has been traced through ANT and post-ANT that inevitably reflects my own interests. For instance, particular texts that would be key or essential in someone else's account, feature in a subsidiary or subordinate role here. The more important aim is to share a positive sense of the way ANT reconfigures our understandings of the processes that shape the social world. To be sure, this reconfiguration is complex and *fluid* and adaptive; nevertheless there is a set of sensibilities that, amorphous though it is, can suggest new ways of thinking about and '*performing*' the social world (and its politics).

I have tried to strike a balance between depth (going into the inner workings and internal dialogues that mark ANT and post-ANT) and breadth (surveying the many empirical, methodological and conceptual routes ANT has taken). I am not at all sure I have succeeded. In any case, the book is a multiple. For some, it might be a resource from which certain concepts can be derived and particular methods mobilized. For others, it might be a text that situates ANT in relation to particular histories of thought, and contrasts it against several countervailing sociological traditions. For others still, the book might feed into an intellectual or personal adventure opening out onto new avenues of thought and practice. But if this book simply sparks, or even deepens, a curiosity in ANT and inspires further exploration of its large and involuted corpus, then I would be pretty happy.

What's in This Book? How Should I Read it?

This book has been designed to provide a sense of the roots of ANT, its earlier versions, the dialogues and diatribes that have surrounded it, the ways in which it was differentiated from other perspectives, its take-up in a number of disciplines, and its continuing development. As such, the structure of the book is fairly straightforward, perhaps even a little too linear.

Chapter 2 considers the roots of ANT in a number of traditions within philosophy and the social sciences: it traces lineages in the philosophy and sociology of science, and the Sociology of Scientific Knowledge (SSK). In stressing the social constructedness of scientific knowledge, SSK serves as a base for ANT's more radical notion of *construction*. A second foundational resource is the work of Michel Serres, whose focus on the role of the nonhuman in the production of social ordering and disordering underpins ANT's analytic focus on *heterogeneity* and the processes of '*translation*'. Alfred North Whitehead's view of the social as the object of 'explanation', rather than the source of explanation (typical of much social science), is also crucial. Foucault's model of power and its productivities will also be seen to be central to ANT, especially to its relational account of actors and their agency. In addition, the debt to microsociology, not least ethnomethodology, which anchors ANT's reluctance to draw on macrosociological categories, will be set out. While this is the general intellectual scaffold from which ANT might be hung, this has been supplemented by various other forebears (Tarde's recruitment into ANT's lineage is especially notable). By the end of this chapter the reader should have a robust view of the various issues (the '*flatness*' of the social, the 'relationality' of the human, the role of the nonhuman, etc.) that these lineages have afforded ANT.

Chapter 3 provides an account of the development of ANT in its early 'classical' phase. It summarizes the key concepts that ANT put into circulation – concepts such as *actor-network, actor, problematization, translation, interessement, enrolment, obligatory points of passage, immutable mobiles, heterogeneous engineering, scripts*. It will also outline the sorts of methodological injunctions that were suggested in order to do ANT research. Throughout the chapter, concepts will be grounded in ANT's classic empirical case studies. However, even as ANT was being 'systematized', so it was being unravelled, reconstituted and diverted. Thus the chapter also traces some of the ways in which the concerns of ANT were being modified and its concepts developed (often through particular case studies) by the key ANT scholars themselves. Approaches to issues around representation, reflexivity, power, modernity and ordering or *durability* began to be rethought, refined or reconfigured.

Chapter 4 traces how ANT has been subjected to numerous – generally 'friendly' – critiques. These critiques tend to focus on making ANT 'better' at what it does or could do, rather than trying to dispute its underlying principles. Amongst these critiques can be counted: ANT's neglect of the other; the constitutive role of *ambivalence* and ambiguity; the need to account for multiplicity and *fluidity* within networks; the empirical and conceptual issues that arise in determining the limits of the network; the role of culture in shaping how networks cohere; the influence of non-experts in the production and circulation of knowledge.

Chapter 5 goes about placing ANT in relation to a number of important traditions in sociology. In particular, its perspectives on the human actor and agency, on the relation between macrosocial and microsocial processes, on the nature of power and interests will be set against three perspectives. These are Elias's figurational sociology, Bourdieusian practice sociology and Giddens' structuration theory. These frameworks seem particularly appropriate in that they too are concerned with 'solving' classic tensions within sociology, such as that between human agency and social structure. This chapter is illustrated with particular case studies chosen because they draw directly on ANT in order to supplement their use of Elias, Bourdieu or Giddens. As we shall argue, these piecemeal appropriations of ANT do not always do justice to its potential.

Chapter 6 further explores the 'appropriation' of ANT, this time by a select group of disciplines. We see how ANT has been adopted and adapted by social theorists John Urry and Nigel Thrift. Crucially, we see how ANT is translated in ways that feed back into what ANT 'is'. Thus, Thrift's non-representational theory highlights the speculative potential of ANT. The same goes for ANT's introduction into parts of geography and management and organization studies: these too have drawn out and elaborated particular dimensions of ANT, in the process shifting it toward new directions.

In Chapter 7, additional 'proliferations' of ANT are presented. Under the auspices of post-ANT, we trace a particular trajectory that brings to the fore inter-related issues of *ontological multiplicity* and *ontological politics*, the relationship between *matters of concern* and *matters of care*, a re-visioning of the world as one of emergence and co-becoming, and a methodological reorientation of post-ANT methods toward speculative practices. Perhaps this traces a peculiar route through recent post-ANT debates – certainly it betrays my interests. Nevertheless, the hope is that it at least evokes the continuing inventive potential of (post-)ANT.

Chapter 8 tries to recalibrate Chapter 7's account of post-ANT. After an initial overview of the book – which includes a commentary on some of the things that have been neglected – the chapter points to a number of other, more or less, fresh developments in post-ANT. Some of these can be linked to particular trends that have gained, or are gaining, prominence, for instance, disasters, dementia and the digital. Some reflect recent interest in empirical topics that have played a relatively minor part in ANT's history – experience, animals and the studio, for instance. In any case, the primary aim is to convey a sense of the expansive liveliness and promise of post-ANT. The chapter ends with a heuristic and tentative list of sensibilities and practical orientations that might help in 'doing post-ANT'.

So, Who's to Blame for This Book, Then?

It is a convention in academic writing that the author takes the blame for whatever is wrong with their text, and redistributes responsibility for all that is good in it over a long list of others. There is certainly no need to break with convention in the case of this book. Over the extended course of my adventures with ANT, numerous colleagues have been hugely influential. While at Lancaster University, Lynda Birke, Nik Brown, Simon Carter, Alan Collins, Susan Condor, Gavin Kendall, Maggie Mort, Rosemary McKechnie, Kath Smart, Vicky Singleton and Brian Wynne were particularly important in shaping my thinking on ANT (and its early drawbacks). While at Goldsmiths, University of London, it was Andrew Barry, Miquel Domenech, Jennifer Gabrys, Bill Gaver, Priska Gisler, Mick Halewood, Maja Horst, Alan Irwin, Tobie Kerridge, Danny Lopez, Celia Lury, Tahani Nadim, Noortje Marres, Finn Olesen, Israel Rodríguez-Giralt, Marsha Rosengarten, Paul Stronge and Alex Wilkie who especially pushed me to develop my thinking in new post-ANT directions. During my time at the University of Sydney, I have been very lucky to have been further inspired by David Bray, Caragh Brosnan, Melinda Cooper, Catriona Elder, Masato Fukushima, Gay Hawkins, Deborah Lupton, Sarah Pink, Kane Race, Robert van Krieken, Sonja van Wichelen, Cathy Waldby, Dinesh Wadiwel. In addition, many friends and colleagues have drawn me into conversations which, in one way or another, refreshed otherwise stale or stuck thinking. A sample would include: Gail Davies, Uli Felt, Sarah Green, Steve Hinchliffe, Joanna Latimer, John Law, Annemarie Mol, Michael Schillmeier, Bev Skeggs, Steve Wainwright, Clare Williams, Steve Woolgar. Needless to say, there are many more. There is a cast of family and friends who also need to be thanked for their support: Tor Brandon, Grahame Jenkins, Steph Macek, Mario Michael, Steve Russell, Chris Todd come immediately to mind. And finally my family – Bethan, Nye and Yanna Rees – must be acknowledged: without their tolerance, humour, love and indifference it would have been impossible to write this book. This book is dedicated to the memory of my aunt, Katerina Michael.

2

ACTOR-NETWORK THEORY: OLD AND NEW ROOTS

Introduction

While ANT has gained purchase in a number of fields, its roots nevertheless can be traced primarily back to the social studies of science. However, this is more of a multidiscipline than a discipline, drawing on various social scientific and philosophical traditions, and extending across numerous empirical areas. Moreover, the pioneers of ANT were not averse to drawing in other intellectual sources, not least from continental philosophy. As such, the intellectual roots of ANT are rather tangled, incorporating, for instance, Marxian, social constructionist and ethnomethodological traditions in sociology; the influence of Whitehead, Kuhn, Serres and Foucault from history and philosophy; elements of Greimas and arguably Barthes from semiotics. Inevitably, some lineages are more obvious than others.

ANT, and its various successors, sometimes collected under the ungainly title of post-ANT, have also accumulated forebears over the years. For instance, Gabriel Tarde is a relatively recent and notable addition. Further, as the term post-ANT indicates, ANT has hardly been static – it has developed in conversation and disputation with scholars from other traditions. For example, the post-structuralist feminist writings of Donna Haraway have been highly influential, challenging several of ANT's early framings.

The upshot is that it would be difficult, if not strictly impossible, to relate a linear account of the roots of ANT (not least when one is in competition with other biographical accountings – e.g. Latour, 2012). Nonetheless, there are key components of ANT that can serve as anchors from which pragmatically to trace 'back' particularly influential traditions (and, conversely, to trace 'forward' some particularly influential criticisms). In what follows, then, we begin with a brief exposition of what is distinctive about ANT. Here I focus on such features as the concern with the constructedness of scientific knowledge, the insistence on the role of the nonhuman in the making of the 'social', the engagement with the microprocesses of relations (of power), the eschewal of distinctions between the microsociological and the macrosociological, and the close attention to empirical study and the commitment to a neutral vocabulary. We then go on to excavate how these have their roots in particular traditions – in SSK, in the philosophies of Whitehead and Serres, in the works of Foucault and those approaches that stress *performativity*, in the epistemology of Tarde, and in ethnomethodology.

ANT – A Sketchy Distinctiveness

ANT arose in the 1980s context of the then new social constructionist analyses of scientific knowledge. In particular, early ANT scholars were concerned to trace the ways in which laboratory practices, and the sorts of materials that circulated through the space of the laboratory served in the accreditation of scientific knowledge as 'objective'. Put another way, the laboratory was seen as a central venue in which texts, materials, skills could be combined to produce primarily texts that were sufficiently potent that they could be used to interest and enrol other actors (scientists, funders, regulators, publics). In this way, these actors would play their part in the extension of the networks of the laboratory scientists.

From this brief sketch we can derive a number of key characteristics of ANT. First, scientists were not seen as having some sort of 'direct' access to nature but, rather, derived – *constructed* – scientific knowledge through activities that marshalled human, nonhuman and textual elements. The privileged space of this marshalling – which included assembling, combining, representing and circulating – was the laboratory. From this space, texts could be sent out into the world to persuade others of the 'objectivity' of the laboratory's scientific knowledge. For ANT, the process of constructing scientific knowledge thus entailed both human and nonhuman elements, and as such stood in contrast from social constructionist perspectives that placed emphasis on social processes. This focus on the nonhuman – a term that covered animals, plants, environments, technologies – would subsequently be generalized to the analysis of the production of 'social' *per se*.

Second, ANT's focus on scientists' circulation of texts, and their use in the 'persuasion' of others amounts to a microsocial view of social ordering. It suggests that others could not be 'impelled' to take scientific findings, arguments, or formulations seriously but had to be coached into doing so. In other words, scientists did not possess some sort of power which could oblige others to align themselves with those scientists (and their projects). Rather, scientists had at their disposal particularly persuasive tools, not least in the form of the scientific paper.

Third, if actors could be successfully aligned – that is, enrolled in the scientists' project – then a network could be established and rendered durable.

So, for ANT, society should not be represented in the traditional social scientific format of a dualism between human actors and social structures (see Chapter 3). Rather, 'society' is comprised of humans (and nonhumans) who are aligned in networks of differing extent. Instead of a qualitative differentiation between human agents and social structures, there is a quantitative difference between the lengths of *associations* amongst greater or lesser numbers of actors. Instead of a model of society organized around levels or in terms of depth (e.g. the infrastructure of the economy and superstructure of culture), society emerges as a flat network of associations.

ANT's insistence on the importance of the nonhuman reflects the fact that it sees the social not as a means to explanation (e.g. social interests explain why some scientific arguments are favoured over others). Rather, the social is seen as the outcome of heterogeneous processes. Human and nonhuman actors together contribute to the production of society. Moreover, in the process of the assembling of a particular network, it is not possible to say *a priori* whether it is human or nonhuman actors that have played the decisive part. Accordingly, it is through close empirical study that it becomes possible to identify the particularly prominent actors, though it is not always easy to determine whether these are social or not. Thus, in order to avoid a sociological leaning toward the social and thereby the prejudicing of analysis, a neutral vocabulary should be adopted. So, alongside close empirical study, ANT draws on a battery of seemingly abstract terms such as actor or *actant*, translation, association, enrolment, problematization, network.

Needless to say, this is the skimpiest of sketches and barely does justice to ANT and its subsequent criticism and extension. What it does do, hopefully, is set up the structure for this and the next two chapters, which addresses the following issues: the constructedness of knowledge; the role of the nonhuman in the making of the social; the way representation serves in the mediation of relations of power; the flatness of networks and the extension of associations; and the emphasis on close empirical study with the aid of a neutral vocabulary.

The Constructedness of Knowledge

At the risk of gross simplification, in the postwar era, sociology's account of scientific knowledge was bifurcated into neo-Marxist and functionalist camps. For neo-Marxist critical theorists such as Marcuse (1964), and Adorno and Horkheimer (1973; see also Collin and Budtz Pedersen, 2015), science was characterized by such processes as objectification, atomization and reductionism. As such, science was a component in a more general bourgeois ideology in which nature becomes 'disenchanted' – a mere object of knowledge and a resource for exploitation. By comparison, for functionalist sociology, in this context spearheaded by Robert Merton (1973/1942), science was seen as pivotal to the post-WWII West insofar as it served to sustain democracy. It was mainly the body of work that reacted against the functionalist model of science that fed into the development of ANT.

a. Functionalism

According to the functionalist perspective, as the source of objective knowledge, science could contribute to the processes of democracy. By presenting the 'facts' of the matter, science could help overcome the divergent ideological positions of conflicting factions. Once the facts were in place, it was possible to proceed collectively along the correct course of action. The other dimension of this account was that such 'real' science, in return, needed 'real' democracy. The freedom democracy provided was necessary so that the norms (see below) that sustain science could flourish. In contrast, for those nation states where democracy was lacking, science was chronically corrupted (the well-known example of this was the Lysenko affair in 1930s and 1940s Soviet Union where a form of Lamarckism led to starvation).

So, science both facilitates and needs democracy. But it also serves as a model for democracy: it was meritocratic; it was a free market of ideas; it encouraged free speech; it was empiricist in that it determined 'how things really are'; and it could thus serve to direct action accordingly.

How did science manage this? According to Merton (1973/1942), science as a system was held together by the four CUDOS norms: Communality, where knowledge is shared unstintingly across the scientific community; Universality, where common standards of scientific practice and judgement apply across the community of scientists; Disinterestedness, where scientists have no personal attachment to their own particular ideas or practices; and Organized Scepticism, wherein all scientific products are subjected to critical scrutiny across the community of scientists. According to this functionalist model, scientists were rewarded or punished according to whether they fulfilled or transgressed these norms. These norms were the social conditions by which true knowledge was generated.

Now, even within the functionalist approach problems were raised: notably, not only did scientists fail to realize these norms, they adhered to their precise opposites (Mitroff, 1974). That is to say, they made mention of a series of counter-norms which justified secrecy (failing to share results meant that one was more likely to make a discovery first), or warranted a profound personal investment in a particular technique or theory (without such 'obsessiveness' one would quickly lose heart given the routine setbacks that beset scientific practice).

Other issues could be raised about Merton's functionalist schema: Is science really a single community, or is it in actuality highly differentiated? Do different disciplines have different standards of proof, or contrasting norms? How do national institutional career structures shape local norms, and thereby impact on the generation of knowledge? How do such norms play out in commercial science where the bulk of scientific work gets done?

Perhaps the most devastating critique of CUDOS comes from Mulkay (1979). Mulkay argued that it is practically very difficult for scientists to gauge whether their peers have adhered to CUDOS norms. Within the main medium of scientific communication – the scientific paper – there is little indication of norm adherence. Indeed, Mulkay contended, scientists acknowledge and reward others primarily on the basis of whether their work is useful. Adherence to norms is immaterial to this process. What then is the value of norms that feature in scientists' own accounts. Mulkay suggests that they operate as ideology: they serve in the representation of science and scientists as disinterested, self-critical, standardized – in a word, 'objective'.

The issue of counter-norms finds a particularly critical echo in the work of Thomas Kuhn. Where Mitroff specified counter-norms which justified the attachment to one's particular theories or techniques, Kuhn's notion of 'paradigm' implied a sort of constitutive 'immersion' in a nexus of theories and techniques. For Kuhn, the idea of paradigm captures the way that in 'normal' science there are commonly held examples of actual scientific practice (e.g. laws, theory, applications, instrumentation, experimentation) that serve as models from which spring coherent traditions of scientific research. In other words, scientists operate within a pattern of practices and ideas – one might say, thought-styles (Fleck, 1979) – which are presupposed. While every so often, there are scientific revolutions in which one paradigm is overthrown by another, generally speaking these background assumptions are rarely subject to critical reflection. Study of these paradigmatic ideas, practices, instruments and so on is what prepares students for membership of the scientific community. In sum, the concept of paradigm connotes rarely challenged ways of thinking and doing which are constitutive of what it means to be a scientist of a particular sort. On this analysis, it would seem that scientists are necessarily 'interested' and, with good reason, practise 'distributed credulity' rather than 'organized scepticism'.

b. Sociology of Scientific Knowledge

Both Mulkay's and Kuhn's perspectives reflect a fundamental shift away from the functionalist approach. In Merton's account, which was in large part derived from the biographies of scientists, once the norms had been identified, these wholly accounted for science's 'success'; only when science went wrong (as in the Lysenko affair) was there anything to explain sociologically. Merton's has thus been called a 'sociology of error'. Mulkay and Kuhn, however, show how even 'true' knowledge is open to social explanation. This sociological revaluation took its most famous form in what came to be known as the Strong Programme. Accordingly, what counted as true or false scientific knowledge could not be worked out in advance (in light of the operation of norms or the application of some technical procedure). It was only in retrospect that data, theories, facts could be seen to be true or false. For such scholars as David Bloor (1976) and Barry Barnes (1977), the factors that led to this or that bit of scientific knowledge becoming established as true should be treated in the same way as those that affected what subsequently came to be known as false. Moreover, it was only through close empirical study of how scientific knowledge was produced in practice that these factors could be identified: what was needed was a Sociology of Scientific Knowledge (SSK).

Crucial here was the analytic focus on scientific controversy: by concentrating on how controversies emerged and were resolved, it would be possible to trace the sorts of factors that were mobilized in order to 'win' the scientific debate. This meant addressing how particular sorts of discourse (Gilbert and Mulkay, 1984) or rhetoric (Myers, 1990) or categories (Gieryn, 1983), and the differential access to various resources such as reputation or opportunity (see, for example, Barnes and Shapin, 1979; Barnes and Edge, 1982) affected the course of a controversy. In all this, the aim was to unravel the means by which one faction of scientists within a controversy discredited their opponents and accredited themselves, and to lay bare how they managed to persuade the 'scientific community' that they were right and their opponents were wrong (for a parallel statement of this analytic sensibility, see Collins, 1985).

Also important were the ways in which the controversy itself reflected divergent interests: interests could explain the composition of the factions even if they could not necessarily tell us which faction ultimately triumphed. These interests were variable and included class positionings and alignments, professional concerns (promoting a specialism, protecting institutional autonomy), and cognitive investments (attachments to particular theories or techniques).

The general SSK approach – also known as 'social constructionism' – to the analysis of science found further expression in empirical studies of scientific laboratories. These revealed how the local disputes – one might say, micro-controversies – that routinely arise in everyday discussions amongst scientists were settled. Variously, this would involve preferences for agreement (Lynch, 1985), or forms of interrogation (Knorr Cetina, 1981), or the calibration of divergent 'modalities', that is, statements of greater or lesser certainty (Latour and Woolgar, 1979). To be sure, these studies did not always sit happily in relation to the Strong Programme (see below) but they nevertheless illuminated issues that were central to it.

The Strong Programme's approach to the Sociology of Scientific Knowledge was distilled by Bloor (1976) into four principles:

- *Causality.* The aim of SSK is to work out which conditions lead to beliefs or states of knowledge. These conditions could be psychological, economic, political, professional, social. As noted above, the notion of interests was pivotal here.

- *Impartiality.* SSK analysts should select case studies irrespective of their perceived truth or falsity, rationality or irrationality. All cases should be subject to the same analytic rigour.

- *Symmetry.* When analysing a particular case of scientific controversy, one should apply symmetrically the same form of social explanation to all sides of the dispute.

- *Reflexivity.* The form of explanation – and the sorts of factors that are deemed to influence the resolution of a controversy – apply as much to SSK as they do to science.

ANT drew upon and adapted many of these principles of the Strong Programme and the sensibilities of SSK. For instance, Impartiality is no less a cornerstone of ANT as of SSK – ANT has applied its own analytic battery to both successful (Pasteur) and unsuccessful (the biologists of St Brieuc Bay) scientific endeavours. And it has examined the means by which factions attempt to 'persuade' one another (though ANT's preferred term is 'enrolment'; see Chapter 3).

However ANT also came to be differentiated from the Strong Programme and SSK. For instance, ANT pioneers like Latour and Callon, drawing on a rather different philosophical tradition, emphasized that the non-social or the nonhuman also has a role to play in the settlement of scientific controversy. Indeed, to *social* constructionism they counterposed constructionism *per se*. As we shall detail in the next chapter, while ANT shared with the Strong Programme a commitment to 'symmetry', this was transformed in ANT into a 'radical symmetry' in which explanation could be social but also non-social, and further, what counted as social or non-social could not be known at the outset. The broader point was that the very idea of the 'social' had to be interrogated (as a construction) rather than assumed (as an explanans, doing all the explaining).

On a different score, there was considerable criticism of the conceptualization of '*interests*' in the Strong Programme. For some writers (e.g. Collins, 1985) this was just too 'clunky': insofar as interests were associated with class or professional position, they failed to capture the fluidity and contingency of interests that emerged through the process of doing science. For others (Woolgar, 1981), doubts were raised over whether interests could be empirically accessed at all: insofar as people routinely talk about interests, how they are rhetorically deployed by scientists should be the first analytic port of call. By contrast, Callon and Law (1982) argued that interests lay somewhere in between these positions – they were fluid and emergent, and they were talked about, and, crucially, they could be instilled in, and attributed to, others. Indeed, they are part of the process of enrolment in that actors' interests are reconfigured – translated – by scientists so that they become attached to scientists' own interests (and networks).

Finally, we can reflect on the principle of reflexivity. At first sight, reflexivity seemed utterly to undermine the epistemological privilege of the Strong Programme (e.g. Woolgar, 1988). Simply put, if the Programme's own accounts of scientific controversy were socially constructed, then why should they be believed? They are, after all, of the same epistemic status as those socially constructed scientific accounts that are subject to the Strong Programme's analysis. For some this was a matter of lament and perhaps required redefinition of 'reflexivity' (e.g. Furhman and Oehler, 1986; Doran, 1989). For others, reflexivity was a matter of celebration and an opportunity to follow the various ironies of applying reflexivity to itself (Mulkay, 1985; Ashmore, 1989). For others still, it meant a retrenchment – an emphasis on the reality and priority of social factors, and their special accessibility to social empirical study (Collins and Yearley, 1992a, 1992b). For Latour (1988a), reflexivity is part and parcel of building an actor-network: to be reflexive is not a negative or celebratory matter, but intrinsic to making texts potent enough to enrol actors. One should be '*infra-reflexive*', acknowledge one's position within and trajectory through a network, and be as canny as possible in writing to one's advantage (after all, even a lament can be haunting – that is, reflexive texts can enrol others to the project of reflexivity).

This should give some indication of this particular lineage of ANT in SSK and the Strong Programme. We shall return to a number of the tensions between these at a later point when, for instance, we contrast their respective versions of politics (see Chapter 4). However, for now, we turn to the roots of perhaps the most distinctive feature of ANT (at least in the context of SSK), namely the analytic concern with the nonhuman and the non-social as central to the 'making' of society.

The Role of the Nonhuman

Actor-network theorists, in contrast to SSK's social constructionist emphasis on the social, have advocated an approach to science that remains neutral with respect to what could 'explain' a particular phenomenon (such as the accreditation of a particular scientific theory, or the failure of a specific technological project). For ANT, to privilege the social in accounting for the production of scientific knowledge seems problematic, not least because what 'makes up' the social includes the non-social and the nonhuman. Society (and various social categories such as interests and discourse but also class, gender or institutions) was something to be explained or accounted for, not just a source of explanation or accounting. As we shall see below, this attentiveness to the nonhuman followed different (but related) paths. On the one hand, at a 'macro' or 'epochal' level, the bifurcation of the human and nonhuman was seen to take form at a particular historical juncture – the birth of modernity (Shapin and Schaffer, 1985; Latour, 1993a). On the other hand, at the 'micro' level of local practice, the nonhuman, in the guise of technological artefacts, routinely shapes the comportment of, and the inter-relations amongst, human actors. Indeed humans and nonhumans are so closely entwined that it is better to think in terms of *hybrids*. The capacity to think of the nonhuman in this way is itself partly a result of the heterogeneous 'products' of science (or technoscience, see Chapter 3) itself: these products – gene sequencers, climate change, digital implants – are so prevalent that we have no option but to try to address their, and our own, hybridity. In post-ANT, this also means trying to think about what it means to do politics – or rather, *cosmopolitics* (e.g. Latour, 2004b; Stengers, 2005a) – that incorporate this crucial role of the nonhuman.

a. Whitehead

Now, the dissatisfaction with the bifurcation between the human and nonhuman, nature and society, was expressed long ago in the work of Whitehead (e.g. 1920, 1929). His work has been a major influence on ANT (see Latour, 1999, 2004a) but has also impacted on intellectual fellow-travellers, notably Donna Haraway (e.g. 2000; see Halewood and Michael, 2008). In addition to the metaphysics of Whitehead, the philosophical anthropology of Michel Serres was also hugely important. Weaving together science and literature, fable and communication theory, philosophy and autobiography, the work of Serres provided a preliminary terminology for capturing the local specificities of human–nonhuman orderings and disorderings.

Key to Whitehead's philosophical project was the circumvention of the 'great bifurcation' between nature and society, that is, a world divided into an external world that can be known and human subjects who know. In Whitehead's schema, 'nature' refers to all existence – after all, it is not possible to 'know' without materiality – in the form of, say, light and sound, body and brain – playing its part. Halewood (2011, p. 85) neatly summarizes Whitehead's view: 'society' denotes 'the achievement of groups of entities, of any kind, in managing to cohere and endure and thus to constitute some kind of unity. ... Rocks, stones, amoeba, books can, thus, be considered to be societies.' Indeed, 'society' as deployed by sociologists is something that we turn to only after we have addressed this broader, heterogeneous version of society that Whitehead proposes. As Halewood puts it: 'any discussions on sociology and of the socio-logical (at the human level) can only be embarked upon after accounting for the wider notions of society and the social which characterise all existence' (Halewood, 2011, p. 86). Unsurprisingly, this prefigures ANT's principle of radical symmetry: we cannot presuppose that 'sociological society' can account for the emergence of this or that phenomenon but must seek to resituate 'sociological society' in relation to this wider Whiteheadian version of society.

This resituating of the 'sociological social' reflects Whitehead's analysis of the world as one in which there is both 'becoming' and the durability of 'stubborn fact'. As such, the world is in process, emergent, unfolding; but it is also popu-lated by entities that endure. To capture this, Whitehead develops a nexus of inter-related terms. Here, I take up only those that seem to me best to illuminate ANT. Central to Whitehead are the concepts of 'actual entities' and 'actual occa-sions'. On the one hand, these denote the durable stuff of the world (stones, atoms, goldfish, people); on the other, they point to the ways in which these are emergent. They are constituted from 'prehensions' – a heterogeneity of elements that span the material and the social, the conscious and the unconscious, the nonhuman and human. These prehensions come together to combine – to 'concresce': in the process of that concrescence, the 'actual entity' is forged. In due course, that 'actual entity' itself becomes a prehension concresced with other prehensions to form subsequent actual entities. That is to say, actual enti-ties have a fleeting existence – a moment of 'satisfaction' where the various prehensions cohere – before, as it were, 'moving on' as the prehensions of other actual entities. The idea of 'satisfaction' reflects a teleological element in Whitehead's analytic – not all prehensions sit happily together in a particular concrescence, some are indeed inhibited, while others are 'welcomed'.

One implication of Whitehead's analytic is that we cannot presuppose unproblematically the human subject or agent when accounting for particular social events. For Whitehead, the subject too is emergent within an *event* – it is thus a 'superject'. As such, rather than preceding, or being the basis of, an event, it is produced through the prehensions 'it' encounters. This point simply serves to underline that just as the 'social' needs to be unravelled in terms of its heterogeneous prehensions, so too does the 'human subject' (or 'human agent').

To be sure, this is a highly selective, and certainly simplified, rendering of (parts of) Whitehead's analysis. Nevertheless, it does have the benefit of allowing us to crystallize three links to ANT. (1) Social events are emergent, in process, composed of a multiplicity of elements (or concresced of prehensions). (2) The prehensions that comprise social events are heterogeneous – the 'social' and the 'human subject' are comprised of elements that include the material, the nonhuman. (3) Once concresced as actual entities, these social and subjective elements become the prehensions of subsequent actual entities. That is to say, one can see in Whitehead the embryo of a model of 'circulation' in which actual entities emerge, are concresced as prehensions into new actual entities, and then 'move on' again as prehensions. In the process of this 'circulation', some actual entities as prehensions can combine with other prehensions to form new actual entities (attain 'satisfaction'), while others are not able to enter particular concrescences. The further point is that actual entities can have a greater 'prehensive reach' – they can be 'satisfactory' to a wider range of concrescences. In ANT this equates with, for instance, the use of certain textual artefacts – such as scientific papers – that are able both to enter into different situations without too much resistance and combine with other forms of texts to produce new knowledge.

b. Serres

Unlike Whitehead, who died in 1947, Michel Serres is an older contemporary of ANT's early pioneers. As such, while his work has developed in ways that diverge from ANT's core concerns, he has also been in direct dialogue with ANT, not least Bruno Latour (Serres and Latour, 1995).

For present purposes, let's focus on Serres' account of the role of the nonhuman in the production of the 'social' and its translation within ANT. For Serres (e.g. 1982a, 1982b; Serres and Latour, 1995), the world is criss-crossed and held together by 'messages'. Serres attempts to get at this process through the mythical character of Hermes – the not always reliable messenger of the gods (hermeneutics derives from his name). Hermes conveys messages, but sometimes they do not arrive in the same form or with the same content as when they were sent, and the relationships they are meant to mediate do not always turn out as intended. In Serres' framework, these 'messages' connect together divergent domains (e.g. poetry and science) to produce particular patterns or orderings. Moreover, these 'messages' are not simply linguistic or semiotic, they are also material. As they move, they can be transformed between, on the one hand, matters, energies, bodies, objects and, on the other, ideas, significations, culture, subjects. And finally, the singular messenger Hermes needs to become a multiple. In the modern digital era, Serres (1995a) suggests that we need a new metaphor – a multitude of angels – to get at the multiplicity of messages that hold the world together (and also, of course, transform it).

The immediate point is that though these messengers – message-bearers – take many disparate forms, they are themselves also the products of message-bearers (which are similarly heterogeneously composed). In other words, whether messengers take the forms of subjects (people) or objects (everyday artefacts that shape our day-to-day comportments and relations), they are themselves constituted out of messages that are similarly disparate. Rather than oppose objects to subjects, there is good reason to blur the difference. To signal their constitutive heterogeneity (while acknowledging their outward appearance), we can, following Serres, refer to them as quasi-objects and quasi-subjects.

These quasi-objects move between humans in ways that shape those humans' relations. One of Serres' favourite examples is that of soccer. As the ball moves, so all the players orient toward it, their movements are fundamentally influenced by the ball's trajectories. Of course, these trajectories are in part affected by the players' kicks and headers, but also by a myriad of other determinants (the length of the grass, the speed of the wind, the build of the ball itself). In all this, the ball is a messenger between the players, and in its circulation amongst those players, it shapes the 'society' of the game. Of course, this 'shaping' is not always faithful: the ball will do things that the sending or receiving player does not expect – it will sometimes 'betray' them.

So, for Serres, quasi-objects are critical for the making of society. Serres writes: 'Our relationships, social bonds, would be airy as clouds were there only contracts between subjects. In fact, the object, specific to the Hominidae, stabilises our relationships, it slows down the time of our revolutions. For the unstable bands of baboons, social changes are flaring up every minute. ... The object, for us, makes our history slow' (1995b, p. 87). But as we have seen with the example of football, quasi-objects' movements cannot be conceived in isolation from human relations. Accordingly, those 'relations at the heart of the group constitute their object; the object moving in a multiplicity constructs these relations and constitutes the group. These two complementary activities are contemporaneous' (Serres, 1991, p. 102).

Serres is acutely aware that quasi-objects vary in the extent to which they can specify the relations between humans. He uses the terms 'jokers' or 'blank dominoes' to signify those quasi-objects that barely influence human relations. However, this is not a stable property: 'Our quasi-objects have increasing specificity' (Serres, 1982b, p. 232). That is to say, as quasi-objects circulate, they can accumulate specificity by specifying social relations which in turn further specify them and so on in a cycle of tighter and tighter coupling. At this point, by being so vital to the production and reproduction of the social, quasi-objects become akin to quasi-subjects.

Above, we remarked that these quasi-object message-bearers are not always faithful. They do not always convey their messages accurately, and sometimes they are simply disruptive, undermining relationships. Serres (1982b) addresses this through the figure of the parasite, which by introducing 'noise', disrupts communication – the movement of a signal – between a sender and a receiver. Given that the world abounds with such parasites, these need to be excluded if the communication is to continue. In British soccer, a series of exclusions have been imposed over time to exclude the disruptions – the 'noise' – of 'hooliganism'. For instance, there has been the banning of alcohol at matches and redesign into all-seater stadiums. ANT is analytically interested in just this process of exclusion. When the interests of actors are translated by a scientist (or some other actor), say from an interest in making transport systems more efficient, to an interest in privately owned electric vehicles, then a panoply of other interests and messages about alternatives, such as more efficient public transport, have to be excluded.

However, as the example of the changes in football hints, parasites are 'productive'. Their presence and exclusion have consequences – the reconfiguration of football stadiums, and arguably of British football *per se*. Serres is thus interested in the way that parasitical disorder is an intrinsic feature of the world, and how its presence and exclusion can trigger a complexification of ordering. Parasites thus have their uses – they generate disordering but also reordering. ANT can be understood as a particular approach to understanding the emergence of these patterns of ordering and disordering (see Michael, 2000).

The final point to make about the parasite is that, like Hermes, it can be either semiotic or material: a disruption can take the form of a physical intervention or an unwelcome story. A physical intervention can lead to new social meanings emerging, an unwelcome story can result in new physical measures being instituted. As with Whitehead, Serres has offered ANT a way of thinking about the relationship between the human and the nonhuman, the subject and object, where these are no longer held to be separate.

Power and Representation

In 1986 Latour wrote:

> No matter how much power one appears to accumulate, it is always necessary to obtain it from others who are doing the action. ... Thus it is always necessary to redefine who is acting, why it is necessary to act together, what are the boundaries of the collective, how responsibility should be allocated. (p. 276)

ANT scholars generally do not assume that actors 'possess' *power*; rather the purpose of analysis is to trace how those actors wield influence, deploy various resources, marshal other actors (human and nonhuman), and establish and make durable a pattern of associations amongst those actors. In this respect, the networks of associations that actors such as scientists generate entail a process of 'translation'. As noted above, this involves a persuasive conversion of people's 'interests' into something that aligns with the interests of those scientists.

To a large degree, this formulation reflects ANT's (often underplayed) debt to Foucault, for whom power does not merely constrain the possibilities for action amongst those who are subject to it. Rather it is 'positive': discourses and practices, not least those related to the 'human sciences' (e.g. medicine, psychiatry, education, the law, social services, prisons), 'make' individuals so that they come to have particular interests and capacities. Foucault (1986; see also 1979a, 1979b, 1981) phrases it this way:

> The individual is not to be conceived as a sort of elementary nucleus, a primitive atom, a multiple and inert material on which power comes to fasten or against which it happens to strike, and in so doing subdues or crushes individuals. In fact, it is already one of the prime effects of power that certain bodies, certain gestures, certain discourses, certain desires come to be identified and constituted as individuals. (p. 234)

Notably this process of 'making people' (see Hacking, 1986) is a circuitous and distributed one. Ways of deriving knowledge about people, society, bodies, minds, morality are developed and implemented within various institutional settings – hospitals, schools, courtrooms, prisons. With these methods of 'power/knowledge' – which migrate across different sites and locales – come our understandings of what it means to be a 'modern individual' with given qualities and concerns. One therefore does not study 'power' but 'relations of power'. In the specific circumstances (of this or that institution at this or that time), one traces the practices and discourses – processes of measurement, testing, observation, or conversation – out of which the individual emerges. From these local instantiations of power/knowledge, Foucault suggests it is possible to move 'upwards', to show how these practices and discourses have been appropriated, elaborated and generalized by larger-scale mechanisms like the state.

With ANT the focus is less on the emergence of an epochal 'modern' individual and more on the local emergence of actors enrolled within a particular network. These actors have their interests translated, their capacities reordered and their relations reconfigured, and as such they are locally 're-made' as individuals. This process entails 'relations of power' but instead of the discourses and practices of the human sciences, it is the natural sciences that are foregrounded. Scientists offer new possibilities to people for realizing their pre-existing goals – whether these be economic security, curing human illness, or saving the environment – by demonstrating, in one way or another, the viability of their versions of nature (or technology). Here, they must 'coax' nature (or technology) into acting in specified ways; they must ensure that electrons or scallops do what is asked of them. Here, not only are people 'made', so too is 'nature'. As John Law (1987) put it, scientists are 'heterogeneous engineers' whose networks have enrolled both humans and nonhumans. Should either of these step out of line, the network falls apart.

Crucial to the enrolment of humans, is the use of representation. Sometimes this takes the forms of scientific papers or reports whose internal composition (e.g. scientific rhetoric, mathematical exposition, graphical depiction) makes the claims they make difficult to dispute. Sometimes it involves forms of demonstration, where experiments are set up to display, for example, how certain interventions in nature yield predictable results. In both cases claims about nature are being staked and, if 'persuasively' rendered, they can serve in the enrolment of actors (including other scientists, politicians, regulators, funders as well as publics) who must thereby adapt their interests and change their relations. As with SSK, ANT analysis traces the rhetorical, discursive and, indeed, semiotic qualities of these texts and demonstrations.

Also central in all this is the 'idiom' (Pickering, 1995; see also Callon, 2007; Nimmo, 2011) of performativity (Austin, 1962). For Austin, to make an utterance is both to intend that something comes about and to have some effect on one's interlocutor. In many ways, then, when ANT attends to the various forms of representation mentioned above, it is interested in the internal workings of these representations mainly insofar as these impact on what those representations can 'do'. As we have noted several times, what these representations do is, ideally, to serve in the enrolment of actors.

Now, in addition to the internal workings of representation, ANT is also attuned to the 'materiality' of these texts and demonstrations. The forging of relations of power (or 'associations' in ANT terms) entails both human and nonhuman elements. Not only must scientific texts be drafted, and scientific demonstrations performed and recorded, they must also be physically displayed, circulated, made available to audiences. These circulations are often managed by scientists: not only do they manipulate the materials of their experiments but they also organize meetings, encourage attendance, arrange chairs and use microphones and PowerPoint displays. These technologies also have their part to play in the relations of power involved in enrolment. The broader point here is that the meanings conveyed by scientists do not simply concern signification, they are also mediated materially: performativity is thus a heterogeneous process.

Flatness and Extension

In the preceding sections there is a singular lack of reference to the categories that routinely feature in the social sciences. No mention has been made of the roles of institutions, class or gender in shaping the efforts of scientists, or the reception of those efforts. Given Whitehead's comments on 'sociological society' this is only to be expected: we cannot presuppose 'the boundaries of the collective' as these need to be unpacked in the specificity of their making.

As we have seen, ANT generally eschews any assumptions about what goes into forging associations between actors. It is by engaging with the empirical specificity of the encounter between actors that we come to an understanding of its character – the elements that comprise it, and the outcome that follows. In this context, to draw on a set of pre-existing categories (e.g. class, gender, institutions or markets) is to be predisposed toward a particular type of analysis that cannot do justice to the nuance and complexity of the encounter. Indeed, it is to fall prey to Whitehead's 'fallacy of misplaced concreteness' defined as 'the accidental error of mistaking the abstract for the concrete' (Whitehead, 1926, p. 64). According to this, classes or institutions are not something concrete that can directly enter into and shape a particular event (of enrolment, say). Or to phrase this in terms of Karin Knorr Cetina's (1988) similar 'fallacy of unwarranted subsumption': we cannot assume 'the argument that once power relations (or structural relations) have been identified, we have discovered the underlying mechanisms which effectively control micro-social transactions, and said all there is to be said about these transactions' (p. 48).

So, as implied in the Whiteheadian notion of 'sociological society', these macrosociological categories are abstractions, constructed and deployed – we could say 'performed' – by the social. Indeed, such sociological categories are resources that actors routinely bring to bear in the course of their everyday interactions. For instance, people regularly deploy different versions of 'society' in managing their local exchanges with others (e.g. Bowers and Iwi, 1993), and it has been argued that some of these versions of society are, at least in part, derived from the social sciences (e.g. Giddens, 1984). In any event, ANT has roots in a lineage of microsociologies which place emphasis on the analysis of discrete occasions of local interaction as a way of grasping the production of social order. Now, there are various ways in which the shift from the 'micro' situation to the 'macro' society is theorized, and we shall explore some of these in relation to ANT in the chapters that follow. For present purposes, however, we can concentrate on the ways in which the microsociological tradition of ethnomethodology has played its part in ANT.

The term 'ethnomethodology' (e.g. Garfinkel, 1967; also Heritage, 1984) can be broken down into its two constituent parts. The 'ethno' refers to the commonsensical, the culturally local and distinctive, the folk: for instance, ethnomedicine connotes medicines and medical practices common to a particular social group. 'Methodology' reflects Garfinkel's observation that people engage in everyday 'methodological' problems: for example, they need to know when someone is being serious or ironic, lying or telling the truth. At base, then, ethnomethodology addresses the body of commonsense knowledge, and the various practical procedures by which people orient themselves to and act within routine social situations. Core to ethnomethodology is the view that dealing with everyday social circumstances is not shaped by a 'beyond' (class, gender, institutional conventions, or social norms) that animates the persons involved. Garfinkel's ethnomethodology was developed against the then predominant functionalist approach, which he regarded as treating people as social 'dopes'. This approach suggested that on entering a particular situation (a hospital, a classroom, an office), people adopted a particular role (a famous example is the 'sick role') and automaton-like followed the norms associated with it. By contrast, Garfinkel argued, people do not simply step 'into' a pre-existing situation, they also have a hand in defining that situation. Moreover, throughout their interactions 'in' that context, they are able to refine, redefine and repair it. Thus people do not mechanically follow norms; rather, people actively engage in such exchanges and reflexively attend to the situation as it unfolds, occasionally drawing on norms to reinforce or redirect the interaction. This way of thinking about social interaction continues to be discussed in con-temporary post-ANT, for instance, via the concept of 'contexting' (e.g. Asdal and Moser, 2012).

For ANT, however, the focus on the local encounter cannot be enough. After all, the point of ANT is to investigate the rise (and fall) of *networks*. On this score, Gabriel Tarde has been reclaimed as an ancestor of ANT. As Latour (2002, p. 122) puts it: 'Tarde can be said to have invented microhistory many decades before its discoverers, in the same way as he has invented ANT long before we had any inkling of what a network looked like.' Not only does Tarde argue for an integration of the nonhuman into the analysis of the social (predating Whitehead by 30 years); not only does he want to account for 'large' phenomena (e.g. social laws, social structures) by way of the small and the 'local' (prefiguring ethnomethodology by many decades); he is also interested in how local events tie up with one another. Latour draws on an example in Tarde: why does a young farmer hesitate in believing his own eyes that the sun, in descending below the horizon, is moving around the earth? It is because he is 'tied' to Galileo via what his school teacher taught him (Tarde calls this an 'imitative ray'). He is changed because he is *in possession* of new properties – 'knowledge' – derived from his prior relations with his teacher. This process of possession, of acquiring proper-ties through relations, is what builds up a network.

In the steps of this belated forebear, ANT scholars have also looked at the relations amongst actors as they are extended 'in' time and space. Or rather, they follow actors, objects and texts as they move around bringing seemingly distant actors closer together in the sense that divergent 'interests' come to complement one another (see above), and disparate practices become cohesive. Here, macrosocial entities do not reside 'beyond' the actors, animating them from above or below as it were; rather they are simply actors that have been resized, extended, enlarged. That is to say, as the 'interests' and the practices (or possessions, in Tarde's terminology) of more and more actors become aligned, so can they act as 'one' larger actor (see, for example, Barry and Thrift, 2007; also Chapter 7).

Method, Vocabulary, Analysis

How does ANT investigate the building of actor networks? One methodo-logical injunction has been to 'follow the actor' (Callon, 1986a; Latour, 1987).

As researchers we need to follow such actors as scientists as they go about making experiments, differentiating facts from artefacts, writing papers and reports, marshalling resources, translating interests, attributing agencies, arranging meetings, circulating texts, etc. This is all in keeping with ANT's roots in microsociology.

But what does all this following of actors yield? First, we need to be clear, actors need not be human. Indeed, Latour has often drawn on the term actant, derived from the semiotics of A.J. Greimas (e.g. 1983), as a way of stressing this (as well as showing how elements within a network become progressively more defined as that network takes shape). As we detail in the next chapter, there are a number of terms that attach to elements that mediate and/or are subject to translation within a network. However, here I simply want to note that the vocabulary that ANT deploys – actor, actant, association, *intermediary*, translation, obligatory passage point, hybrid, immutable mobile – aims to be an abstracted, neutral one. To be sure, the neutrality of these terms has been contested (see Chapter 5), but the reasoning behind such a terminology is clear: it serves in avoiding presuppositions over the 'what', 'who' and 'how' of network-building. What or who are the actants? How has an association been established? Who or what has been translated by 'whom' or to 'what'? We can only answer these questions once we have engaged empirically with the unfolding of an actor-network.

Bluntly, this terminology does not, or so it is claimed, predispose ANT accounts toward general (sociological) explanatory frameworks. The terms are simply 'vessels' for tracing out the complexity and detail of network-building. As such, ANT engages in ethnographic fieldwork to produce a version of 'thick descriptions' (Geertz, 1973) of the events into which its actors enter, and out of which they emerge.

The upshot is that ANT accounts aim to be stories full of detail. As Latour (1988b, p. 174) puts it:

> ... we have to write stories that do not start with a framework but that end up with local and provisional variations of scale. The achievement of such stories is a new relationship between historical detail and the grand picture. Since the latter is produced by the former, the reader will always want *more details,* not less, and will never wish to leave details in favour of getting at the general trend. ... Every time we deal with a new topic, with a new field, with a new object, the explanation should be wholly different. Instead of explaining everything with the same cause and framework ... we shall provide a one-off explanation, using a tailor-made cause.

On one level, all this can be read as falling in line with the long interpretive tradition in the social sciences in which the meanings that circulate within the social world are crucial to understanding it (we could also have pointed to the works of Shutz, Goffman or Cicourel). However, as we have hinted above, and shall see in detail in the next chapter, 'meaning' is itself reinterpreted so that it accommodates the role of the nonhuman.

Conclusion

In this chapter, we have attempted to locate ANT in relation to a number of intellectual lineages. However, as the latter parts of this chapter hint at, a pre-history is itself a performance – a means of reinforcing old, or establishing new, associations. And new forebears can be accumulated as new associations are made. Thus Tarde allows ANT to be represented as the inheritor of a tradition of sociology alternative to that of Durkheim. Recent alignments with the works of Gilles Deleuze and the American pragmatists, also serve to resituate (post-) ANT. All this goes to demonstrate again that ANT is a fluid beast, that has undergone, and is undergoing, many translations. This chapter serves mainly to orient the reader toward a limited number of historical lines that are entangled in early – or, what we shall call in the next chapter, 'classical' – ANT. As we shall see, many more lines will be gathered together and woven through ANT's subsequent unfolding.

3

'CLASSICAL' ACTOR-NETWORK THEORY

Introduction

In this chapter, we outline actor-network theory in its initial – 'classical' – iterations. In some ways this is not such a difficult task. There are a series of generally recognized 'key texts' that have been central in delineating the 'core' features of ANT. Having said that, and as noted in the previous chapter, ANT has been anything but static – its original advocates, as well as later spokespersons, have responded to a series of criticisms, and engaged in new empirical studies, that have nuanced and broadened ANT. The upshot is that drawing a line around 'classical' ANT is perhaps more difficult than might at first appear. In any case, there are enough divergences to suggest there will be no universal agreement over precisely what 'classical' ANT might be.

So, accepting that the 'classical' ANT presented here is inevitably a particular, contestable version, the advantage is that we can explicate a series of elements – not least, tenets – that distinguish ANT as an approach to the study of 'the social'. To delineate a 'classical' ANT will also allow us to trace, in the next chapter, how ANT has developed in reaction to numerous criticisms. This chapter also sets the scene for later discussions of how ANT maps onto several 'standard' sociological frameworks, and has been appropriated and applied by various disciplines and sub-disciplines. The present chapter will thus serve to highlight just how far ANT has travelled.

In what follows, we begin with a discussion of a number of key pre- or proto-ANT texts in which some of the key sensibilities of classical ANT were set out. We then discuss a range of writings through which ANT came to be formalized or systematized, and where the vocabulary familiar to the ANT stalwart took shape. In the rest of this chapter, we follow the last chapter's general schema, and move through the same five headings. In 'The Constructedness of Knowledge' we consider how ANT studies the ways in which scientific knowledge 'emerges' – that is, is rendered credible, durable, transportable – through agonistic processes that echo SSK, but also go beyond its social constructionism.

In the section 'The Role of the Nonhuman' we consider how nonhumans are attributed agency in the building of a network, but also how their 'stubbornness' or 'recalcitrance' can also undermine such network-building. Importantly, the extent of nonhumans' embroilment in the social means that our 'units of analysis' might need to change. The next section, 'Power and Representation', looks at the ways in which representation serves in the mediation of relations of power. For instance, we explore how particular discourses – or what John Law calls *'modes of ordering'* – affect who comes to be 'empowered' within an institution. In 'Flatness and Extension' we reiterate ANT's insistence that the social world needs to be understood as a flat network of associations, and focus specifically on the problem of network durability. What needs to be in place so that associations are kept in place? Finally, in the section 'Method, Analysis, Vocabulary' we look at some ANT methodological strategies, taking note of their partiality, and how this feeds the reluctance to provide explanations for – as opposed to descriptions of – networks.

ANT-in-the-Making

a. Laboratory Life

As a key text in the emergence of ANT, *Laboratory Life* (Latour and Woolgar, 1979) is an obvious place to start this introduction to 'classical' ANT. Based on a two-year study of Roger Guillemin's laboratory at the Salk Institute, in it we see ANT beginning to take shape. While there is little mention of translation, many elements of ANT are present in embryo. First, in contrast to the Sociology of Scientific Knowledge, the authors profess an 'interest in the details of scientific activity (as it) cuts across the distinction between "social" and "technical" factors' (p. 27). They 'want to pay attention to "technical" issues in the sense that the use by scientists of "technical" and "intellectual" terminology is clearly an important feature of their activity' (p. 27). To address this they do not wish to 'depend in any significant way on the uncritical use of the very concepts and terminology which feature as part of that activity' (p. 27). In these brief extracts we see that Latour and Woolgar wish to trace both how the 'technical' and the 'social' are resources for the scientists in the laboratory as they go about constructing their facts through arguments, texts and experiments, and how in tracing the use of these terms, they themselves do not resort uncritically to those very terms (for example, by privileging the role of 'social' in their accounts). This shift in emphasis to embrace both the 'social' and the 'technical' was perhaps most famously signalled in the second edition of *Laboratory Life* where the subtitle was changed from 'The Social Construction of Scientific Facts' to 'The Construction of Scientific Facts'.

Laboratory Life's case study entailed a process of making the laboratory appear ethnographically strange. In any case, it quickly became apparent that key to the doing of science is text: 'it strikes our observer that [the laboratory's] members are compulsive and almost manic writers ... [there] is the proliferation of files, documents, and dictionaries' (p. 48). The production of these texts is a matter of what the authors call 'literary inscription': 'The function of literary inscription is the successful persuasion of readers, but the readers are only fully convinced when all sources of persuasion seem to have disappeared. In other words, the various operations of writing and reading which sustain an argument are seen by participants to be largely irrelevant to "facts" ' (p. 76). In sum: a text is seen to contain a fact once readers no longer feel the need to interrogate how that text was put together; conversely, to question the processes of literary inscription by which a text was produced is to query its 'facticity'. The authors examine how inscription takes place in relation to such activities as the exchange of arguments at the lab bench (and the changing degree of certainty in the scientists' statements), through to the use of '*inscription devices*' such as bioassays or NMR spectrometers which generate inscriptions 'which can be used to write papers or to make points in the literature on the basis of a transformation of established arguments into items of apparatus' (p. 66).

Unsurprisingly, given the foregoing, a key theme in the analytic schema of *Laboratory Life* is that of 'agonism'. Scientists are involved in a struggle to ensure that their statements and arguments (about the little bit of world they are studying) are accepted as 'true'. Latour and Woolgar write: 'The solidity of the argument is always central to the dispute. But the constructed character of this solidity means that the agonistic necessarily plays a part in deciding which argument is the more persuasive' (p. 238).

This agonism reflects the position of scientists in what the authors call 'cycles of credit' in which the production of new facts yields credit (including resources) that allows investment for the production of further facts. 'If a scientist stopped doing new experiments, occupying new positions, hiring new investigators, and generating new statements, he [*sic*] would very quickly become a "has been." His grant money would be stopped, and, save for any tenured position or niche he had previously established for himself, he would be wiped out of the game' (pp. 229–30). But the scientist is not a free-standing agent, as it were. She is caught between the dual demands of the 'cycle of credit': she must be both an 'investor', 'continually obliged to reinvest if [she] does not want to lose [her] capital' and 'an employee constantly required to account for the money lent [her]' (p. 229). Put another way, she is embedded within different networks – those of funders, policy makers, regulators, and her own growing scientific networks. In this respect, any facts that she constructs must stand the test of these different networks. Or, to put it in Latour and Woolgar's terms: 'a network [is] a set of positions within which an object such as TRF [Thyrotropin Releasing Factor] has meaning, it is clear that the facticity of an object is relative only to a particular network or networks' (p. 107). These networks can be relatively 'large' – say composed of those – including the media – interested in science in some general way. Or they can be relatively 'small' – say comprising several thousand medical practitioners or a select handful of specialists associated with a particular sub-field of endocrinology. In other words, the scientist must orient toward various networks, if she is to establish the 'facticity' of her objects.

b. Pasteurization

This expansion of the scientist's network-building activities is brought into focus in Latour's (1983) famous chapter 'Give me a laboratory and I will raise the world'. In this piece, Latour wants to 'propose a simple line of enquiry: that is, to stick with the methodology developed during laboratory field studies, focusing it not on the laboratory itself but on the construction of the laboratory and its position in the societal milieu' (p. 143). As such, the boundary between the 'laboratory' and the outside world is assumed to be highly porous. Drawing on his case study of Pasteur's work on microbes (see also Latour, 1988a), Latour (1983, p. 143) writes:

> ... in the year 1881, the French semi-popular and scientific press is full of articles about the work being done in a certain laboratory, that of Monsieur Pasteur at the Ecole Normale Supérieure. ... journalists, fellow scientists, physicians and hygienists focus their attention on what is happening to a few colonies of microbes in different mediums, under the microscope, inside inoculated animals, in the hands of a few scientists. The mere existence of this enormous interest shows the irrelevance of too sharp a distinction between the 'inside' and the 'outside' of Pasteur's lab.

Now, this process of straddling the laboratory and the 'outside world' is not fortuitous or inevitable. And the 'interest of outsiders for lab experiments is not a given: it is the result of Pasteur's work in enrolling and enlisting them' (p. 143). How is this accomplished? By translating the interests of these 'outsiders' so that they conform with what Pasteur can do – namely, science. In 'The translation that allows Pasteur to transfer the anthrax disease to his laboratory in Paris. ... He takes only one element with him, the micro-organism, and not the whole farm. ... With the microbe, however, he also draws along with him the now interested agricultural societies. Why? Because having designated the micro-organism as the living and pertinent cause, he can now reformulate farmers' interests in a new way: if you wish to solve your anthrax problem you have to pass through my laboratory first' (p. 146).

As Latour traces, this translation remains weak not least because the ways in which the anthrax infection behaves are too disorderly. But Pasteur is able, through his laboratory techniques, to mimic that behaviour, firstly by 'reproducing epizootics in the lab' then 'varying at will the virulence of the microbes' (p. 148). With this comes a variation in scale: what the various actors (e.g. hygienists) concerned with anthrax are trying to do at the macro-scale of farms and herds, cities and countries, Pasteur is doing at the micro-scale of his laboratory. The hygienists are faced with the following translation: 'If you wish to understand epizootics and soon thereafter epidemics, you have one place to go, Pasteur's laboratory, and one science to learn that will soon replace yours: microbiology' (p. 149).

Still, the lab remains 'small' – Pasteur needs to move beyond the laboratory not least because those who are passing through his laboratory are unlikely to remain there. Though the farmers' interests are translated into those of Pasteur, they eventually must return to their farms. So Pasteur moves onto a larger scale, that of a field trial. In doing so, he is reinforcing the attention paid by farmers, but also others (veterinary scientists, hygienists, medics), and indeed 'France', who now, after the success of the trials, are part of a 'network much like a commercial circuit' (p. 152) through which Pasteur's laboratory products can move more or less unimpeded.

There are three key points we can draw from Latour's chapter. First, there is the dissolution of the inside and outside of science, replaced by 'long, narrow networks that make possible the circulation of scientific facts' (p. 167). Second, science plays havoc with differences of scale – it moves between the macro and micro, and it uses the micro to reshape the macro, while orienting toward the macro to affect the micro. Third, we cannot base our accounts of these transformations on the social sciences' usual 'categories and concepts' which 'reconstruct the "social context" inside which science should be understood' (p. 160). After all the microlevel of the laboratory serves to 'redefine and displace' (p. 158) the macrolevel of French society. It is microanalysis that best accesses the complex shifts between micro and macro-scales because it is here that we can trace how, for instance, 'the scientist doing lab experiments on microbes ... ends up modifying many details of the whole of French society' (p. 169).

c. The Big Leviathan

This view of the movement between scales finds more general expression in Callon and Latour's (1981) 'Unscrewing the big Leviathan'. Here, the idea of 'translation' receives a more detailed definition:

> By translation we understand all the negotiations, intrigues, calculations, acts of persuasion and violence, thanks to which an actor or force takes, or causes to be conferred on itself, authority to speak or act on behalf of another actor or force. 'Our interests are the same', 'do what I want', 'you cannot succeed without going through me'. Whenever an actor speaks of 'us', s/he is translating other actors into a single will. ... S/he begins to act for several, no longer for one alone. S/he becomes stronger. S/he grows. (p. 279)

In this definition we get a sense of the translational processes by which the individual actor grows: the more the number of successful translations, the larger the actor becomes. But translation also has a negative connotation – it diminishes competing actors, making them 'small and provisional in comparison' (p. 284).

To translate and recruit actors into one's own network is to disengage them from other networks which thereby shrink. Further, to translate another's interests into one's own, one needs to ensure that those translations, say into the procedures of a laboratory (as we saw with Pasteur above), are 'solid', robust, ideally so obvious that they are automatically accepted. Thus an 'actor grows with the number of relations he or she can put, as we say, in black boxes. A *black box* contains that which no longer needs to be reconsidered, those things whose contents have become a matter of indifference. The more elements one can place in black boxes – modes of thoughts, habits, forces and objects – the broader the construction one can raise' (pp. 284–5). A macro-actor is thus 'a micro-actor seated on black boxes, a force capable of associating so many other forces that it acts like a "single man" ' (p. 299).

Association is a key term in all this. In discussing the struggle between Electricité de France and Renault over the viability of an electric vehicle and its fuel cells (see below), Callon and Latour, ask 'Who will win in the end? The one who is able to stabilize a particular state of power relations by associating the largest number of irreversibly linked elements. What do we mean by "associate"? ... Two actors can only be made indissociable if they are one. For this their wills must become equivalent. He or she who holds the equivalences holds the secret of power' (p. 293). In sum, 'in order to grow we must enrol other wills [make durable associations] by translating what they want and by reifying this translation in such a way that none of them can desire anything else any longer' (p. 296).

Once more, Callon and Latour bypass the usual analytics of sociology to focus on the processes by which the 'growth' of actors is accomplished – how they translate more and more actors, craft more and more associations, collect more and more wills. Key to this 'growth' is rendering those translations and associations 'obvious' – black-boxed to the point where they cannot be problematized: 'Only the differences between what can be put in black boxes and what remain open to future negotiations are now relevant for us' (p. 285). This is a far cry from the usual practices of sociologists. Indeed, sociologists are translators in their own right 'using polls, quantitative and qualitative surveys [to translate] what [actors] are' (pp. 296–7). Callon (e.g. 1998a; see also Chapter 6) brings the same sensibility to bear on the discipline of economics. Suffice it to say here, that the methodological and analytic operations of sociology serve to prioritize the role of macrosociological factors (what above were called 'social contexts'). However, we can still deploy sociological analysis so long as it follows how 'actors can bond together in a block comprising millions of individuals ... enter alliances with iron, with grains of sand, neurons, words, opinions and affects. ... Sociology is only lively and productive when it examines all associations with at least the same daring as those actors who make them' (p. 292).

In this section, we have traced many of the elements of what subsequently became Actor-Network Theory. In the next section we see ANT find a fuller expression, not least through a systematization of its terminology and its underpinning principles.

Systematizing ANT

Taken as a whole, the systematization of 'classical' ANT has been a rather piecemeal affair (which is another way of saying there is not really a concerted systematization). Even so, there are a number of canonical texts that are key to any grasp of 'classical' ANT. Latour's *Science in Action* (1987) and *Reassembling the Social* (2005) are two such texts (and highly recommended). However, here I focus on a number of shorter texts that seem to me particularly helpful in setting out the main parameters of 'classical' ANT.

a. Tenets

As we noted above, an actor-network 'emerges' when a key actor successfully aligns a series of other elements that do that key actor's 'bidding'. Those elements are heterogeneous – they include both the human and the nonhuman. Crucially, that process of alignment is heterogeneous too – signs and materials are put into circulation, and experiments, technologies and texts 'shape' nature, technologies and people. For John Law (1986, 1987), this reflects a process of 'heterogeneous engineering' 'in which the stability and form of artifacts should be seen as a function of the interaction of heterogeneous elements as they are shaped and assimilated into a network' (Law, 1987, p. 113). Such networks are rarely easy to put together or sustain: 'heterogeneous engineering may be treated as the association of unhelpful elements into self-sustaining networks that are, accordingly, able to resist dissociation' (p. 114).

There are a number of points to draw out here. First, to reiterate, there is the heterogeneity of the network. This reflects, as Law points out, Michel Callon's (1986a) generalized principle of symmetry. This along with Callon's other two tenets extend the principles of SSK's Strong Programme (see Chapter 2) to address the issue of the heterogeneity entailed in the production of 'accredited' scientific or technical knowledge. The principle of *generalized symmetry* demands that the actor-network theorist analyses in the same way – using common analytic tools – the disparate elements that make up a network. For ANT this has entailed the use of an abstracted, neutral terminology that grasps the roles played, and the struggles between, those elements without prejudice (specifically without privileging the human over the nonhuman). This analytic eclecticism was reflected in Callon's remaining tenets. The principle of *generalized agnosticism* advocates impartiality with regard to what or who are embroiled within a particular controversy. Thus, in contrast to the Strong Programme's framework, not only should the human winners and losers of a controversy be subjected to equivalent forms of analysis, but so too should the nonhumans that are lined up on either side of a scientific or technological dispute. Finally, the tenet of *free association* refused any *a priori* distinctions between what could count as social, natural, or technological. These collapse into each other in innumerable combinations – and indeed are routinely mixed up by scientific and technological actors themselves as they go about the business of translating humans and nonhumans, and lining up materials, publics, funds, scientists, regulators, etc. into networks.

With this focus on the heterogeneity of scientific practice, it becomes more fruitful to speak of '*technoscience*' instead of science and technology separately. This is because, in Latour's (1987) hands, in the study of science – not least in the study of the laboratory science and the possibilities it offers to 'raise a world' (see above) – 'technoscience' directly addresses this heterogeneity. It helps to capture 'all the elements tied to the scientific contents no matter how dirty, unexpected or foreign they may seem' (Latour, 1987, p. 174). Of course, the building of networks is not confined to technoscience – after all, politicians, entrepreneurs, bureaucrats are no less intent on aligning others to their cause. But this heterogeneity is particularly elaborated for technoscience: insofar as it draws on a much broader array of entities it is especially potent in network-building (Latour, 1990).

The second point is that the 'precipitating' or 'animating' actor is not some sort of 'prime mover' behind the emergence of a network. This is not always as apparent as it could be in the corpus of early ANT writing. Nevertheless, we get hints of this in Latour's notion of technoscience: if other 'non-scientific actors' are busy building their own networks, it would not be surprising to find that bureaucrats, politicians or entrepreneurs sometimes attempt to recruit scientists into their particular networks. Law (1987, p. 113) is especially clear on this point. Both 'the *conditions* and the *tactics*' need to be taken into account when trying to work out how a particular technology (or scientific fact) came to be stabilized. He goes on to write that his study of the various elements (technological artefacts, skilled bodies, bits of nature) that contributed to Portuguese expansion in the fifteenth and sixteenth centuries involved following 'one system building effort – that of the Portuguese maritime planners'. As he notes, this is a matter of pragmatism, and a means to contain the analysis which could otherwise be extended indefinitely (as more and more elements are brought into the analysis). Specifically, for the sake of making his analysis manageable, he treats certain actors – 'system builders' – as 'givens' but this does not mean that they are 'primitive entities that are themselves unamenable to analysis. Just as vessels or navigators are fashioned out of the interaction between networks of forces, so too are heterogeneous engineers. ... [Even] the king of Portugal is just as much an effect as a cause' (p. 132). In sum, to the extent that the analytic narrative of ANT orients around a 'prime mover' this is a matter of convenience – a practical condition for rendering an account manageable. As we shall see in Chapter 4, this 'manageability' is not necessarily innocent.

A third point concerns the ways in which the filaments of a network are established and maintained. In Law's case study, communication between Lisbon and India could be maintained because a series of elements were in place. There were the rule books of navigation – these were stable and highly mobile. Yet these could only be followed if the right technologies such as the astrolabe were in place to apply those rules. In addition, the navigators had to be trained so that both document and device would be put to appropriate use. Law notes that each of these three elements – 'documents, devices and drilled people' (p. 254) – had to be aligned. However, each of these also had to be 'stabilized', that is 'black boxed' – 'placed in the right circumstances, fed the right inputs' (p. 254), each (and together) yield expected results (a measure of latitude).

In Law's account, the navigational network of which the above three elements were key was the result of the efforts a small Commission convened by King John II of Portugal in 1484. This had been charged with developing navigational methods that enabled travel beyond European waters. So, for this network, the King of Portugal and the Commission are 'primary actors'. They must draw together associations across a series of other elements to generate a network.

Now, how such associations are drawn might appear to differ in different circumstances, and indeed different epochs. In the circumstances of fifteenth-century Portugal, it might appear that the King and the Commission possess the power simply to forge ahead and construct their network (especially by 'obliging' their various human underlings). However, as Law documents (1987, pp. 128–9), such a process of 'forging' can rest on copious amounts of good fortune (through which various elements luckily fall into place). Equally importantly, as noted above, these 'primary actors' are themselves 'effects' – emerging from other networks. Moreover, as we noted in Chapter 2, the apparent potency of these actors cannot be attributed to their 'possession' of power. Both King and Commission are relatively small, yet the array of actors they must marshal in order to build their network is enormous. How do they go about the task of marshalling, or building the associations that allow the network to hang together? Here we turn to the processes of enrolment (and the various intervening steps).

b. Terminology

On this score, in two influential articles, Michel Callon (1986a, 1986b; see also, 1987) describes two case studies that he uses to lay out the process by which 'technoscientists' go about building their respective networks. I present thumbnail sketches of these en route to laying out Callon's particular account of ANT and its terminology.

First we have Callon's (1986a) study of biological researchers' attempts to persuade the fishing community of St Brieuc Bay that it should commit to the researchers' project of scallop farming. In this, the biologists ascribed a range of roles to the actors that they hoped would make up their projected network. The local fishermen's interests in scallop fishing were translated into interests in restocking the local scallop beds, and sustaining those beds through the various cultivation techniques being developed by the researchers. The scallops were also given roles: through the biologists' various scientific techniques they were represented as potentially 'farmable'. The wider scientific community also had a role to play – that of being in general agreement with the researchers' project and methods, of accrediting their technical competence and scientific expertise. The biologists thus represented themselves and their experiments as what the fishermen had to pass through in order to realize their (translated) interests. The biologists and their experiments comprised what Callon calls 'obligatory points of passage'. In other words, the farmers needed to offer up their consent and trust to the biologists if they were to realize their interests. As long as they supported the researchers, then the network held. This was no less the case for the scallops. As long as they played their role as cultivable within the technical system developed by the researchers, the network would hold. Unfortunately, in both cases the researchers were 'betrayed'. The levels of cultivated scallop larvae were simply not sufficient enough to signal persuasively either the success of the project, or the continued competence of the researchers. The fishermen also failed in their allotted roles: rather than continuing to subscribe to the long-term sustainability of the scallop beds, they over-fished. No longer could the biologists claim to represent the interests of the fishermen, their position as an obligatory passage point dissipated.

Callon's (1986b) second case study addresses the attempts of Electricité de France in 1973 to build an actor-network concerned with the development and construction of electric vehicles, with itself as the obligatory passage point. Electricité de France began by producing a plan which set out the necessity for an electric vehicle, a plan which allocated roles to a series of components that would feature centrally in its network. These included, for instance: the French public (who were represented as urban post-industrial consumers); French society (depicted as disillusioned with consumer society in general, and antagonistic toward the internal combustion engine in particular); the car manufacturer Renault that was to become devoted to building the chassis of the new electric vehicle; and the French government which would enthusiastically provide subsidies and a supportive regulatory environment for the development of the electric vehicle. Of course, Electricité de France also had to allocate roles to various nonhumans that needed to behave in certain ways if the electric vehicle network was to be viable: batteries, electrolytes, accumulators – all these had parts to play too. In pulling all these elements together as a network, Electricité de France was in effect describing a 'geography of obligatory passage points' through which all these elements had to pass. To combat pollution and the waste of consumer society, it was imperative to design and produce an electric vehicle; to develop an electric vehicle, new fuel cells capable of running it needed to be invented; the innovation of such fuel cells required experiments, experiments that were best carried out at the laboratories of Electricité de France; to conduct these experiments, Electricité de France needed the assent and support of the newly committed Renault and French government. As the *spokesperson* for the electric vehicle, Electricité de France also attempted to be the spokesperson for Renault, the government, the French public – that is, the translator of their interests – as well as for electrons and batteries. Importantly, Electricité de France's plan was put into operation through a number of activities, for example, circulating various texts (reports, surveys, memoranda, academic articles), and organizing and running various events (colloquia, meetings).

This allocation of roles to various prospective components of Electricité de France's network was also, as Callon demonstrates, a process of simplification, or *black-boxing*. The complexity of each was reduced, not least through their careful juxtaposition with one another: the public wants clean air, therefore France needs electric vehicles, thus Renault can best serve as a chassis builder, and all this is possible because we, Electricité de France, can produce a fully functional fuel cell. But these simplifications could not hold once it became apparent that Renault would fight hard to sustain its position as a major manufacturer of cars (it did not want to see its own extensive network contract), or that the French public might be more disposed toward better public transport, or that Electricité de France's scientists were struggling to discipline electrons and build workable fuel cells. In the end, Electricité de France's network collapsed when it turned out that the right sort of fuel cells were not attainable, and that Renault was full of canny technoscientists who could cleverly dispute Electricité de France's account of the desires of the French public and the trajectory of French society.

Callon provides a terminology that describes the various steps in the (attempted) building of an actor-network. First, an *actor* (which might be a composite like the three scientists of St Brieuc Bay, or Electricité de France) needs to 'interest' others in its project. This '*interessement*' implies 'actions by which [an actor] ... attempts to impose and stabilize the identity of other actors it defines through its *problematization*' (Callon, 1986a, pp. 207–8). So, questions are raised about the identities and interests of actors. The fishermen of St Brieuc Bay, or the farmers faced with anthrax, are represented as concerned with sustaining scallop stocks and protecting their animals, respectively. But (and here is the problematization), these actors cannot realize these identities and interests. What the technoscientists do is thus interpose themselves between the current unsatisfactory state of affairs and a future where interests can be satisfactorily realized. Clearly this entails the translation of interests and production of new associations. But it also involves a process of dissociation, that is, disconnection from those pre-existing associations that would detract from the technoscientists' project (and projected network): fishermen have to be dissociated from their usual fishing practices; Renault needs its identity as a major car manufacturer recast (which amounts to a disruption of all those associations that feed into that identity).

As we have seen repeatedly, others' interests are then translated: to deal with anthrax, you need to commit to Pasteur and his experiments; to realize French environmental aspirations, you need to support Electricité de France's experiments on fuel cells; to realize sustainable scallop stocks you need to back the three biologists' scientific work. Insofar as these actors take up these translated interests, they can be said to enrolled within the actor-network. That is to say, in each case, this *enrolment* orients toward the technoscientists – they are the *obligatory passage point* through which the translated interests attached to these new roles can be realized. However, as we have also noted, such enrolments are in need of maintenance: fishermen, car manufacturers, farmers can all be distracted, or become associated with other actors. Their consent to be in a network is always already contingent: it is not as if the technoscientist has power 'over' these enrolled actors – any such power is relational. In other words, the technoscientist must work at keeping the enrolled actor's (translated) interest. Callon suggests that this process can be thought through the notion of **displacement**: this term indicates the many means by which technoscientists go about directing information, people, materials, resources. Organizing meetings with key communities, setting up public experimental displays, establishing and reinforcing contacts with central actors such as administrators – all these serve in the maintenance of enrolments and the durability of a network.

Hopefully, the foregoing gives a reasonable sense of the flavour of 'classical' ANT. However, there are a number of additional concepts and sensibilities that also fall under this heading.

'The Constructedness of Knowledge'

In the foregoing we have seen that knowledge is constructed as a heterogeneous process (of engineering as Law would put it) and entails the marshalling of a panoply of human and nonhuman elements, each of which are ascribed particular roles. This ascription involves the translation of the 'interests' of those elements, a translation which rests on *associating* those elements to one another. For the fishermen of St Brieuc Bay to realize their interests, the scallops must 'learn' how to be farmed; for the scallops to be farmed, the fishermen must 'learn' to resist the temptation of fishing too enthusiastically. The crafting of these roles needs to be seamless: they need to appear unproblematic, self-evident. In other words, the work that goes into crafting such (relational) roles should become invisible – these elements need to be black-boxed, their inner workings hidden from view, with only their input and output visible.

Where does all the hard work of black-boxing take place? Latour suggests this happens primarily at '*centres of calculation*', such as laboratories. It is in this domain of the technoscientists that many heterogeneous components of the emergent network are brought together, combined and rendered into resilient representations. These representations can then be sent back out into the world, describing a network in which each element has its role to play and its relations to reproduce.

At centres of calculation 'specimens, maps, diagrams, logs, questionnaires and paper forms of all sorts' (Latour, 1987, p. 232) are collected and tied together as new 'compressed' two-dimensional representations. As Latour (1987, 1990) traces, the combinability of these elements through, say, the Cartesian coordinate system means that figures, graphs, numbers, tables can be merged into a single, simplified representation. Through such mechanisms the inscriptions of more and more events, and classes of event, are 'cascaded' and condensed into simpler and simpler inscriptions. Crucially, these increasingly simplified representations yield increasingly stable knowledge, that is, harder and harder facts. As Latour (1990, p. 38) illustrates, a measure such as the Gross National Product entails the 'cascading' of all manner of inscriptions: lists of receipts, tax returns, company records, ministerial reports, all processed and combined. In this way, it also becomes possible to 'talk about the economy of a nation by looking at "it" ' where the 'it' has become black-boxed, and all the work that has gone into constructing 'it' has become hidden.

Now, knowledge is not only stabilized through these cascades of inscriptions but also becomes more and more resilient – there are greater and greater costs for those who would wish to problematize the representation at the end of a cascade of simplifications. We shall return to the issue of representation below. Here however, we can summarize by noting that knowledge – as something that is stabilized, resilient, credible – rests, in part, on complex practices of representation that take place in 'centres of calculation'. However, whether such knowledge can hold, that is, whether it conveys some 'reality', depends on whether it can withstand 'trials of strength' (Latour, 1987) – 'whatever resists is real' (Latour, 1988a, p. 158). The practices of representation might afford advantages in trials of strength, but this requires certain skilled bodies that read condensed inscriptions in the 'correct' way (as we saw in John Law's account of Portuguese navigation), and where those bodies are not disciplined, then, as we have seen in Callon's cases studies, technoscientific inscriptions can collapse catastrophically.

'The Role of the Nonhuman'

The role of the nonhuman is central to ANT. As we saw in the last chapter, this draws on philosophical perspectives which regard the events that comprise social life as necessarily inhabited by all manner of nonhuman (as well as human) elements. On this score, the processes by which scientific knowledge becomes 'true', or, for that matter, technological artefacts come to be seen as 'working', are a subset of processes by which the 'social' world in general is constituted.

a. Necessary Nonhumans

So, for Latour (Latour and Strum, 1986; Latour and Johnson, 1988; Strum and Latour, 1988; Latour, 1992), what is distinctive about human societies is the necessary co-presence of nonhumans: 'We are never faced with objects or social relations, we are faced with chains which are associations of humans (H) and nonhumans (NH)' (Latour, 1991, p. 110). However, we should not essentialize humans and nonhumans – they are relational. They emerge as the effects of networks: each is subject to the ways in which these networks are heterogeneously engineered, and thus each is composed of particular admixtures of humans and nonhumans. Any specific human individual or collectivity, any given technological artefact or system, has resulted from the configurations of associations that draw in both the human and nonhuman.

Now, we have seen how in the making of actor-networks, processes of translation, association and enrolment need to be wrought. Drawing associations across human and nonhuman actors involves a variety of exchanges that might be material as well as social, physical as well as semiotic. Akrich and Latour (1992; see also Akrich, 1992) discuss the '*sociomateriality*' of associative processes by rethinking the idea of 'meaning' so that it can encompass the human and nonhuman. In this respect they expand the idea of semiotics so that it becomes:

> The study of how meaning is built, [where] the word 'meaning' is taken in its original nontextual and nonlinguistic interpretation: how a privileged trajectory is built, out of an indefinite number of possibilities; in that sense, semiotics is the study of order building or path building and may be applied to settings, machines, bodies and programming languages as well as texts. (p. 259)

A key phrase here is 'how a privileged trajectory is built, out of an indefinite number of possibilities': when one studies a network one is seeking to understand 'how a privileged trajectory is built' through heterogeneous processes of translation and association.

The part played by technological nonhumans in the building of a privileged ordering reflects both their emergence from, and their position in, particular actor-networks. Latour notes that the many technological artefacts with which we cohabit are often invisible to us. They do their job quietly and unobtrusively, at the same time facilitating all manner of privileged orderings. Latour (1992) tells us that technical objects have been designed to do certain jobs because they can do them more efficiently and effectively than humans, who inconveniently require training, supervision, surveillance and discipline. By comparison, technological artefacts barely need any oversight. The functions once carried out by tiresomely needy humans are 'ex-corporated' out of people and in-corporated into efficient, uncomplaining technological artefacts. In the process new paths are built: the technologies require new skills and capacities of their users.

To clarify, let us draw on one of Latour's (1992) illustrations, that of the door-closer or groom (the mechanism, affixed by an articulated arm to door and wall, which slowly closes the door without slamming). This replaces what might have once been a porter or a concierge, and at a stroke gets rid of all the inconvenience that such human figures imply. Yet, 'inscribed' (Akrich, 1992) in these technologies are particular '*scripts*' or rules of use: in order to get them to 'work', particular capacities and skills need to be in place. In other words, human comportment needs to adapt to the demands of the technology. In the case of the door groom, its hydraulic mechanism might be such that particular levels of strength and mobility are necessitated.

So, here we have what would appear to be a 'physical translation' of the user: in order to get through this door, this is how you must use your body. This process of shaping of bodily comportment has been called *prescription* or *proscription* (cognate terms include affordance and allowance). At base, these technological artefacts act as 'conduits' of morality or politics. By prescribing what is do-able in order to realize one's goals through the 'use' of a technology, that technology can enable some users, but discriminate against others.

However, the prescriptions and proscriptions associated with technological artefacts are not always faithfully followed. Akrich (1992) documents that the photoelectric lighting kits that were made available in French Polynesia, while prescribing certain actions, had features that were not appreciated by users (to protect the battery, the current would cut off when the battery ran low; or the current would be switched on to avoid overcharging the battery). Akrich suggests that the design of the kits entailed a 'grooming' of the user: the kits enacted 'a set of rewards and punishments that is intended to teach proper rules of conduct' (pp. 218–19). Given that the battery's charge could not be easily determined, for its users, the kits' 'actions' – indeed 'sanctions' – seemed arbitrary and its users 'denounced it and expressed their displeasure every time the system cut off the current while they were quietly sitting watching television. The electrician, who quickly became tired of doing repairs in the evening, tricked the system by installing a fused circuit in parallel with the control device. When the control device shut off the current, users could bypass it with the fuse' (p. 219). The point is that in spite of all the prescriptions built into a technology, it can nevertheless be undermined or subverted. Or to put this another way, the designers of technological artefacts cannot fully determine the goals and uses that attach to their technologies – these are not always predictable or 'prescribable'. To draw on Latour's phrase: 'we are exceeded by what we create' (1996b, p. 237) – the stuff we produce often has consequences beyond what could be predicted.

b. Hybrids

In Latour's account of the door groom we have a picture of the constitutive embroilment of the human and the nonhuman. Strip a person – a doctor, a teacher, a factory worker, a politician, a scientist – of their technologies and they cannot operate as such. As Law (1994) has noted, remove a manager's technologies whether 'high' (mobile telephone, computer, smart printer, data projector) or 'low' (desk lamp, desk, chair) and she is no longer a manager. Put another way, perhaps we need to change our units of analysis from 'human' and 'nonhuman' to 'hybrids'. For Latour (1993a, 1994), hybrids are everywhere – indeed they always have been – and are proliferating at an accelerating rate. The problem is that we 'moderns' have been blind to them, attached as we have been to what Latour has called the 'Modern Constitution'. This Modern

Constitution, which has its roots in seventeenth-century debates over the standing of empirical science (Shapin and Schaffer, 1985), keeps distinct – 'purifies' – on the one side, subjects, values, beliefs (the domain of politics) and on the other, the natural, the objective (the domain of science). Latour's contention is that this divide, this *purification*, is peculiar to a particular historical, 'modern', moment that has detracted from our '*amodernity*', that is our chronic immersion with nonhumans and our constitutive hybridity. Importantly, this purification is reproduced by science, even as it constantly traverses the human and nonhuman in the process of building its networks and ensuring its 'objectivity'. Such purification, while constantly enacted, say in the media (with its compartmentalization of news as 'about' politics, versus science, or technology versus morality), is under pressure. In light of the contemporary proliferation of hybrids – frozen embryos, sensory-equipped robots, gene synthesizers, nanobots – it becomes harder and harder to sustain the divide between the natural and the social, the scientific and the political.

One implication of this erosion of the Modern Constitution is that we have become sensitized to the mundane hybridities that have always inhabited the 'amodern' everyday world. In hybrids, human and nonhuman components exchange properties, mutually translate one another, shift their capacities. Latour illustrates this process through the example of the citizen-gun. In contrast to both right-leaning views that it is 'people that kill', and left-leaning views that 'it is guns that kill', Latour argues that bringing gun and person together yields a new hybrid – 'the citizen-gun' – with its new associations, emergent goals, unfolding translations. Both gun and person have mutually become something different – it is this new entity that needs to be evaluated, not subject or object separately. Latour (1993b, p. 6) writes:

> The dual mistake of the materialists and of the sociologists is to start with essences, either those of subjects or those of objects. ... Neither the subject, nor the object, nor their goals are fixed for ever. We have to shift our attention to this unknown X, this hybrid which can truly be said to act.

In summary, in this section we have traced some of the means by which technologies have been chronically influential in shaping humans (our comportments, behaviours, bodies, social relations), even as these technologies have been shaped by humans (engineers, designers). Our longstanding neglect of technology's role in making society is, according to Latour, down to our embeddedness within the Modern Constitution. It is the technoscientific proliferation of hybrids that sensitizes us to this constitutive role of technology in society (also see Waldby, 2000).

'Power and Representation'

In the preceding sections we have seen how actor-networks are constituted through the circulation of certain texts and materials. To render associations, to translate interests, to enrol elements, an actor must engage with them. Through processes of interessement, problematization and displacement actors are 'persuaded' to pass through the main actor who acts as an obligatory passage point. Crucial to these moments of 'persuasion' is the centre of calculation at which are generated the two-dimensional texts which characteristically entail cascades of simplification and combination, and thereby resist criticism. Because of these qualities of semiotic resilience, Latour (e.g. 1987) has called these texts *immutable mobiles*: their meanings tend to remain stable, and they are highly transportable. Again, power here is distributed because, for all their immutability, these texts must still undergo *trials of strength*. It is not difficult to imagine how one immutable mobile can be confronted with another: Electricité de France's plan is juxtaposed to Renault's report, and some of the simplifications so carefully crafted in the former (e.g. the desires of the French public, the prospects of a viable fuel cell) are unravelled and undermined by the counter-simplifications in the latter. As Law (1994) notes, the immutability of these mobiles is not guaranteed; as with the technologies with their embodied scripts, immutable mobiles can be purposefully misread – it all depends on the state of the network into which they have been entered and through which they circulate.

Of course, representation (to recall, understood performatively) does not simply take the form of text or technology – it also circulates as talk (though this tends to be less durable, see Law, 2009). In Law's (1994) ethnographic study of Daresbury Laboratory he pays particular attention to the discourses that circulate within the organization). Thus he traces how Daresbury's participant actors drew on a number of distinct discourses in trying to characterize the organization as a whole (along with its history). For instance, there was an 'evolutionary' discourse in which Daresbury is characterized in terms of 'a reasonable and unfolding evolution of scientific and technical concerns moderated more or less by financial constraints and the need to maintain the Laboratory on an even keel in a difficult world' (p. 55). This discourse performs Daresbury as an organization that is bureaucratic and measured. By contrast, the 'heroic' discourse enacts Daresbury as emergent from discontinuous processes of struggle in which 'heroic' characters play a major part. Accordingly, 'Heroism told of the way the Laboratory had gone through good periods and bad. And, most of all, it talked of revolutionary change and the role in such revolutionary change of crucial individuals' (p. 56). These were not the only discourses (Law also identifies visionary and charismatic ones), but they all contribute as 'ordering resources for working on and making sense of the networks of the social. ... They shape (and are embodied in) action' (p. 71).

For Law, these discourses can be regarded as elements in the *modes of ordering* by which Daresbury comes to be shaped in both its stability and fluidity (see below). Here I focus on Law's account of the way that these discourses feature in the enactment of hierarchies. He notes that in the commission of a new linear accelerator, scientists excluded technicians, much to the latter's chagrin. This was 'managed' through the physicists' discourse which performed 'a version of vocational stories of hierarchy ... between creative puzzle-solvers on the one hand, and those who are passive, uncreative and unskilled on the other' (p. 123). As such, the technical crew were being discursively situated into roles that were comparatively restricted. To be sure, as Law documents, the members of the technical crew were not happy about this 'translation', but they nevertheless seemed to accept it. Or rather, they had available alternative discourses that dissociated them from Daresbury. Unlike the physicists whose associations bound them tightly to Daresbury ('they tell of wanting to excel in their science and engineering' – p. 125), for the technical crew, achievement and agency are not to be sought in their role as employees of Daresbury. Drawing on what might be termed discourses of desire, in which their aspirations are performed as lying elsewhere, work becomes a means to something else, something more valuable. In the case of the leader of the technical crew, this 'something more valuable' is linked to the project of becoming the skipper of a boat. This means that he must 'work, at least for a time, to sustain this project. So he sits at the controls [at Daresbury] ... and performs a kind of hierarchy' (p. 126).

What we see here is how discourses serve in the microprocesses of power, specifically in the enactment of hierarchy within a particular network, that of Daresbury. However, as hinted in the above account of multiple discourses (and modes of ordering), even an apparently singular entity such as the Daresbury Laboratory is evidently multiplicitous. We shall elaborate on this point in future chapters where we tackle the issue of the 'multiple ontologies' that comprise 'networks' (though, as a result, the term 'network' itself becomes problematic). What is immediately pertinent is that Law's analysis foregrounds the complex ways in which the durability of networks – above linked to hierarchy – is accomplished. In this respect, discourse is only one means by which durability is established, and other elements are often more potent than discourse simply because they can have greater longevity (e.g. the *sociomaterial* organization of spaces within Daresbury). We turn to this issue of durability in the next section.

'Flatness and Extension'

Actor-network theory is renowned, even notorious, for its in-principle eschewal of macrosocial scientific categories. It was noted above how ANT scholars are not interested in explaining social ordering through an exclusive focus on social processes – these too must be analysed. What ANT aims to show is how the non-social (or rather, the 'non-sociological' social) and the nonhuman are central to social ordering. Moreover, in ANT there are tools for treating social ordering as a process of 'extension'. So, instead of holding that an 'external factor' such as class or gender, however subtly or reflexively (see Chapter 5) deployed, is 'responsible' for this or that social ordering (e.g. patterns of food preference, schoolroom behaviour, or everyday violence), ANT aims to trace how such 'external factors' might themselves emerge. As such it focuses on the associations forged amongst network elements and the ways in which these can eventuate as such 'external factors'. On this score, it is also important to keep in mind how the work of sociologists (with their surveys, studies and graphs – see above) also operate to establish the 'facticity' of these 'external factors'. For ANT 'external factors' are not, of course, external in the sense of lying somehow above or below the relations amongst actors. Rather, they are particular representations of the social deployed in the processes of problematization, interessement, translation, enrolment and so on, that serve in establishing associations amongst actors. Here, the spatial metaphor is less one of 'depth' in which social phenomena are animated by 'factors' that lie beyond their plane, as it were, and more one of flatness and extension in which phenomena are composed of associations extended on a single plane.

In light of this formulation of social ordering in terms of flattened, extended networks, an obvious question is: how are the actors that make up these networks held in place? Flatly, how do networks endure? How are networks rendered durable? Durability denotes the continuation of a network: such a network is comprised of actors whose roles are 'stabilized', of black boxes which remain firmly closed, of immutable mobiles that are indeed immutable, of associations that resist betrayal. In tackling durability, Callon (1991) draws out a number of conceptual tools, in particular, intermediaries, actors and *convergence*. For Callon 'intermediary' refers to 'anything passing between actors which defines the relationship between them' (p. 134). Intermediaries can take on myriad forms, including 'scientific articles, computer software, disciplined human bodies, technical artefacts, instruments, contracts and money' (p. 134). And they are crucial to the composition of the network insofar as 'they define and distribute roles to humans and nonhumans' (p. 137). Now, intermediaries are themselves, not unexpectedly, networks. They are heterogeneous – hybrid – admixtures of such elements as artefacts, texts, human bodies. For instance in many durable networks – such as a university or a hospital – there is the circulation of forms, physical or online, that measure and review people's performance. These are 'textual' – made of particular, often black-boxed categories; but they are 'physical' too – limited by paper size (Bowker and Star, 1999), the parameters of an online system, or the timings within which they must be completed; and they entail 'humans' – forms are intimately attached to advisors, supervisors, reviewers. As they move they serve in the (continued) delimitation of associations and the distribution of roles (between, say, 'advisor' and 'advisee', or 'supervisor' and 'supervisee'), a delimitation and distribution that can tend toward standardization and normalization (Callon, 1991, p. 151).

In the wake of this definition of intermediaries, we might ask: what then is an actor? While, an actor can be defined as 'any entity able to associate texts, humans, nonhumans and money' (Callon, 1991, p. 140), this does not seem so different from Callon's 'intermediary'. For Callon, the division between 'actor' and 'intermediary' lies in the former's capacity for 'authorship'. As such, actors 'conceive, elaborate, circulate, emit or pension off intermediaries'. Simply put, 'an actor is an intermediary that puts other intermediaries into circulation' (p. 141) and therefore 'the division between actors and intermediaries is a purely practical matter' (p. 141). It is through empirical investigation that we can identify who/what is acting as an actor, or serving as an intermediary. Such actors can take many forms: individual humans, nonhumans, groups, institutions – all these can be actors and the empirical task is to trace how they have 'put other intermediaries into circulation'. Having noted all this, Latour (2005a) develops the idea of the 'intermediary' in contrast to that of the *'mediator'*. Where the former captures the ways in which meaning can be faithfully conveyed in the forging of associations, the latter addresses the ways in which meanings are reconfigured as they are passed along, thereby proliferating and complexifying associations (as opposed to simply reproducing them).

Clearly, Callon's framing of network-building in terms of actor and intermediary raises the thorny question of 'agency'. Does this definition of actors as 'authors' – a definition that includes nonhumans – mean that they 'possess' agency, that actors have a capacity to make wilful interventions in 'social' processes? Complex and convoluted arguments have been made in relation to the formulations of agency in ANT (and post-ANT's subsequent refinements), formulations which are essentially 'distributive' ('agency' is associated with an actor's heterogeneous composition or 'network-ness') and 'attributive' ('agency' is something that is ascribed to actors, rather than 'possessed' by them). I will reserve discussion of this until the next chapter where we will see how the lines of debate have been drawn up, and how the issue of agency has played itself out.

For now, I want to discuss how the relation of actor to intermediary, and of author to circulation, is instrumental in making actor-networks durable. In this respect, Callon (1991) develops the notion of 'convergence'. This refers to the ways that the elements in a network – elements which might be marked by dramatic difference and divergence – nevertheless 'work together'. If the roles of all these heterogeneous elements can be rendered complementary – that is, they can be ascribed, aligned and harmonized – then the network of which they are a part becomes durable. An institution such as Daresbury Laboratory can be stable if its elements – physicists, technicians, managers, accountants, buildings, linear accelerators and so on – all do their ascribed jobs. Indeed, with an 'appropriate' degree of convergence and coordination, an institution such as Daresbury can itself become a durable cogent actor, affecting and effecting other networks (say in relation to industry or government). However, as we have seen with Law's account of hierarchy above, what counts as 'appropriate' convergence in the making of durable networks can be rather fluid, and a matter of empirical investigation. In the next chapter, we will see how networks can hold fast, despite what appear to be all manner of internal 'divergences' or 'multiplicities'.

Callon also goes on to suggest that the complication of a convergent network can work to its advantage. As he writes: 'the more numerous and heterogeneous the interrelationships the greater the degree of network co-ordination and the greater the probability of resistance to alternative trans-lation' (p. 150). For such highly complicated networks, arrays of associations can become increasingly densely bundled together. The tight coupling and knotting of associations that this entails means that to attempt to reconfigure any one association, or to reshape a particular role, is likely to be costly because it will be unlikely to be effective: any change is likely to require the simultaneous reworking of many associations. Thus, changing any one ele-ment, by virtue of its thoroughgoing interconnectedness, would require a major intervention, and the upheaval of a generalized retranslation of the net-work as a whole. The upshot is that such networks are likely to be resistant to such meddling. To return to our example of the durable networks of hospitals or universities, to question the value, utility or role of performance review is simultaneously to problematize the roles of manager, supervisor, advisor, doc-tor, administrator, lecturer, cleaner, security personnel, programmer. If all these roles are 'convergent', and assuming that the performance review form serves in the delineation of these roles, such a question will likely be dismissed, even incomprehensible.

Callon (1991) proposes that these convergent networks can become irre-versible. If the forms of performance review can become standardized, then they can routinely delineate the roles present in a university or hospital net-work. This is undergirded by normalization in which, in our case, the rules pertaining to performance review, such as the design of forms themselves, the timing of their implementation, their generalized application across staff and so on, 'become constraining norms which create and control deviance' (p. 151). To the extent that a network is 'irreversibilized' it acts as a black box that behaves predictably – generating specifiable outputs from given inputs. As a black box, it can associate with other black boxes; that is, it can become an element in another network. In that respect it can be said to be 'punctualized' and thus become 'an entire network [that is] a single point or node in another network' (p. 153). Conversely, as the local standardized mechanisms (forms, timetables, roles) of performance review begin to move from one network to another – from hospital to university, from corporations to local government institutions – these become punctualizations within a large network, or what has been called 'Audit Society' (Power, 1999). Here, again, we are witness to the 'flattened and extended' transition from the microsocial to macrosocial, from local practices to social epoch.

'Method, Analysis, Vocabulary'

Let us begin this section with the issue of vocabulary. ANT has been couched in highly abstracted terms. The aim of this is to ensure that no assumptions are made about what can 'fill' them. Concepts which address the components of networks, concepts such as actor, mediator, intermediary, immutable mobile or hybrid, do not give much of a clue as to what can actually serve as an actor, mediator, intermediary, etc. Similarly, concepts which address the processes out of which networks emerge and are sustained – problematization, enrolment, translation, ordering, prescription, circulation, convergence – do not tell us much about what can count as an example of such processes. This is because what can fill these categories is a matter of empirical investigation. The fundamental point of ANT is that no *a priori* assumptions – especially those which privilege either 'natural' or the 'social' factors – are made about what has gone into the emergence of this or that network (and the associated production of 'facts' and 'falsehoods'). As Latour (1987, p. 258) sets out in his Rules of Method:

> *Rule 3* Since the settlement of a controversy is the cause of Nature's representation, not its consequence, we can never use this consequence, Nature, to explain how and why a controversy has been settled. ...

> *Rule 4* Since the settlement of a controversy is the cause of Society's stability, we cannot use Society to explain how and why a controversy has been settled. We should consider symmetrically the efforts to enrol human and non-human resources. ...

> *Rule 5* We have to be as *undecided* as the various actors we follow as to what technoscience is made of; every time an inside/outside divide is built, we should study the two sides simultaneously and make the list, no matter how long and heterogeneous, of those who do the work.

How then does a practitioner of ANT empirically access the ways in which networks are manifested. Taking a leaf out of the Sociology of Scientific Knowledge, a key methodological tactic is to focus on those networks when they are relatively weak – either in the early stages, when the efforts at enrolment are still in process, or when there is some sort of crisis within the network as seemingly faithful elements do not do what they are 'supposed to'. As Latour (1987, p. 258) puts it in relation to technoscientific networks: 'Rule 1 We study science in action and not ready made science or technology; to do so, we either arrive before the facts and machines are blackboxed or we follow the controversies that reopen them.' Akrich (1992) echoes these points in relation to technology when she comments: 'The difficulty with vocabulary is the need to avoid terms that assume a distinction between the technical and the social' (p. 206) and 'The methodological problem is that ... We need to find disagreement, negotiation and the potential for breakdown' (p. 207; see also Latour, 1996a).

If these methodological recommendations facilitate our entrée into the workings of a network, what do we do once we get there? We describe. As we have seen above, Latour (1988b) is not especially interested in deriving grand causal explanations – we produce a *description* of what is happening in order to get a handle on the specific role the different elements are playing. Causality here is highly localized and contingent on the particular state of a network. In a similar vein, Callon (1991) writes:

> Some will say I have offered a method for describing [networks] ... but not a theoretical framework for their explanation. ... Talk of explanation assumes that network evolution can be described using a small number of variables or concepts. But this requires a very strong assumption about the shape of the network and the convergence of its translations. ... But anyone who looks for explanations ... will learn nothing about the mechanisms by which irreversibility is created ... to search for laws and regularities is to overlook the way in which networks are not in actors, but are produced by them. And they ignore the way in which networks only stabilize at certain places and at certain times. (pp. 154–5)

As any ethnographer knows, description is not a transparent process. In the field, the elements that are encountered can rapidly proliferate out of control. How does one draw boundaries so that one can make some sort of judgement between that which is 'relevant' and that which is not? Callon (1991, p. 149) suggests that in seeking to demarcate a network, those elements that 'weaken [its] alignment and coordination – that is the convergence' can be regarded as lying outside it. Even looking 'within' a network, there are challenges as to what it is necessary to describe: if every actor is a network too, to what extent does one unpack this 'network-ness'? Callon and Law (1995) discuss this in relation to '*hybrid collectifs*', a version of actor-networks broadly defined as 'relations. Links. Interpenetrations. Processes. Of any kind' (p. 486). They suggest that, in the end, it is a matter of taste (and, we might add, practicality) as to the variety, the number and the length of associations that are described. That is to say, in an actor-network 'analysis' some associations will feature more prominently, and in more detail, than others. In some ways this is inevitable simply because of the empirical access granted, or available to, the actor-network analyst. As John Law (1994) once put it in relation to his study of Daresbury, 'I had a terrible anxiety about being in the right place at the right time. Where I happened to be, the action was not' (p. 45).

The point is that to engage empirically with 'a' network is to confront the partiality of that engagement. As we shall see, this partiality reflects not simply empirical exigency (what one can or cannot access), but also the 'interest' and the 'situation' of the researcher which serves to emphasize some elements over others (which are thereby occluded to some degree or other). Privileging and othering are chronic dimensions of all research practice, and in what follows we shall see how ANT has been accused of neglecting these dimensions of its practice (see Chapter 4), but also how, in later post-ANT guises, it has responded to these criticisms creatively (see Chapter 7).

Conclusion

In this chapter, I have set out some of the key elements (and there are several that have been missed for ease of exposition – for instance, Callon's early notion of 'actor worlds') in what I have called 'classical' ANT. As noted, this is hardly a satisfactory moniker. The term 'actor-network theory' can be disputed, and Law (2009), for example, sees ANT as a sub-set of practices that fall under the broader category of '*material semiotics*' (which encompasses the work of Donna Haraway, for instance). Like ANT, but with a wider range of tools, material semiotics studies the 'enactment of heterogeneous relations that produce and reshuffle all kinds of actors, including objects, subjects, human beings, machines, animals, "natures," ideas, organizations, inequalities, scale and sizes, and geographical arrangements' (p. 141). Further, 'classical' is problematic too not least because, from its earliest days, ANT has been in process as new associations were forged in response to various criticisms, complexifying ANT in numerous ways. We turn to a number of these critiques and complications in the next chapter.

4

CRITIQUES, CONCERNS AND CO-PRODUCTIONS

Introduction

To the extent that ANT could be said to have taken on a 'classical' form, this was even at the outset accompanied by a series of concerns, commentaries and criticisms. At one end of a notional scale of critique, there were those reactions that were outrightly hostile, questioning ANT's fundamental premises, notably, the pivotal role allocated to the nonhuman and its indifference to standard sociological analytic categories. At the other end of the scale were relatively friendly rebukes which accepted ANT's key tenets while querying, for example, the nature of the associations that 'held' a network together – did translations really need to be so solid and convergent? In between were accounts that pointed to major shortcomings while nonetheless sympathetic to the general thrust of ANT: for example, ANT routinely relegated the role of culture, or failed to reflect on its neglect of the 'other'.

These more or less critical engagements with 'classical' ANT arose in a variety of ways: through comparison to alternative intellectual traditions (e.g. the works of Deleuze and Guattari); through empirical case studies for which ANT's accounts seemed inadequate; or in light of political anxieties about ANT's capacities to redress the partiality of both its networks and its analyses. Needless to say, these were often mixed up. In any case, in order to manage the complexity of both the criticisms and the sources of those criticisms, the chapter will follow the format of preceding chapters and use the same headings as before. In 'The Constructedness of Knowledge' we ask: is the 'facticity' of knowledge really settled through trials of strength? And can expert knowledge be 'uncertain' yet still central to a durable network? In 'The Role of the Nonhuman' we consider the legitimacy of giving 'voice' or attributing 'agency' to nonhumans. Further, how might ANT deal with the ostensible variations of 'a' nonhuman across networks? In 'Power and Representation' we address ANT's treatment of patterns of inclusion and exclusion of actors from a network. In 'Flatness and Extension' we reflect on the limitations of ANT's account of extension. In 'Method, Analysis, Vocabulary' we discuss the supposed neutrality of ANT's terminology, as well as the status of its analytic accounts.

Yet again, these headings are barely satisfactory but they serve the heuristic purpose of allowing us both to pinpoint a number of key criticisms of ANT and frame subsequent developments in what we shall call post-ANTs. In keeping with this, I end the chapter with an extended discussion of 'agency'. Not only has 'agency' been a hot topic of debate in relation to the value of ANT, it also spans the different headings (e.g. the agency of nonhumans, the agency of some humans versus others, the agency of the ANT analyst, etc.).

'The Constructedness of Knowledge'

In the previous chapter we explored the ways that 'classical' ANT accounted for the production of scientific knowledge. We noted the ways in which a number of elements needed to be in place for 'accredited' knowledge successfully to emerge and stabilize. The interests of various human actors had to be translated; the process of translation and enrolment was mediated, in part, by resilient representations; these representations were rendered resilient both because of their internal structure and because they were victorious in trials of strength with alternative versions of the relevant bit of the world; human and nonhuman actors had to be enrolled into the network as promoted by a key actor linked to a centre of calculation; the convergence of the various elements of a network afforded it durability; the extensiveness of a network as it is described by an analyst is potentially unending.

In relation to 'the constructedness of knowledge', we can abstract from these various elements a nexus of overarching motifs that structure this early enactment of ANT. First, as mentioned above, there is the motif of 'agonism' – to build a network is a matter of struggle, 'persuading' (problematizing, translating, enrolling) others, not least through 'trials of strength'. Second, there is a motif of 'centre and periphery': scientists have a series of tools to hand that afford them a peculiar advantage – they have laboratories (centres of calculation) and from these they send out textual intermediaries (immutable mobiles) that are crucial to the processes of network-building. Third, there is the motif of, let us call it, 'cogency': every relevant actor – whether human or nonhuman – must play its discrete part if the network is to persist. As we have seen, however, even early on there were suspicions that ANT tended to neglect subtler processes through which relations emerged.

a. Boundary Objects

For example, texts might associate actors without being 'immutable'. In the work of Star and Griesemer (1989), drawing on 'social worlds theory', the emphasis is less on agonism between actors and more on coordination of social worlds. Social worlds are more or less coherent social units marked by internal and regularized forms of communication or discourse. Examples of social worlds might include a scientific community, a lay local community, a business community. These are the building blocks of wider society which is, accordingly, composed of a 'mosaic of social worlds that both touch and interpenetrate' (Clarke, 1990, pp. 18–19; see also Clarke and Fujimara, 1992; Clarke and Montini, 1993). These 'social worlds' are sufficiently divergent in their characteristic forms of discourse and practice that a central analytic problem for social worlds theory is how communication and interaction between them is made possible. Crucially, rather than seeing this interaction in agonistic terms where one social world translates and enrols another, the emphasis is placed on coordination. As such, members of social worlds need means of interaction that allow them to 'work together' with members of other social worlds, while retaining their own distinctive identity. It follows that the media of such communication – whether texts or physical entities – must enable mutual use even while that use will reflect the characteristics of each social world. Such media have been called **boundary objects**. As Star and Griesemer (1989; see also Bowker and Star, 1999; Star, 2010) put it:

> Boundary objects inhabit several intersecting worlds. … Boundary objects are objects that are both plastic enough to adapt to local needs … yet robust enough to maintain a common identity across sites. … They have different meanings in different social worlds but their structure is common enough to more than one world to make them recognizable, a means of translation. (p. 393)

In their germinal paper, Star and Griesemer apply this formulation to the efforts of the Berkeley Museum of Vertebrate Zoology to establish itself as a research-oriented natural history museum by, for instance, securing a flow of specimens and information from such social worlds as those of collectors and trappers. They note that boundary objects come in various forms (e.g. ideal types such as 'species'; coincident boundaries such as the 'state of California'). Thus, the state of California was represented through maps which shared borders, but whose contents differed according to the particular social world (for collectors maps contained representations of roads and camp sites; for professional biologists, 'life zones'). While the different work practices of social worlds are reflected in the maps, the common referent of 'California' enabled cooperation. The concept of boundary object has been applied to a number of areas, notably biomedicine, where the social worlds of disparate disciplines are coordinated to facilitate 'research centres' or emerging research programmes. Thus Bazanger (1998) analyses how the 'Gate Control Theory of Pain' served as a boundary object that enabled cooperation across the members of a multi-disciplinary pain team. For Williams et al. (2008) it was the 'embryo' that facilitated mutual translation across the social worlds of pre-implantation genetic diagnosis and embryonic stem cell research.

The point here is that there are other ways of thinking the construction of scientific knowledge that do not necessarily rest on agonism. Indeed, the idea of the 'cogency' of actors within a network also seems spurious in light of the above example: are trappers and collectors fully immersed in their 'roles' – or is something more complicated going on? Their roles seem to be multiple – they are attached to different networks or social worlds, and particular associations seem to be multiplicitous, that is to say, they are made up of several elements. To explore this, we can consider how associations can be 'ambiguous', and an actor's enrolment can be marked by 'ambivalence'.

b. Ambivalence

Vicky Singleton (Singleton and Michael, 1993; also Singleton, 1996) addressed the part played by ambivalence in the associations between General Practitioners (GPs) and the UK state-sponsored Cervical Screening Programme (CSP). By paying close attention to the various accounts of the GPs, she argued that the role of the GP within the CSP network was a multiple one: GPs were variously ambassadors of medical science, expert practitioners who conducted the cervical smear test, and promoters of the CSP, persuading and recruiting women to the programme. Alongside the GPs, a range of other entities were attributed particular roles – nurses, speculums, fixatives, cervical secretions, for instance. However, the GPs both attached themselves to, and distanced themselves from, particular representations of the CSP network. So, while the GP role was partly enacted through the CSP, it also embodied a problematization of that CSP. This ambivalence finds expression in, for example, both a commitment to the black-boxed laboratory-based production of cervical smear results *and* an emphasis on GPs' specialist, skilled interpretation of those results (which thus un-black-boxes the lab). Ambivalence was also evidenced in GPs' commitment to the government's 'patient' recruitment targets, and the problematization of those targets (as unattainable given the many other pressures faced by women).

Singleton argues that this ambivalence actually played its part in sustaining the CSP network by addressing divergent elements within it. On the one hand, there is a need to support and simplify the CSP network and the GPs' roles within it (for medical, financial, institutional reasons); on the other hand, there is a need to problematize the network and unravel the GP roles as complex and multiplicitous (which also served to underline the autonomy of the GP). On the one hand the CSP is reinforced by a 'reiteration' of its handed-down parameters; on the other hand, the CSP is reproduced through 'non-prescribed' ways of working. As Singleton (1993), puts it, the Cervical Screening Programme can be seen as the GP's 'benevolent adversary': to un-black-box the governmental Cervical Screening Programme would endanger both it and the GP role; yet, to follow it blindly would effectively make both the CSP and the GP role impracticable.

In this section, we have seen how for an 'actor-network' to cohere and to attain some sort of durability, it is not necessary for there to be 'comprehensive' translation and enrolment. Enrolment can be productively partial. In later sections, we shall pursue this partiality further when we elaborate on how actors can be enrolled into multiple networks. For now, we turn to some of the ways in which the place of nonhumans within networks has been challenged.

'The Role of the Nonhuman'

In the previous chapter we saw that nonhumans play a critical role in the emergence and durability of actor-networks. If the scallops fail to attach themselves to the biologists' scaffolds, if the electrons don't behave as they should in Electricité de France's batteries, if Pasteur's microbes don't follow his predictions – the network so carefully crafted by the main protagonists disintegrates. However, sometimes nonhumans were performed ambivalently – cervical cells could both be understood only through lab work, and only interpreted by GPs. Turning to technologies, we saw how these have pre- and proscriptions built into them – they 'oblige their users' to act in particular ways. Yet we could read the case study of the photoelectric lighting kits installed in French Polynesia as an example of 'technological ambivalence' – users both used the kit and subverted it.

a. 'Fluidity'

We can elaborate on this ambivalence and ambiguities toward the nonhuman in terms of the contrasting, multiple roles nonhumans can play within a network. So, in the case of cervical cells, these are both transparently readable by the GPs (through the lab reports), or opaque and indeterminate (requiring skilled interpretation by the GPs). In the case of the 'Map of California', its meaning is both common across the different social worlds involved with the Museum of Vertebrate Zoology, yet also specific to those disparate social worlds. The types of nonhuman that were enacted (transparent versus opaque; common versus divergent) depended on what sorts of associations are emphasized. In the case of the cervical cells, to be transparently readable is to bond the GP more tightly to the CSP, where they are opaque this emphasized the GP's autonomy; in the case of the Museum of Vertebrate Zoology, the common meaning of the map indicated a shared attachment to 'California', whereas divergent understandings indicated professional specialization. The broader point is that what the nonhuman 'is' depends on the nexus of relations of which it is a part, and out of which it emerges.

This has been brought out with particular forcefulness in the work of Mol and Law (1994; Mol, 2002; and see Chapter 7). For Mol and Law, the 'thing' that is anaemia is something that varies across the associations that enter into its making: accordingly as 'anaemia' travels across different 'regions' such as the 'Netherlands' and 'Africa' what it means changes. 'It' is thus characterized by both fixity and fluidity. As they write: 'if we are dealing with "anaemia" over and over again, something that keeps on differing but also stays the same, then this is because it transforms itself from one arrangement into another without discontinuity' (p. 664). To expand, the configuration of associations that comprise an entity such as anaemia might change, but this does not necessarily imply the 'agonism' of 'classical' ANT. Rather, as the 'entity' moves, it is 'enacted' in ways which do not entail a betrayal or disruption of prior networks. Indeed, as Mol and Law (2004; see also Law, 2002a) propose, the fluidity of, and differences within, an enactment of an entity can yield a sort of ordering. So, in considering an entity such as 'hypoglycaemia', it is clear that this is manifested in bodies in multiple ways – it is enacted through biomedical practices of course, but additionally through domestic, labouring and aesthetic activities, for instance. This means that sustaining the hypoglycaemic body is a process that straddles many associations (and networks). Despite this, the body retains its integrity. As Mol and Law (2004) write:

> So long as it does not disintegrate, the body-we-do hangs together. It is full of tensions, however. These are tensions between the interests of its various organs; tensions between taking control and being erratic; tensions, too, between the exigencies of dealing with diabetes and other demands and desires. In the day-to-day practice of doing bodies such tensions cannot be avoided. Like it or not they simply must be handled. (p. 57)

Taken together with the foregoing, what this quote usefully highlights are the disparities and tensions within and across networks, that these networks are not always distinct, or are distinct but linked in ways that are simultaneously contrary and cogent.

Law and Singleton (2005) elaborate on the fluidity and multiplicity of objects in their analysis of alcoholic liver disease. In the cases of anaemia and the hypoglycaemia, we have seen how these objects at once manifest stability and display instability: as they traverse different sets of associations, they both retain their identity and undergo gentle (and sometimes, not-so-gentle) changes. In the case of alcoholic liver disease, Law and Singleton detect similar dynamics. There is fluidity of meaning across the different parts of a hospital and even within textbooks. However, they also point out that these transitions are not necessarily gently fluid – they can be abrupt. Alcoholic liver disease can take on highly divergent shapes. In terms of its links to alcohol consumption, it might not signify the need for abstinence (as it does in the hospital) but a preference for moderation that allows for improvement in family communication. Under other conditions, it might be seen as a more acceptable alternative to drug dependency. Put another way, alcoholic liver disease in the hospital also comprises a series of absences (or absent presences, or otherings).

What alcoholic liver disease 'is' thus also rests on what it is not, or what it might be. To capture this abruptness and difference that is constitutive of objects, Law and Singleton (2005, p. 347) propose the image of *'fire objects'* (as in bush fire):

> In this way of thinking, alcoholic liver disease becomes an object that jumps, creatively, destructively and more or less unpredictably, from location to location.

In sum, networks might be better understood in terms of their messiness and compromise, fluidity and difference. This has implications both for the very viability of the idea of 'network', and for methodological perspectives on studying 'networks' (see below).

b. Complex 'Functions'

If the nonhuman is better understood in terms of multiplicity, fluidity and difference, we can pursue this further in relation to what the nonhuman 'does'. Specifically, we can examine the extent to which the 'scripting' of a technological artefact affects what that artefact does and what can be done with it. Above, we noted Latour's argument that technological artefacts 'exceed' their designers' intentions, that is, the 'scripts' that have been incorporated into them and which must be followed for those artefacts to 'work'. However, this 'excess' does not simply reflect how users use artefacts in unscripted, surprising ways, or how the scripts precipitate 'unintended' effects. Rather, the scripts that are embodied in technologies are multiple and map onto, and reflect, different networks, some more extensive or less obvious than others. For example, in their discussion of the Zimbabwe Bush Pump, de Laet and Mol (2000) list a number of its manifestations: 'A water-producing device, defined by the mechanics that make it work as a pump ... a type of hydraulics that produces water in specific quantities and from particular sources ... a sanitation device' (p. 237). Of course, because it is a network, also included in the pump's constitution are 'manuals, measurements, and tests ... [and maybe] the village community' too. Crucially, 'perhaps the boundaries of the Bush Pump coincide with those of the Zimbabwean nation. For in its modest way this national bush pump helps to make Zimbabwe as much as Zimbabwe makes it' (p. 237). Here, then, materially and semiotically – sociomaterially – these technological nonhumans complexly mediate other sorts of 'meanings' (in the sense of 'privileged ordering' set out in Chapter 3), including overtly political ones (cf. Winner, 1985; Pfaffenberger, 1992).

Now, it might also be the case that some of these 'wider meanings' slip past 'classical' ANT. Let me illustrate by returning to the example of the 'door-closer'. According to Latour (1992), this object has the apparent advantage of 'convenience' and 'efficiency' when contrasted to unruly, undisciplined humans with all their unpredictability and recalcitrance. However, convenience and efficiency are not self-evident qualities – they vary according to the networks in which they are situated. Under relevant 'conditions', disciplining human bodies might be more convenient and efficient than in-corporating their capacities into technologies. Where labour is cheaper, then a door-closer is perhaps not so convenient. Even when labour is expensive, for certain 'elite' establishments the absence of a door-closer and the presence of a concierge is a matter of maintaining a network where conspicuous consumption is paramount: in other words, 'waste' signifies luxury and luxury forms a basis upon which associations to a particular clientele are wrought (Michael, 2000). The point is that the door-closer's 'meaning' is exhausted neither by its scripting and immediate use, nor by its non-use or mis-use. The door-closer, as a cipher for many other technologies, is an object that both in its presence and absence mediates different sorts of larger, more convoluted and layered 'networks'. Arguably, we are now beginning to approach the limits of the 'network' metaphor (see below).

c. Hybrids and their Problems

Finally, in this section, I want briefly to consider another element of ANT's treatment of the object – namely, the argument that humans and nonhumans are, in the contemporary world, entering into ever more numerous, complicated and intimate relations. In Chapter 3 we followed the claim that the unit of analysis should shift from the contrast between humans and nonhumans to the combination of the two – the hybrid. According to Latour (1993a), hybrids have always been present but have, through the Modern Constitution, been neglected (though, as Lee and Stenner, 1999 show, the nature of this misrecognition can be disputed). The point here is that versions of the hybrid are rather more in evidence than Latour allows. Objects are attributed agency (i.e. human characteristics) on a regular basis, not least in everyday life (Pickering, 1995; Hekman, 2010). The example of John Cleese as Basil Fawlty screaming at his car 'you vicious bastard' before giving it a 'damn good thrashing' with a branch is funny in part because we recognize in his actions our own responses – our attributions of a humanity of sorts – to such nonhumans as computers, printers, photocopiers and so on.

Indeed, in popular culture, it is not uncommon to find commentaries on combinations of people and technologies deemed to be, in one way or another, morally problematic. Michael (2000) provides the example of the 'couch potato' that, as a combination of person, couch, remote control and TV, is condemned because the human component is corrupted by its embroilments with its nonhumans, and fails to live up to certain citizenly, economic or medical virtues. Moreover, we can observe that the status of animals and environments as objects or subjects has been highly pliable: modernist views of their object-ness has routinely been accompanied by ascriptions of subject-ness. By way of illustration, witness the early modern vermin trials (e.g. Leeson, 2013) through to the 1916 lynching of 'Murderous Mary the Elephant' in Erwin, Tennessee. In sum, within 'modernity', at the level of everyday culture, the divisions between subject and object, human and nonhuman, are far more blurred than Latour credits.

'Power and Representation'

In Chapter 3, we saw how the emergence of networks rested, according to Latour, in substantial part on the circulation of texts which were deemed to be both highly mobile and resilient in their meaning. By contrast, above, we saw how the 'power' (with all the provisos that attach to this, see Chapter 2, and Latour, 1986) or potency of 'immutable mobiles' nevertheless depended on whether their readers were predisposed to read them in ways desired by their producers. In this chapter, we have discussed how the notion of immutable mobiles might be linked to a particular model of the network – one in which enrolment, rather than coordination, is privileged, where the emergence of a singular dominant network is what is of analytic interest, rather than the interdigitation of numerous networks (or social worlds).

a. Marginality

We can further elaborate on the role of representations in tying together actors to form a network if we shift our focus from dominant or primary actors and networks – say that of Pasteur – onto those persons who fit 'uncomfortably' within a dominant network. Star (1991, p. 33) writes: 'We know how to discuss the process of translation from the point of view of the scientist, but much less from that of the laboratory technician, still less from the lab's janitor.' In other words, we need to move away from the managerialist or 'heroic' perspective of the 'enroller'. John Law (1991) makes a similar point. So while 'for Latour, Pasteur is an effect, a product of a set of alliances, of heterogeneous materials' (Law, 1991, p. 12), nevertheless, too much attention on the mobilizing actor detracts from those who are, seemingly, enrolled. Along with Star, Law asks how ANT might bring those who are marginal to, or excluded from, or subordinated within, networks to the centre of an actor-network analysis. One advantage of this is that it throws into relief those marginal or excluded networks that nevertheless 'inform' – or, better, partially shape – those actors who are enrolled into the network that is the primary focus of an actor-network analysis. After all, as Star states, 'People inhabit many different domains at once … and the negotiation of identities, within and across groups, is an extraordinarily complex and delicate task. It's important not to presume either unity or single membership, either in the mingling of humans and nonhumans or amongst humans. We are all marginal in some regard, as members of more than one community of practice (social world)' (Star, 1991, p. 52).

b. Culture

This focus on the 'primary' network, so to speak, has also been critiqued from a rather different, though linked, perspective. Emily Martin (1998) argues that what has been called 'classical' ANT was underpinned by a particular metaphor in which science sits in a 'Citadel' dispensing knowledge to its potential enrollees – to the ' "untutored" public' (p. 30). For Martin ' "science" and "society" ' should both be seen 'as categories ... produced inside the heterogeneous matrix of culture, the missing term in ANT' (p. 30). To unpack this a little, the flow of knowledge is not one way – from science to the 'untutored' non-scientist. Instead, through shared cultural resources, there is also simultaneously an opposite flow from non-scientific culture to science. In Martin's view, immutable mobiles should be disconnected from ANT's linear accounts of enrolment: accordingly, they do not always enrol, or they enrol partially, or they enrol in ways that are not expected by the Citadel. Further, the complex, ambivalent, conditional ways in which immutable mobiles are received reflect 'the imagery, language and metaphor operating in ... culture' (p. 33). That is to say, given that science and the 'untutored' share (to some degree or other) a culture, an immutable mobile might work because of commonly held cultural elements – 'imagery, language and metaphor' – whose origins are by no means 'in', or exclusive to, science. We see this exemplified in Martin's own classic work (1989, 1994) on the underpinning scientific metaphors for the female reproductive system (as a factory) and the human immune system (as an army in the Cold War era, and a flexible labour force in the late modern, post-Fordist era). These shared metaphors might render the representations and the practices around female reproduction more resonant – that is, more liable successfully to enrol women to particular biomedical networks – by virtue of being widespread within a culture. Of course, as Martin goes on to show, these metaphors might also prompt resistance: the menopause is not a matter of 'factory breakdown' implying the need for hormonal supplementation, but an opportunity for celebrating the female life course.

In summary, representations' mediation of relations of power cannot be attributed solely to their immutability and mobility (even when they are studiously scientific or highly technical). The 'potency' of these texts lies as much in their extended cultural embeddedness. In any case, we need to be circumspect about the potency of such representations, especially when we take into account that 'classical' ANT analyses have tended to focus on primary networks (and actors who are 'prime movers'), while neglecting actors excluded from those networks, and the marginal networks which they inhabit.

'Flatness and Extension'

In the last chapter we noted how networks were built, extended and stabilized through the delineation of associations amongst various human and nonhuman entities. Crucial to this definition and distribution of roles is the circulation of intermediaries – immutable mobiles, highly disciplined humans, algorithms, money, contracts, standardized technologies and so on. Time and again we have seen the process of rendering actor-networks is altogether messier than initially portrayed in ANT. Boundary objects, ambivalent associations, inter-digitations of different networks, marginalities and exclusions, common but contested culture across science and its audiences, smooth fluidities and abrupt disjunctions in the shapes of objects – together these suggest that in describing the production of knowledge, and indeed, 'society', there is needed an expanded range of concepts in ANT.

a. Topology

Law (2002a; also Mol and Law, 1994) proposes that in contrast to 'network' a better – or at least supplementary – model that grasps the fluid movement of entities across different patterns of associations, is that of topology. Accordingly, Law suggests that as an entity 'moves' it is co-constituted with its spaces (spatiality is emergent rather than presupposed or imposed), even as that entity is partially and fluidly transformed. That transformation entails both change and continuity – in the terms of topology, there is homeomor-phism between different versions. An example of this is the homeomorphism between the letters 'A' and 'R'. In those cases where the rules state that shapes belong to the same set if they possess one hole and two tails, then as A is transformed into R, it is both the same and different (see Michael and Rosengarten, 2012a). As Law notes, this sort of simultaneous sameness and difference is possible only if the network boundaries that an entity travels across are fluid, allowing the transformations of an entity while also enabling the retention of identity in spite of that transformation. This can be con-trasted against rigid boundaries where to cross is to be changed in some fundamental way. What happens to the notion of network when we start thinking in terms of a boundary's fluidities, and an entity's combination of transformation and continuity?

Law (2002a, p. 102) argues that we should not imagine that networks 'fail' just because some of 'their' objects are fluid. To be sure, different manifestations of an object might appear very different and very distant when considered in terms of the network metaphor (e.g. divergent versions of anaemia in the Netherlands and Africa, or alcoholic liver disease in a central hospital and a local GP surgery). Yet these can also be seen to be topologically connected if the appropriate (e.g. homeomorphic) characteris-tics are emphasized. This reflects the idea that within topology space is foldable – that seemingly distant entities and regions can be shown to be, under certain conditions, closely related (and conversely what are proximal turn out to be distal). For instance, the CSP is both welcomed and criticized by GPs, and the laboratory is both close (credible) and far away (needing supplementary expertise).

b. Rhizome

These arguments about the limitations of the network metaphor find an echo in Emily Martin's (1998) critical remarks on ANT's top-down or centre-periphery motifs. As we saw above, she disputes the linear movement of 'knowledge' (or rather knowledge claims) from scientific Citadel to untutored public, preferring a model in which both are embedded in a shared but contentious culture. Any movement is always liable to entail some form of change but also some degree of continuity. On this score, Martin refers to Haraway's (1994) concept of the cat's cradle which, in being passed from one 'player' to another, undergoes transition while still retaining elements from previous patterns. For Haraway, 'one does not "win" at cat's cradle; the goal is more interesting and open ended than that. It is not always possible to repeat interesting patterns, and figuring out what happened to result in intriguing patterns is an embodied analytical skill. ... Cat's cradle is both local and global, distributed and knotted together' (Haraway, 1994, p. 70). Cat's cradle works through 'global', that is shared, conventions while also yielding new possibilities – it is not passed on as a static pattern (as if it were an immutable mobile).

Martin like Law also seeks an alternative to the network metaphor, and to this end she draws on Deleuze and Guattari's (e.g. 1988) notion of the *rhizome*. The rhizome is contrasted to the root and both are particular configurations of an *assemblage* comprised of bodies, actions, passions, enunciations and statements (the human and nonhuman). Where the assemblage is rootish, its elements align in linear relations to one another, bifurcating like the branches of a tree, or indeed, network. Where the assemblage takes on the form of a rhizome, any part of the assemblage can connect with any other part. Importantly (and this point is made by Law too), root and rhizome are not mutually exclusive: 'there are knots of arborescence [roots] in rhizomes, and rhizomic offshoots in roots. ... The important point is that the root-tree and the canal rhizome are not two opposed models' (Deleuze and Guattari, 1988, p. 20). Thus the imagery that rhizomically flows into science from broader cultural trends can afford it a particular potency that rootishly builds networks.

c. Mediators

Latour (2005a, p. 9) has also suggested that we abandon the terminology of actor-network theory – one of his options was 'actant-rhyzome ontology' (he decided against this for the typically ironic reason that the 'acronym A.N.T. was perfectly fit for a blind, myopic, workaholic, trail-sniffing, and collective traveler. An ant writing for other ants, this fits my project very well!').

Latour has also moved away from the idea of the intermediary, perhaps best exemplified by the immutable mobile, to introduce the notion of the mediator. Thus whereas an intermediary faithfully conveys a meaning, slippery mediators 'transform, translate, distort, and modify the meaning or the elements they are supposed to carry' (p. 39). Importantly, Latour uses this distinction to reinforce the ANT argument of 'flatness' – that we need to examine the 'how' by which elements (human and nonhuman) become associated to constitute the 'social'. Latour gives the example of stockings whose nylon or silk sheen faithfully reproduces pre-existing social phenomena, respectively low- and high-brow culture (or cultural capital – see Chapter 5). In contrast, rather than treat nylon as a faithful intermediary of the low-brow, we should examine the many mediators that have contributed to its making (technological as well as social), and the ways these might have impacted on the very construction of 'low-brow'. For Latour's ANT, the world is full of mediators and a core task of ANT is to trace how they become intermediaries: 'there exist endless number[s] of mediators, and when those are transformed into faithful intermediaries it is not the rule, but a rare exception that has to be accounted for' (Latour, 2005a, p. 40). So, here we have shifted toward a more dynamic version of the network in which stability is a relative rarity rather than the commonplace of a durable actor-network.

But let us take another step back here. As actor-network analysts, are we intermediaries faithfully depicting a network, or are we mediators transform-ing and translating it? Are we not ourselves embroiled in the fluid, multiple and marginal networks suggested by Star, Law and Martin? For a writer such as Donna Haraway, the actor-network analyst cannot be removed from their own networks (or situation, as she would call it): the actor-network analyst cannot stand 'above' a network, objectively tracing its associations. This would be another instantiation of what she famously called the 'God trick' – being simul-taneously everywhere (one can empirically access everything) and nowhere (there are no interests or investments in particular networks that might skew or bias that access).

On top of this, unlike 'classical' ANT, Haraway has had no problem with drawing on standard social scientific categories such as corporations, racism, sexism, ideology and so on. However, these categories are always treated circumspectly – there is no simple, transparent access to them, for they are both the conditions and outcomes of networks, including those networks in which we as analysts are 'situated' (Haraway, 1997). To speak of class, or gender, or race, etc. is, at once, to insist both on their reality and on their constructedness, of their actual complex inter-relations and their storied-ness. As Haraway (1994) has put it:

> For the complex or boundary objects in which I am interested, the mythic, textual, political, organic and economic dimensions implode. That is, they collapse into each other in a knot of extraordinary density that constitutes the objects themselves. In my sense, story telling is … a fraught practice for narrating complexity in such a field of knots or black holes. In no way is story telling opposed to materiality. (p. 63)

As we shall see below, this concatenation of the real and the constructed finds expression in Latour's (1999, 2010b) notion of the factish – the combination of fact and fetish. The crucial issue here is that if we are to take seriously the ethos of flatness, this must be applied no less to the operation of ANT itself: it too has emerged out of a nexus of associations, it too is a mediator.

'Method, Analysis, Vocabulary'

a. Baggage

The preceding, albeit condensed, commentary on Haraway should give us pause. For Haraway, her terms (cyborg is pivotal in this respect) are always deeply rooted in particular (circumspect) histories. ANT's abstracted terms, however, are presented as if they come without baggage. Of course, that is precisely the point, to address the emergence of networks without presuppositions (not least with regard to what is human and what nonhuman). Haraway's point is that this is simply not possible. Even a seemingly innocent term such as 'hybrid' turns out to have complex connotations. For Latour (1993a), hybrids are the chronic (amodern) admixtures of human and nonhuman that have been neglected under the Modern Constitution, and which need to be attended to if we are more consciously to engage with, and make judgements about, their proliferation (and wider impacts). Yet, according to Elam (1999), this management of hybrids is of a piece with Western security experts' sustained concern with the 'careful monitoring and management of hybrid networks' (p. 16). On this account 'Latour cannot help re-enacting the imperial ambitions that infuse the networks he charts' (p. 21).

These arguments – that there is a need to situate ANT's, supposedly presupposition-less, terms in relation to their specific contexts – take several forms. For some authors, a number of ANT's terms tend to import contexts that muddy its analytic promise. Take the term 'actant'. As we saw in Chapter 2, this derives from semiotics and is designed to show how a particular entity – human or nonhuman – operates within a narrative of network-building. Pasteur is such an actant (Latour, 1988a) – a signifier derived from various texts – that can be narrated, in its changing guises, as central to the emergence of Pasteurism. Yet, the application of 'actant' (along with its semiotic context) can detract from the analysis. Thus Lynch (1993) writes that '[Latour's] historical narratives are difficult not to read as, for example, realistic accounts of how a person named Pasteur managed to build alliances and proselytize a particular research program' (p. 109, fn. 88). Similarly Pickering (1995) states, 'even when Latour claims to be doing semiotics he often seems to forget, and to speak directly of laboratory practices' (p. 15, fn. 20). Pickering prefers John Law's perspective which does not take 'any detours through semiotics' (p. 15, fn. 20). Put bluntly, it is not clear how the term 'actant' adds anything to the analysis of how an individual comes to be placed in so powerful a position.

b. Otherness

Over and above the problems associated with particular terms within ANT's vocabulary, criticisms have also been levelled at the very idea of a 'network'. We have already noted several above: the notion of 'network' fails to accommodate various processes that range from multiplicity and fracture (Star, Law, Mol) to underpinning cultural commonality (Martin). If these are 'substantive' failings insofar as specific empirical findings escape the 'net' of the network, there are also 'formal' critiques that reveal how the application of network analysis can be profoundly limiting. Lee and Brown's (1994) analysis provides just such a critical account: ANT is apparently so all-encompassing that it seems to cover everything, it has no 'Other'. As they write: 'no topic, no objects or arenas of inquiry, can escape redescription or assimilation within [ANT] ... ANT risks the production of yet another ahistorical grand narrative and the reproduction of the concomitant right to speak for all' (p. 774). If it is the case that every form of analysis, by virtue of framing issues in a particular way, misses or 'others' something, 'classical' ANT has been neglectful. In an echo of Martin's analysis, Lee and Brown go on to note that 'ANT focuses firmly on the striated' (that is the rootish version of the assemblage) thereby othering the smooth (the rhizomic). As we noted above with reference to Deleuze and Guattari (1988), the smooth (or rhizomic) and striated (or rootish) coexist: 'in any particular multiplicity [such as a "network"] the actions of striation and smoothing are both at work' (p. 785).

We can also address 'classical' ANT's neglect of 'Otherness' through the lens of methodology. To read Latour's (1987) rules of method in *Science in Action* is to be struck by their overt 'empiricism': ANT analysts will follow the actors wherever they lead and whatever they are, making a list 'no matter how long and heterogeneous' (p. 258) it is. Nothing, it seems, will escape the ANT analyst's gaze. Yet, as John Law (2004a) has argued, every methodology operates in relation to 'others' – those that fail to enter within its frame of reference. In that respect, methodology is necessarily performative insofar as, for instance, in engaging with the empirical world certain parts of it will be missed (fail to be recorded or accounted) while other parts will be registered and emphasized. We shall take up the idea of the performativity of method in Chapter 7, when we address recent attempts to develop 'speculative' or 'careful' approaches to the other.

c. Property

Finally, we turn to Marilyn Strathern's complex commentary upon ANT (1996, 1999; also Gad and Bruun Jensen, 2010). She notes that ANT operates with a model of networks that are potentially infinitely extendable internally (or fractally – every entity that is a component within a network is itself a network) and externally (as entity after entity is identified, enumerated and added to an outwardly extending network). Her argument is that such extension does not simply peter out by a 'cessation of the flow of continuity' (1996, p. 524) in which we run out of elements to add. Rather, the limits of a network analysis are shaped by extraneous factors, most especially those associated with property and forms of ownership. She gives the example of a biomedical invention many of whose authors are cut out when that invention is patented by a few of their colleagues (and the same truncation applies to the human source of the tissues in which the invention is based – see also Calvert, 2007). What is also important here is the way that the network, made up of heterogeneous elements (human ingenuity, technology, corporeal matter) culminating in a hybrid invention, is also truncated: the establishment of a patent reintroduces human–nonhuman divides in the form of humans-who-own-things.

This operation of property is brought into further relief when Strathern (1999) considers the use of intellectual property rights (IPRs), specifically the International Convention on Biodiversity, to defend the local knowl-edges and practices of people in Papua New Guinea. Here, local traditional models of personhood do not hold to a Western distinction between humans and things – 'there is no predetermined discontinuity between people and the products of their efforts' (pp. 166–7). The application of IPR protections ironically cuts this hybridity by imposing a Western version of ownership with its distinction between the owning human and the owned nonhuman. Put very simply (for the situation was considerably more convoluted), if Papua New Guinea was to sign up to the Convention's network, it might be at the cost of 'truncating' its own internal 'networks', partly evacuating them of their own particular and constitutive heterogeneity. Not only is the net-work metaphor found wanting, according to Strathern's analysis, but so too is a term such as hybridity – again this is not neutral, but found to take dif-ferent forms, with different implications, in different cultures.

ANT and Agency

Throughout this chapter there has been a more or less explicit bracketing of the 'problem of agency'. Each of the preceding discussions could have turned to the thorny issue of agency – Who or what can shape the construction of knowledge? Does the nonhuman 'possess' agency? Do representations have an autonomous 'capacity' to shape their readership? How does agency fea-ture in the extension of a network? Is agency an artefact of the way that associations are shaped by 'higher' forces (e.g. class structures)? In 'doing' ANT, how does the analyst trace and 'perform' agency? The deferral of the discussion of agency to this section is, in part, a pragmatic matter – it is so complex an issue (not least in terms of the many debates within ANT and SSK) that to have pursued it at every turn would have muddled previous discussions. While I cannot hope to do justice to this complexity here, I can at least aspire to give an indication of some of the themes that have arisen over the course of ANT's evolution.

a. Distributive Agency

In Callon's (1986a, 1986b) accounts of the electric vehicle and the biologists of St Brieuc Bay, we saw how in the analysis of the emergent networks, electrons and scallops were both attributed agency – they had to act in certain ways in order to realize new networks, but also ended up subverting the roles they were ascribed and betraying those networks. This is the radical symmetry that has long lain at the core of ANT – that in explaining the emergence (and collapse) of networks of elements, we need also to trace the 'agencies' wherever they lead, whether to humans or nonhumans. However, for some writers, this is illegitimate. In perhaps the most famous attack on ANT's tenet of radical symmetry, Collins and Yearley (1992a, 1992b) dispute that a common agential status is applicable across humans, technologies and animals. For these authors, technological and 'natural' entities can never have an unmediated voice in our analytic accounts – they never speak directly to us. Rather, they are always mediated by humans – scientists – who tell and show what they can do, or are capable of doing. In other words, nonhumans are necessarily socially constructed through the socially derived categories and practices of science. It is the role of social science (in the guise of the Sociology of Scientific Knowledge) to unravel these social processes – after all, it is only to these social processes that we have direct access. So, in contrast to ANT's ecumenical perspective on what is pertinent to the construction of scientific knowledge, Collins and Yearley advocate a 'social realism'. As Pickering (1995) notes, this social realism is a bulwark against yielding 'our analytic authority to the scientists themselves' (p. 12): to give voice to nonhumans (and their agency) is in actuality to capitulate to scientists 'who have the instruments and conceptual apparatus required to tell us what material agency really is' (p. 12).

Pickering goes on to point out that Callon and Latour's (1992) riposte draws on semiotics to deny the contrast between SSK and technical accounts that Collins and Yearley set up. Even if there are problems with this use of semiotics (see above), Callon and Latour's counter-argument nevertheless holds. In brief, they note that the 'social' is not pure – it is composed in part of technologies (and other nonhumans) that contribute to that social's durability. As such, in the case of scientists, their constructions are shaped by prior technologies which are shaped by prior humans – it is chains of humans and nonhumans that make up the social. Let us recall Law's (1991) figure of the manager who could not function as a manager were her telephone, computer, scanner and so on not to hand. It would seem then that agency is distributed in this schema. This distributive conceptualization of agency also finds a home in Callon and Law's (1995) notion of hybrid collectifs (see Chapter 3). As they comment, in Western discourse it is more common to attribute agency to singularities rather than interactions, fields or networks.

This distributive version of agency can also be seen as 'flowing' or circulating amongst different elements of network (or collectif) – or rather as enacted in the relations 'between' entities. The agency of nonhumans 'enables' the agency of humans which enables the agency of nonhumans and so on. Andrew Pickering (1995) pays particular attention to this temporal dimension of agency. His approach takes the following summary shape:

> My basic image of science is a performative one, in which the performances – the doings – of human and material agency come to the fore. Scientists are human agents in a field of material agency which they struggle to capture in machines. Further, human and material agency are reciprocally and emergently intertwined in this struggle. Their contours emerge in the temporality of practice and are definitional of and sustain one another .... [there is] a reciprocal tuning of human and material agency, tuning that can itself reconfigure human intentions. (p. 21)

This is a 'dance of agency' in which scientists as 'active, intentional beings ... tentatively construct some new machine. They then adopt a passive role, monitoring the performance of the machine to see whatever capture of material agency it might effect. Symmetrically, this period of human passivity is the period in which material agency actively manifests itself' (pp. 21–2). In this way, there is what Pickering calls 'a dialectic of resistance and accommodation' where material agency can manifest unexpectedly (say, an experiment fails) and scientists accommodate this by, for instance, intentionally reshaping their goals (it's the wrong hypothesis), redesigning the experiment (and the technologies involved in that), and even the social relations (getting rid of that inept post-doc).

b. Attributive Agency

In the foregoing we have touched on a version of agency that is distributive – agency 'circulates' spatially and temporally. But agency is also attributive – it is ascribed to particular entities and this is part and parcel of rendering associations and building networks (or collectifs). In Pickering's dialectical model, as scientists adapt to resistant material agency, they might also ascribe agency to those colleagues who failed to overcome that resistance through misfortune or incompetence in setting up experimental equipment (see, for example, Knorr Cetina, 1999). A different example of this attributive version of agency can be found in the work of Charis Cussins (1996) who speaks of 'ontological choreography' (rather than the 'dance of agency'). In her study of women in hospital wards, she found that women could move adroitly between 'being' objects (where they were simply examined and told the medical truth) and subjects (where they were addressed as knowledgeable persons). In other words, they were ascribed, and tactically accepted for the purposes of diagnosis and treatment, the different ontological statuses of object (as a passive body devoid of agency) and subject (as a human actor imbued with agency).

Latour (2005a) similarly deploys the ascriptive as well as distributive model of agency. As ever, this is a complicated process, not least because the actors that are followed are themselves engaged in processes of heterogeneous ascriptions of agency (as Pickering's and Cussins' examples illustrate). That is to say, in doing agency, one is also ascribing and distributing it. So for Latour, when we study agency in networks, we must remain agnostic as to its 'place'. Unlike the 'mainstream' sociologists against whom he is arguing, we should not be tempted to situate agency in a few pre-specified elements, whether they be infrastructural (e.g. late capitalism, neoliberalism), superstructural (e.g. ideologies, imaginaries), or phenomenological (e.g. individuals' rational strategies, persons' situated reflexivity). Rather, we should engage with the specific agencies as they are ascribed in the emergence of network. As such, he asks:

> Which agencies are invoked? Which figurations are they endowed with? Through which mode of action are they engaged? Are we talking about causes and their intermediaries or about a concatenation of mediators? ANT is simply the social theory that has made the decision to follow the natives, no matter which metaphysical imbroglios they lead us into. (Latour, 2005a, p. 62)

Let us unpack this a little. The term 'figurations' relates to the figure that has been endowed with agential force. This ranges from (at least) a person all the way to a full-scale society (these are of course simplifications insofar as the figurations detract from their own network-ness). And when he compares causes and their intermediaries to concatenations of mediators, Latour is asking us to be circumspect about assuming that singularized agential figurations like a class or a community generate many effects. Rather, the analyst should engage with the many complex and unpredictable causes that are collapsed in various ways to effect a network. In following the latter, we are simply following the 'natives', as he puts it, who pay no heed to the neat figurations of sociologists, and mix up all sorts of agencies that cut across categories of human and nonhuman, social and material, real and constructed. Even when people do invoke 'society' to account for their actions, as Bowers and Iwi (1993) show, they have at least eight different versions to draw upon, and they do not necessarily deploy these in neat or discrete ways.

However, let us reflect further on this. From very different perspectives, both Giddens (e.g. 1984) and various Foucauldian scholars (e.g. Osborne and Rose, 1999) have argued that the social (and human) sciences do not simply describe society, they also contribute to its making. 'Sociological' categories and techniques enter through various routes into networks (e.g. through university education, social services, government and commercial systems for assessing the 'state' of society) acting as mediators that inform actors' attributions of agency. It might be the case that when, following Latour, we follow the natives, they are, in part at least, natives of the social sciences. Perhaps, insofar as the social sciences resource natives' understandings and ascriptions of agency, the imbroglios into which those natives lead us are not as complex or messy or interesting as Latour imagines.

c. Agency as 'Method'

The issue of agency remains very much a live one in ANT and its derivatives (see Passoth et al., 2012), but here we end with an approach to agency that frames it in terms of 'method'. Accordingly, the analytic attribution of agency can serve as a means of exploring networks and associations. In keeping with the general distributive thrust of ANT, Michael (2000) has suggested that hybrids are 'co-agents' that are caught up in a melee of co-agency, that is, circulations of agency. On the basis of this, he suggests that the analyst can concoct such hybrids that despite their distributed-ness can nevertheless be treated as if they were cogent, in the sense of possessing a certain unitariness or singularity. Putting together co-agent and cogent, Michael suggests the term co(a)gent to describe these distributed and distilled agents. These co(a)gents can be derived from popular culture (e.g. the couch potato) or the analyst can make them up (e.g. the hudogledog – comprised of human, dog and doglead). Michael uses these as a pragmatic means for opening up associations that might otherwise remain hidden.

For instance, Michael (2004) derives the co(a)gent 'pitpercat' from the combination of pitbull terrier, cat and person in order to show how animals can play an agential part in the enactment of larger-scale social entities. Thus, he relates an episode in which a research interview was disrupted by the actions of the cat and terrier, together with the human participant's resistance to the research topic (she would rather talk about her recent employment in a major fast food chain than respond to questions about local radiation risks). The 'pitpercat' suggested that cat, dog and human worked together to undermine the interview; as such, the nonhuman animals contributed to the situated differentiation of university from corporation. The objective of such a technique is to avoid, or at least, problematize, the usual ascriptions of agency to the more or less standardized 'intermediaries' of the social sciences (class, gender, institutions, human individuals, etc.), but also, as mentioned, to explore unusual or unlikely places where agency might be said to lurk.

Conclusion

In this chapter, we have collected together a number of more or less sympathetic criticisms of 'classical' ANT. Even if this collection has not been exhaustive, it should nevertheless have signposted a number of the main routes that post-ANT has taken in the last 20 years or so. Lying behind many of the discussions in this chapter has been the impetus to address the 'others'

of 'classical' ANT – whether these be the actors at the margins of the network, the not-so-agonistic processes by which associations are forged, the
neglected popular cultural resourcing of a network, the performativity of
ANT's methods, or the fluidities of boundaries and the related ambiguities of
actors, mediators and intermediaries. In Chapters 7 and 8, we begin to
explore how many of these themes have played out in post-ANTs. But before
that, we consider how ANT compares and contrasts to other perspectives
that share with it a concern with how 'society' is made.

5

ANT AND SOME BIG SOCIOLOGICAL QUESTIONS

Introduction

In the last chapter, we traced a number of criticisms of ANT. As we saw, while these raised specific issues about ANT, they also held to a generally similar analytic and empirical ethos. So, while some writers were critical of the 'managerialism' or 'heroism' of actor-network accounts, they were sympathetic to ANT's avoidance of macrosociological categories; or if exception was taken to ANT's seeming God-eye empiricism, there would nonetheless be a shared attention to the role of the nonhuman. These criticisms are not simply a matter of nuance and, as we shall see in Chapter 7, they underpin a number of substantive changes in the intellectual shape of ANT.

However, for all its heterogeneity, ANT still falls within the purview of the social sciences: it is routinely read as a major intervention in the sociological understanding of society and social processes, and an alternative to more 'mainstream' approaches to 'the social'. It is therefore important to get a sense of how ANT relates to well-established sociological perspectives. Of course, there have been many ways in which society has been theorized, but for present purposes I have chosen to focus on three well-known sociological traditions. These are derived from the work of Anthony Giddens ('structuration theory'), Pierre Bourdieu ('practice theory') and Norbert Elias ('figurational studies'). Each of these bodies of work has, in their own ways, attempted to deal with the divides between agency and structure, and object and subject. In part this choice is a matter of convenience – there is only so much one can know or do. More positively, I have chosen these three approaches because there are existing writings in which scholars have drawn out some of the perceived advantages and shortcomings of ANT in the context of Bourdieu's, Elias's and Giddens' respective frameworks.

In what follows, I begin with a short reflection on ANT's general antipathy toward grand social theorizing, and the periodization of social history into distinctive epochs. This leads into our discussion of three grand social theories. In the three subsequent sections, a brief outline of each perspective is presented, paying particular attention to the categories through which 'society' is understood, and the associated attempt to account for the inter-relations between human agents and larger-scale social processes and structures. Each section also contains examples of how authors have used Elias, Bourdieu or Giddens to develop commentaries on ANT, while also drawing on ANT in order to supplement those theories. In this way, we shall again address what is distinctive about ANT, but also how it intersects, in part at least, with each of these social theoretical standpoints.

A Brief Note on ANT's Anti-Social Theory

Before we proceed, it might be useful to reiterate that ANT has not evolved in direct relation to social theory. Its roots, as we have seen, lie in particular philosophical and historical traditions (for example, Whitehead, Serres, history and philosophy of science), and in certain still comparatively minor frameworks of sociology (e.g. SSK, ethnomethodology, Tarde). Of course, there are points of common empirical concern (say, the way that 'science' interacts with 'society'), the formulation of environmental issues, the nature of globalization. Yet even in these cases, ANT has drawn on sources other than those that usually appeal to social theorists. Or rather, ANT can be said to be characterized by an insistence on empirical specificity. In other words, prior to the move to a generalized account of society and the social, we first need to ask how society, sociality and the social themselves emerge.

Here are three brief examples to illustrate.

a. The Posthuman

Numerous authors have suggested that the 'posthuman' signifies an epochal change in human societies. According to Fukuyama (2002), the posthuman marks a fundamental shift from the liberal possessive individual. Thus, the posthuman is seen to involve a major transformation in the capacities of the human by virtue of various biomedical, biotechnological and digital interventions: for example, these will impact on consciousness, longevity or health. The implication is that the stable, agential, responsible self is endangered by these transformations, and with it the social systems through which rewards and blame are distributed, and which in turn depend upon that stabilized individual. Bryan Turner (2007) provides further detail to this picture of the future. He suggests a panoply of widespread changes that range from enhanced inequalities between rich and poor regions of the world (the populations of the former become 'immortalized', those of the latter would be further impoverished) leading to greater resentments, through various economic and environmental impacts (longer-lived populations lead to greater stress on labour markets, food supply systems, the environment), and on to the remaking of the responsible self (if biomedicine can cure anything why bother to look after one's own, or others', health?).

For ANT, as we have seen, human enmeshment with the nonhuman is fundamental to the human condition. In this respect we have always been posthuman. Peculiarly, in 'modernity' (the irony of this is not lost) we have neglected to pay due attention to this embroilment, thus incongruously enabling a largely unchecked broadening and deepening of these multifarious and constitutive relations between people and technologies (Latour, 1993a). What the new technologies of the 'posthuman' do is serve to sensitize us to these complex embroilments, while also insisting on the transformation of the human (see Waldby, 2000). ANT's response to these dramatic claims about posthumanism is sceptical – for ANT posthumanism is, by and large, business as usual. Ironically, the claims made by advocates of specific posthuman developments can likewise emphasize 'business as usual'. For instance, the sociology of expectations – which draws heavily on ANT – attends to how specific technoscientific innovations and, crucially, their related futures, are constructed, enacted and circulated in order to establish associations. Brown and Michael (e.g. 2003) have traced the rhetorical means by which advocates of xenotransplantation (in simple terms, xenotransplantation is the transplantation of animal organs and tissues into human bodies) attach it to particular futures that promise a solution to the chronic dearth of transplantable human organs, but also a revolution in human healthcare systems. Yet they also stress the ethical mundanity of xenotransplantation: accordingly, to have a pig heart transplant is the ethical equivalent of eating a ham sandwich. The point is that in treating innovations in their empirical specificity we uncover the complexities of the so-called posthuman – complexities which include the reinforcement of the relatively mundane and boringly human. We see this also in patients' responses to the prospect of xenotransplantation: for them, this biotechnology is one amongst several prospects, including more 'traditional' health promotion interventions. When thinking about the posthuman, we need to take into account that specific technological innovations are enacted as both transformative (in order to garner funding and regulatory support) and ordinary (in order to allay perceived public anxieties – see Michael, 2006). In any case, these posthuman innovations vie for the future within a world full of mundane technologies (shoes, paperclips, Velcro, which, to re-quote Michel Serres, make our history slow).

b. Governmentality and Neoliberalism

Woolgar and Neyland, in their book *Mundane Governance* (2013), also draw on ANT (as well as ethnomethodology) to query the generalizing 'social theoretical' statements made by a number of writers on governance and governmentality who have been influenced by the works of Michel Foucault (e.g. Rose, 1996; Rose et al., 2006). For such writers, through complex systems that span penal, medical, educational, etc. institutions, particular types of self, or subject position, are rendered normal and natural. Such selves include the psychological, biosocial and calculable – in sum, neoliberal – self. As Woolgar and Neyland put it: 'The subject positions are articulated and reaffirmed through discourses such that individuals come to think of themselves as, for example, calculable individuals – appropriately subject to assessment and evaluation for our productivity and creativity' (p. 27).

However, these neo-Foucauldian perspectives on neoliberal governance tend to present too 'general and smooth' a picture, especially if these selves are seen to be coherent and to manifest uniformly across diverse social settings. By contrast, individuals might find the discourses that mediate these selves problematic, unclear, internally contradictory, and so on. This Foucauldian account of governmentality appears to leave 'little room for irony, or for resistance [which might be messy, unmotivated and mundane], interpretation, recursion or reflexivity' (p. 27). In other words, Foucauldian 'technologies of self', rather than 'more or less straightforwardly provid[ing] the conditions of possibility within which conceptions of self are enacted' (p. 30), should be regarded as subject to interpretative flexibility, ongoing contestation, negotiated implementation and so on. Woolgar and Neyland's book is a sophisticated charting of the many ways in which these variegated and messy processes take empirical form across the numerous instantiations of governance – from policy-making (e.g. struggling to choose a 'scientific' method for measuring waste disposal compliance) to local mundane practice (e.g. struggling to understand the instructions on recycling bins).

c. Risk Society

Finally, we turn fleetingly to another major social theoretical framing – that of Ulrich Beck's (e.g. 1992, 2000; Beck et al., 1994) risk society and reflexive modernity. Crudely condensed, this perspective addresses major transitions in contemporary societies toward a world shaped by the global distribution of 'bads' (as opposed to goods), the emergence of ambivalent relationships to scientific institutions, and the transformations of the individual and their intimate relations. The risks of reflexive modernity have become hybrids of constructed-ness and reality, and the awareness of this dual status has led to a heightened social reflexivity in which there is a 'peculiar synthesis of knowledge and unawareness' (Beck, 2000, p. 216), and a complex dynamic of increasing control and increasing uncertainty.

Bruno Latour's (2003) commentary on reflexive modernity is that ANT is a 'social theory' too, but one which operates at the much finer level of granularity – that of associations. He notes that for Beck the changes that typify reflexive modernity are real ones 'out there'. Latour is happy enough with social theory (and master narratives of epochal change) but sees these as resources in the making of society by 'thrashing out, through a lasso-like movement, constantly new interpretations of what gathers us together' (p. 41). For Latour, Beck, along with other social theorists of society as a whole, is confronted by the requirement to ground his account in empirical data. Yet this is impossible given the complexities and contingencies of both the social world and the data-gathering process. By comparison, social theories can be treated as a resource (Latour, following Garfinkel, also calls them ethnomethods). Accordingly, sociology (and social theory) is a source of alternative propositions about society, a source that is 'just one among others' (p. 40), in competition with other actors' accounts of society, accounts that are often more powerful and resonant (e.g. those of economists, politicians, etc.). Beck's work thus stands as 'a powerful proposition that ... shifts attention from the mainstream ... to discrepancies, cracks, failures and side-effects ... [that] claims that ... it can produce a coherent picture of a European world which has outgrown progress' (p. 46). On this score, Saito (2015) proposes a rapprochement between ANT and risk society theory in which the latter takes on board the former's focus on performativity, in order to pursue, through dialogue, preferred political ends.

To summarize, in relation to claims about new eras – the posthuman, the neoliberal, the risk society – we have seen how ANT-tinged commentaries lay emphasis on empirical complexity. But we have also seen how social theory is itself performative, enacting particular versions of society that feed into the very processes of making society. We shall return to this in Chapter 7.

Bourdieu, Practice and ANT

a. Overview

Pierre Bourdieu has exercised a major and growing influence on sociology and increasingly on the sociology of science and technology (e.g. Albert and Kleinman, 2011; Hess, 2011). His framework – sometimes called 'field theory' (as well as practice theory) – has evolved and been refined over many years and his own empirical research has touched on the education system, forms of consumption, artistic and scientific production, emerging forms of poverty, and sociology itself to name but the more obvious. It goes without saying that it is not possible to do justice to such an extensive and varied oeuvre, though we can at least sketch the bare bones of his perspective, not least in order to highlight where it maps onto and diverges from ANT.

At the core of Bourdieu's framework is a triumvirate of interwoven terms: habitus, capital and field. Habitus straddles the agential and structural insofar as it entails a conditioned, embodied set of dispositions. Habitus can be adapted to take into account the structured circumstances in which agents find themselves, though that adaptation is not a simple matter of exercising agency. For Bourdieu (1990, p. 53) habitus is therefore a structure structured by various social conditions, but also a structure that structures an individu-al's practice and representations.

However, this does not mean that habitus is mechanistically generative of pre-determined practices and representations. Rather, it yields a limited diver-sity comprised of 'all the "reasonable", and "common-sense", behaviours' (Bourdieu, 1990: 56) which make sense and are socially permissible within a particular context, or what Bourdieu called a field. Though this might give the impression that habitus entails coherence or unity, Bennett (2007) points out that there is considerable debate over this, not least insofar as it can be 'split' (see Friedman, 2016).

In any case, we can frame habitus in another way: agents have a conditioned 'feel for the game' that characterizes a field or social space within which they are embedded, a feel that at once reflects the presuppositions or *doxa* of the game, and an investment in those presuppositions – the *illusio*. So, the practices of agents have impacts within the field even as those impacts are partially obscure to them: 'It is because agents never know completely what they are doing that what they do has more sense than they know' (Bourdieu, 1990, p. 69). This does not mean that the field is simply reproduced by these prac-tices, for the field is marked by change (though conversely, habitus can lead to 'misadaptation' to the field). At this point we need to specify in more detail what is meant by 'field'.

Field refers to a constructed, structured space marked by a particular set of presuppositions or beliefs that demarcate what practices can feel 'right' or 'natural' within that field. However, as Thompson (2012) notes, fields are rela-tionally highly complex. They are thus 'internally multiple' (in that they are characterized by hierarchies in which some agents are more 'privileged' than others), they are 'externally multiple' (in that fields are related to others – educational to cultural fields for instance – so agents can straddle several fields simultaneously), and they are 'externally hierarchical' (in that what happens in one field can be subordinate to what happens in another). Thompson gives the example of the housing field shaped by state and financial fields, and the cul-tural field in its entirety 'dominated by the economic field' (p. 71). Within this complexity, it is still nevertheless the case that any given field is the 'site of a logic and of a necessity that is specific and irreducible to those which regulate other fields' (Wacquant, 1989, p. 39).

Put simply, a field is a social terrain organized by positions occupied (or potentially occupied) by agents; it is differentiated by the type of habitus those agents are possessed of; and it is reflective of the differential sorts of 'capital' available to those agents. As such, fields are structured by relations of inequal-ity and domination. However, each field needs to be related to other ones, not least to what Bourdieu calls the 'field of power' in which the dominant actors in various fields struggle for the supremacy of their particular form of capital (Wacquant, 1997).

In the end, however, Thompson argues, field is a heuristic concept – there to be realized through empirical engagement. Key to charting a field is mapping the positions within it, the types of habitus that attach to those positions, and the sorts of power or relative privilege or dominance that typify those positions. Key in all this is the notion of 'capital'.

For Bourdieu capital denotes 'the set of actually usable resources and powers' (1984, p. 114). However, capital takes several distinct forms – economic, cultural, social and symbolic are the most general, though it can take forms specific to a particular field (such as scientific capital). The volume and composition of capital mark the relative power of the agents within a field (see Weininger, 2005). Thus within the 'field of power' there might be dominant groups from other fields (e.g. university professors, industrialists, high level managers) but the relative composition of their capital favours some factions over others – industrialists generally have higher economic capital and this tends to trump professors with their relatively greater cultural capital.

A distinctive contribution is Bourdieu's emphasis – conceptual and empirical – on the variety of capitals. Regarding cultural capital, this can take various forms. As summarized by More (2012), it can be objectified in galleries and museums, enacted through a particular habitus (e.g. a sense of what is 'right' or 'good' in the arts) and embodied as corporeal predispositions (e.g. taste, poise). The differential play of cultural capital – the ways that buying and consuming a particular item can be seen as sophisticatedly ironic for some groups of consumers, while vulgarly gauche for others – reflects the field's hierarchy and the struggle for 'distinction' (Bourdieu, 1984). As part of these sorts of dynamics, economic capital (money) is converted into symbolic capital which can then be subsequently transubstantiated back into economic. Bourdieu's point is that some groups by virtue of their position within a field are able to capitalize on their cultural capital – further entrenching their advantages. For Bourdieu, these cultural distinctions are arbitrary in the sense of being the product of human categorization and valuation. Insofar as these distinctions are naturalized, and there is a common 'misperception of social space – which characterizes both the dominant and the dominated, albeit to the advantage of the latter', this is an instance of what Bourdieu calls 'symbolic violence' (Weininger, 2005, p. 145; Bourdieu, 1989).

Now, what is missing from the account is a sense of how social dynamism is captured. Agents move within the field 'partly because they are subject to forces which structure the social space and partly because they resist the forces of the field with their specific inertia' born of their entrenched habitus, for instance (Bourdieu, 1984, p. 110). But such movements or trajectories are not random, they adhere to the 'field of possibles' within the field that is configured by agents' 'given volume of inherited capital' (p. 110). The animation of these trajectories has various sources both collective (wars, crises) and individual (encounters, benefactors), even as these sources and their mobilization (e.g. access to, and skills in nurturing, certain social connections) reflect the existing capital and position of agents.

In sum, in Bourdieu's work (and the above is a highly condensed rendering – many of Bourdieu's terms remain unexplicated), we see a sustained endeavour to overcome the micro/macro divide: agents have the capacities to move within a field in their attempts to accumulate or hold onto capital, even as the moves they are making are shaped by both the relationalities within a given field and between fields, and by the sorts of capital and habitus with which they are historically and biographically endowed.

b. Bourdieu and ANT

According to Albert and Kleinman (2011), what Bourdieu adds to ANT (as well as other similarly 'micro'-oriented strands in science and technology studies) is what might be called a sense of the 'outside' or the 'behind'. Thus, while they acknowledge that 'conflict is central to Latour's vision, and it is clear that the construction of networks and obligatory passage points enable some actors to the disadvantage of others, it is not evident from where the initial source of this capacity comes. We cannot satisfactorily ... understand the intersection between science and social inequality in a Latourian framework, and we cannot gain purchase on the relationship between power and the social organization of science' (pp. 264–5). At base, the structure of a field of science (and its relations to other fields) shapes what actors are empowered, and demarcates who is better resourced in the struggles that characterize that field.

On a rather different note, Guggenheim and Potthast (2012) point out that there is a similarity between Latour and Bourdieu in that both address the conflict at the heart of scientists' (and indeed all agents') movements in relation to a field or network, and both think of this as a matter of strategy. Yet, if for Bourdieu strategy inflects with the subjectivity of 'what feels right' and the objectivity of 'the field of possibles', for Latour 'the forces of fields' do not operate behind the backs of the actors but are entangled in 'scientific objects, laboratories and texts' (p. 160) that are central to scientific activity. The 'strategies of scientists are therefore not determined by scientists' position in the field; rather their position is a result of their scientific actions ... [stripped] of their structural properties' (p. 160). This reflects Latour's, and more generally ANT's, denial of 'any strong differentiation within society' into fields. Indeed, as Guggenheim and Potthast put it, Bourdieu's version of sociological differentiation is a mere artefact 'of sociology to produce an orderly account of society' (p. 162).

Let us address some issues surrounding 'differentiation' in a little more detail. For Bourdieu there seems to be a 'behind' that animates agents – 'quasi-mechanistically' as Camic (2011, pp. 279ff.) details. For ANT, this 'behind' is anathema: whatever form it takes – norms, institutions, fields, or society as a whole – it is necessarily something to be enacted whether by scientists, bureaucrats, 'ordinary people', or sociologists. The 'behind' is a generic resource (and it doesn't have to be sociological, it can be genetic, or psychopathological) available to actors as they go about making associations. Part and parcel of the mobilization of a 'behind' is to generate critique – to show how those who are being criticized are being animated by that which they do not grasp. As Schinkel (2007, p. 711) notes, Latour is critical of Bourdieu precisely because he has taken

> ... a rather paternal and arrogant attitude of the social scientist who sees things as they really are, and who sees it as his duty to speak on behalf of all ignorant souls, suffering under the strain of social mechanisms they are themselves unaware of, but which the sociologist can capture in his metalanguage.

So, it would seem that ANT attempts not to make such presumptions: it does not differentiate between what is accessible to actors and what lies beyond them. However, this does not mean that it has nothing to say about the operations of power 'through' larger-scale actors. As we have seen in Chapter 3, Callon (1991) describes some of the broad principles by which networks can become durable. To the extent that a network has a durability comparable to that of a field, then what is of interest to ANT is how this is accomplished – how have associations been crafted and converged in order to afford a network its durability? Having said that, the durability of these networks (or assemblages) rests on the multiple and heterogeneous activities of multiple and heterogeneous entities. In other words, what precisely a network 'is' is not something so readily grasped or mapped in the way that a Bourdieusian field appears to be. Networks are made and remade through the ongoing forging of associations in their local specificity. As a matter of 'heterogeneous engineering', the making of associations requires that all manner of skills, resources, texts, artefacts and so on are brought to bear, only some of which fit neatly within the field of 'science'. The notion of 'technoscience' also captures this heterogeneity (see Chapter 3), not least because it encompasses the disparate range of actors that contribute to the making of a scientific network (e.g. bureaucrats, ethicists, administrators, patient groups, etc.). This point is neatly captured by Schinkel (2007, p. 725): 'Bourdieusian sociology sees one kind of relation; Latourian sociology sees many kinds of assemblages.' The further point is that ANT cannot capture or expose complex, emergent networks so much as add to the accounts that already circulate (not least within those networks).

Now, ANT's focus on heterogeneity and contingency applies no less to the body. Bourdieu's notion of habitus – embodied, transposable, corporeally durable – is said to structure (along with the field) what is possible as practice. The resilience of habitus lies in part because it is conditioned (or socialized) into the individual from a young age. Yet this model of embodiment is perhaps a little too static – it neglects the body as something that is 'done' and whose coherence (and, indeed, non-coherence) needs to be enacted and accomplished, not least as it encounters all manner of affects that impact upon it (Latour, 2004c). So, against the coherence implied by habitus, this alternative model of the body is riven by heterogeneous tensions. As we have already mentioned with reference to Mol and Law (2004), the non-coherent body entails an ongoing compromise between different interests (amongst organs), and between orderings (say, medical self-discipline) and disorderings (say, indulging in potentially damaging pleasures). Embodiment, according to this model, is not simply something that 'does', but that is variously and continuously done and redone.

Finally, we need to turn to the role of the nonhuman. While objects, technologies and artefacts have been addressed by Bourdieu, as Prior (2008, pp. 303–4) writes: 'the problem of technology does not feature highly enough in Bourdieu's work to give it the strategic status it deserves; at worst its inclusion stretches his arguments to the limits of credibility'. Prior discusses the rise of 'Glitch' from the late 1980s, a genre of music in which composition draws on 'a series of micro incidents – bleeps, cuts, clicks and pulses – rendered by digital techniques and tools' (p. 306). At first this was rooted in experimental music but increasingly entered the mainstream and 'crystallized as an established genre' (p. 307).

Prior provides a Bourdieusian account of the way in which Glitch was a sub-field, practised by a faction with privileged cultural capital and supported by high theoretical criticism. Over time, this was taken up by more mainstream or popular artists and producers who appropriated its 'cool-ness' and 'edginess'. This precipitated a reaction in which the original protagonists of Glitch were obliged to 'call for continuous experimentation to stave off the risk of becoming an orthodoxy' (p. 310). For Prior, here is an account that details the 'ongoing struggles over classification, practice and use [which] are the very stuff of cultural fields' (p. 310). Yet, technology is largely missing from this account. Most especially it (and various attempts to think technology through a Bourdieusian framework) fails to appreciate the 'multifarious modifications and translations that technologies afford ... beyond reproduction, to what they make possible' (p. 313). This means that technologies need to be understood as mediators, and 'human and nonhuman materials as co-producers of the field, as heterogeneous assemblages on-goingly exchanging properties in relatively structured settings: to open the black box of technology as well as the well-regulated ballet of the field' (p. 316). According to Prior, what this treatment of technology does – and we may apply this argument to many sorts of nonhumans (even the most mundane) – is 'allow for moments of disruption and the unscripted, for the non-human and transformative' (p. 317).

To sum up: if Bourdieu's work displays a complex interweaving of bodies, practices, relations and hierarchies, it nevertheless, according to an ANT perspective, lacks analytic suppleness. It is difficult to see how it can account for the heterogeneity of fields, the non-coherence of bodies, or the fluidity of relations (or associations) not least as these are partially shaped by technologies and their not always predictable affordances.

Structuration and ANT

Anthony Giddens' (e.g. 1984) theory of structuration has been an influential and controversial framework (e.g. Turner, 1986) for thinking about the ways in which microsocial and macrosocial processes relate to one another. In what follows, I provide a brief and predictably selective outline of some of the key features of Giddens' perspective. However, the focus is primarily on the reworking of structuration as 'strong structuration theory' which has been developed by Rob Stones. The reasons for this are twofold. First, Giddens' work does not lend itself readily to empirical application (though it has been taken up in such broad areas as management and organizational studies, e.g. Englund et al., 2011; Hond et al., 2012). By comparison, Stones' strong structuration has been designed to do just this – to be used in the analysis of specific cases. Second, strong structuration theory has critically engaged with, and strategically borrowed from, ANT. This allows us to trace some of the convergences and divergences, and respecify some of the peculiarities of ANT. It goes without saying that I do justice to neither Giddens' nor Stones' analytic subtleties.

a. Giddens

Probably Giddens' most famous statement of structuration theory is found in *The Constitution of Society* (1984). This is part of a sustained endeavour to get beyond the structure/agency divide. Giddens places great emphasis on the reflexive capacities of the agent who is thus capable of assimilating and responding to analytic, social scientific, accounts. As such, agents can affect the reach and relevance of those accounts. The implication is that social scientists cannot provide an overarching account of society: indeed, in keeping with an ethnomethodological sensibility (shared with ANT), structuration theory can at best provide only sensitizing concepts.

Key to structuration theory is the concept of the duality of structure: 'Accordingly ... the structural properties of social systems are both medium and outcome of the practices they recursively organize' (Giddens, 1984, p. 25). Giddens insists that structure needs to be understood as internal to individuals, 'as memory traces, and instantiated in social practices' (p. 25). Moreover these structures are both constraining and enabling, and can contribute to the 'structured properties of social systems [that stretch] away in time and space, beyond the control of individual actors' (p. 25). So, while structure 'has no existence independent of the knowledge that agents have about what they are doing on the level of discursive consciousness ... [nevertheless those agents] may know little of the ramified consequences of the activities in which they engage' (p. 26). This boundedness of knowledge means the unintended consequences of human action 'may form the unacknowledged conditions of action in a feedback fashion' (p. 27). That is to say, actions yield conditions which serve in the repetition of those actions: this is a sort of homeostatic system that entails 'the operation of causal loops, in which the unintended consequences of action feed back to reconstitute the initiating circumstances' (p. 27). However, there are also 'strategically placed actors [who] seek reflexively to regulate the overall conditions of system reproduction either to keep things as they are or to change them' (pp. 27–8). Crudely, some actors might have more influence than others, affecting more conditions and shaping larger social systems (e.g. a media mogul's impact on electoral preferences and government policies).

It is clear from this all too brief overview that actors' 'knowledgeability' of their structural context plays a key part in Giddens' schema. Agents tacitly know how to 'go on'; that is, they have 'practical consciousness' through which they monitor their own and others' activities. But they are also able to 'monitor the monitoring' in 'discursive consciousness' – to bring to consciousness, articulate and sometimes contest what Stones (2005) calls these 'structures-within-knowledgeability' (p. 17). In addition, Giddens' theory allows for an unconscious (in part to address the matter of motivation), though as Stones suggests, how this is precisely demarcated is probably best left open (p. 25).

Giddens differentiates three broad (analytically separate but practically inter-twined) types of structures: signification (meaning structures), legitimation (normative structures) and domination (power structures). The former two involve rules of language use and rules of social behaviour. They can be illumi-nated respectively by theories of coding and theories of normative regulation, and they find institutional expression respectively in symbolic orders and legal institutions (Giddens, 1984, pp. 28–34). In keeping with the duality of structure, enacting such rules, the agent is also reproducing these structures. In the case of domination structures, Giddens regards these in terms of resources: domination 'depends upon the mobilization of two distinguishable types of resource. Allocative resources refer to types of transformative capacity – generating com-mand over objects, goods or material phenomena. Authoritative resources ... [generate] command over persons or actors' (p. 33). These are respectively real-ized in economic and political institutions. However, to reiterate, each of these institutional orders in actuality incorporates the other structures: illustrated simply, it is difficult to imagine political institutions not 'drawing on' symbolic, economic and legal orders.

Stones (2005) draws together numerous commentaries to provide a sum-mary of the many criticisms levelled at Giddens' structuration theory. These include: its abstract-ness, its unclear or varying definition of several concepts, its over-emphasis on the agent to the exclusion of external structures, a level-ling of agents that excludes recognition of inequalities amongst agents, the poverty of its conception of the unconscious, the oversimplified relation between rules and structures. Stones also notes the de-coupling of Giddens' work on structuration theory from his more substantive studies (1990, 1991) of, for instance, late and reflexive modernity. This is partly because, as Stones reads it, Giddens' structuration is an 'ontology-in-general', that is, a statement of the nature of the social world that is not designed to be 'applied' to specific cases. By contrast, Stones (2005, p. 8) wishes to develop a strong structuration theory that can operate as an 'ontology-*in-situ*' that 'is directed at ... particular social processes and events in particular times and places'.

b. Strong Structuration Theory

Strong Structuration Theory (SST) focuses especially on matters of methodology and epistemology. These can be approached through the reconfigured ontology of SST. Stones (2005) develops a three-level ontology: an abstract level of ontology that serves as a general 'guide to empirical researchers'; a 'concrete' or ontic level that addresses the 'empirical evidence of actual social relations in particular times and places'; and a meso-level that cuts across the other two and makes it 'possible to talk about at least some abstract ontological concepts in terms of scales or relative degrees' (p. 77). In particular, this meso-level comprises a means of analysing the *relative* interactions of agency and structure: for instance, the greater or lesser knowledgeability or critical reflection of actors; the fewer or greater opportunities for making choices that are available to actors; the lesser or greater durability of external structures; the variability in number and impact of unintended consequences. As such, a particular *in-situ* case study of a sequence of actions (Stones gives the example of a gay Chinese man coming out to his father and the threatening unintended consequences of this) can be related to the meso-level where one can begin to trace what might be called the set of possible variations (or perhaps the room for manoeuvre) within that sequence of actions. For instance, the consequences of the gay man's 'admission' 'whether few or many, are identifiable and particular, with more or less significance to specified agents' (p. 81). Here, through the meso-level, we see how the abstracted ontological concepts of, for instance, duality of structure and unintended consequences are linked to the specificity of the particular sequence of actions.

Stones deepens his meso-level analysis by situating the agent within a field of position–practice relations. In essence, this refers to the networks of 'social positions' that entail social identity, obligations and prerogatives. The upshot, in brief, is that these relations hold in place what it is possible to practise within any position, though there can still be enough 'give' within a position so that the web of relations is not totally deterministic. As we would expect, the precise character of these relations will be illuminated through *in-situ* empirical analysis. Conversely, and iteratively, how the analyst directs her empirical analysis will be shaped by the web of position–practice relations.

Jack and Kholeif (2007) have asked whether this framing in terms of 'field of position–practice relations' is so different from that of ANT. They answer that Stones remains attached to a duality of structure whereas ANT refutes the divide between structure and agent. As they put it, 'for actor network theorists organizations (and, one might add, individual humans) are networks which come to look like single point actors …; for structurationists, agency and structure are always present together, separately identifiable but not identical' (p. 213).

Now, Stones (2005) relates the web of position–practice relations to what he calls the quadripartite nature of structuration. First there are external structures conceived as 'independent forces and pressuring conditions that limit the freedom of agents to do otherwise' (p. 109). Second, there are internal structures that are subdivided into two categories. On the one hand, there are 'general dispositions' which explicitly echo Bourdieu's habitus (see above). On the other hand, there is 'conjuncturally-specific knowledge of external structures' which equips agents to respond to the perceived particularities of given situations and settings. Third, there is 'active agency', which includes 'the ways in which the agent either routinely and pre-reflectively acts, or strategically and critically, draws upon her internal structures' (p. 85). Finally, there are 'outcomes', which encompass a wide variety of effects on both internal and external structures, effects that can entail more or less reproduction of, or change in, those structures.

This conceptualization of structuration also underpins the overarching approach toward empirical analysis, though never at the cost of *in-situ* specificities. So, there are two key dimensions of structuration analysis. First, there is analysis of agents' conduct – how agents reflexively monitor their actions and concerns in the interaction sequences. This permits analytic entrée into actors' knowledgeability as enacted through internal structures (as described above). By comparison, agents' context analysis again follows knowledgeability but 'outwards into the social nexus of interdependences, rights and obligations, asymmetries of power and the social conditions and consequences of action' (p. 122), that is to say, external structures. This empirical strategy both 'respect[s] the hermeneutics of the lay actors' while also identifying 'the range of relevant causal influences, the potential courses of action, and the probable consequences of both' (p. 122).

c. Strong Structuration Theory and ANT

We now turn to a specific example of the application of SST – one in which there is a direct engagement with ANT. In their analysis of the implementation of large IT programmes in healthcare, Greenhalgh and Stones (2010) cautiously incorporate elements of 'classical' ANT into SST. In particular, they are interested in ANT's conceptualization of 'technologies and human actors as part of the same network' (p. 1289). On this score, both can be accommodated within the network of position–practice relations. However, they reject the principle of symmetry where humans and technologies can both be regarded as actors or actants: for Greenhalgh and Stones, there are differences in the ways humans and technologies act. Second, following ANT, they treat technologies as being inscribed with elements of the social order and thus technologies can be said 'to some extent "freeze" certain position–practice relations' (p. 1289). As such, to investigate the origins and interests that underlie the codes and standards relevant to big IT is to shine a light on how such technologies might serve in, for instance, the reproduction of certain social structures. However, the extent to which technologies embody social orders can be highly variable, not least insofar as this embodiment might be unintended. Third, while Greenhalgh and Stones agree that socio-technical networks shape human action, they are unwilling to see human agency reduced to mere network effects. For them, the 'classical' ANT processes of translation would benefit from more complex treatment of structure and agency wherein technology is also understood in terms of its specific use in relation to the task at hand (rather than a reflection of the scripts inscribed in the technology). For SST, this also means that technologies-in-use also have a role to play in the dynamics of social structures. Over and above the way that these scripts are 'baked into' technologies thereby potentially constraining action and thus reproducing social structures, social structures are also affected by the way people choose to interpret and deploy technologies, including refusing them. In SST's terms 'the recursive relationship between structure, agency and technology evolves continuously at the micro-meso level … [and] also played out at meso-macro level and on a longer timescale' (p. 1290), that is, at a structural level.

It is certainly possible to dispute some of Greenhalgh and Stones' characterizations of ANT. After all, as we documented in Chapters 3 and 4, the scripts incorporated into technologies are hardly deterministic in the way these authors portray: in ANT terminology, technologies are mediators as well as intermediaries. More importantly, ANT is resistant to any *a priori* distinctions between humans and technologies because it is interested in pursuing *empirically* 'whatever' is instrumental or influential in the making and remaking of networks. To make such distinctions, fine-grained as they are in the case of SST, is potentially to miss out on the complexity of the actants and their hybridity, 'no matter which metaphysical imbroglios they lead us into' (Latour, 2005a, p. 62). One might say that there is nothing in ANT that precludes the uniqueness of human agency *per se*; it just has to be empirically demonstrated in its specificity.

Greenhalgh and Stones (2010) briefly illustrate their ANT-informed SST with a number of examples. I focus here on their analysis of the 'Choose and Book' technology introduced as a means to enable GPs and patients more easily to arrange appointments at hospital outpatient departments. This analysis was subsequently elaborated, as well as conceptually supplemented, in Greenhalgh et al. (2014). In this latter paper there is a sophisticated theoretical and methodological account of the study, but for present purposes I will focus on a selection of the findings. The 'Choose and Book' system was part of the New Labour government's early 2000s promise to afford patients the opportunity to choose the place, date and time of their hospital appointments. 'Choose and Book' was a software package installed onto the desktop computers of GPs and administrative staff which, in brief, could be used to offer a choice of clinical providers (e.g. hospitals).

Greenhalgh et al. found that GPs were initially reluctant to use the system. Many found the notion of offering 'choice' absurd: patients routinely expected to be sent to the closest hospital – choice more often than not led to confusion. The system was also resisted because: it was not fit for purpose (it generated more work); interfered with GPs' knowledge, skills and judgement (in relation to patients' conditions and circumstances, or to the exigencies of local clinical provision); altered the relation of GPs to management (GPs were assessed in terms of the implementation of the system rather than how they cured, cared for and comforted patients). Nevertheless, GPs did use the system in a minimal manner, chiefly because there were financial incentives attached to it, but also because it began to yield service improvements.

In terms of SST, we might say, albeit simplistically, that there was a disjunction between (the 'policy') version of 'Choose and Book' and the GPs' internal structural knowledgeability (about how the system worked) that manifested in the form of GPs' active agency, that is, their resistance to the system. Or, we could note that structural attempts to introduce 'Choose and Book' were an unwelcome 'perturbation' in GPs' network of position–practice relations. From a 'classical' ANT perspective, however, we do not presuppose that the nodes that are part of the network of position–practice relations can be so readily differentiated into human and technology as they are in Greenhalgh and Stones' schema (2010, p. 1289). The GPs' active agency of resistance is partly born of their embroilment with the mundane technologies of GP practice: rather than see the GP as the externally and internally structured 'seat' of this resisting action, the GP might be understood to be necessarily hybrid, partially enacted through such artefacts as stethoscopes and thermometers. This hybridity applies no less to the administrators, the 'Choose and Book' system, or the NHS managers (at whatever level). The point is that this allows for a more nuanced description of the 'network'; at best, only very local 'causal explanations' can be derived (see Chapter 3).

In addition, for ANT, these actors are seen as emergent from their relations. The ANT equivalent to SST's network of position–practice relations is far murkier and more fragmentary. In the case of the GPs, their co-present 'resistance to' and 'implementation of' 'Choose and Book' directly parallels the ambivalence evidenced in Singleton's study of the GPs' relation to the Cervical Smear Programme (see Chapter 4). One upshot of this is that GPs, emergent from their nexus of relations, are, to draw on post-ANT's emerging vocabulary, 'non-coherent' or 'ontologically multiple' (Mol, 2002; Law, 2004a). That is to say, the putative cogency of GPs is an accomplishment that holds together fragmentary, ill-fitting elements and multiple, divergent relations. This model applies no less to technologies, of course: the 'Choose and Book' system is likely to encompass a panoply of disparate elements (e.g. aspirations to efficiency, greater patient choice, interface design fashions, unwieldy workarounds, and so on and so forth). To reiterate, to come to grips with this mixing of fragmentary technological and human elements requires close empirical study. Indeed, when we trace the embroilments – the multiple and piecemeal entwinements – of the human and nonhuman that make up the relations of a network, we might wonder whether the concept of agency as depicted in structuration theory has sufficient purchase.

Elias, Figuration and ANT

As before, I proceed cautiously: what follows is undoubtedly an incomplete account of Elias's figurational (or process) sociology. Its relevance for ANT lies in, variously, the novel way in which it addresses structure/agency divides (e.g. van Krieken, 2002), its application in concert with ANT to empirical cases (Michael, 2000; Newton, 2002), and the fact that it has been directly allied with ANT (e.g. Law, 1994). Regarding the last, Elias's notion of figuration refers to the interdependencies amongst individuals who are understood to be constitutively open rather than closed in on themselves – something that is clearly shared with ANT (e.g. Callon, 1999, p. 185).

a. Elias

While Elias was not keen on the label social theorist, he did nevertheless address the ways in which microdynamics linked to macrosocial processes. As van Krieken (2001) puts it: 'His analysis of the historical development of emotions and psychological life is particularly important in relation to the connections he established with larger-scale processes such as state formation, urbanization and economic development' (p. 353).

Elsewhere, van Krieken (1998) suggests that there are (at least) five key inter-related principles that underpin the sociology developed by Elias. The first is that while people act intentionally, the cumulative effect of such human action is nevertheless unintended and unplanned. So while groups of people might aim to reproduce a state of affairs, they can nevertheless instigate change. The reverse also holds: 'something comes into being that was planned and intended by none of these individuals, yet has emerged nevertheless from their intentions and actions' (Elias, 1994/1939, p. 389; see also 1978, p. 147).

Elias's second principle is that of figuration: the fact that individuals need to be conceptualized in terms of their interdependencies with one another. These interdependencies are patterned as networks, and incorporate both the individuals but also their dynamic patterns: the dance, as Elias (1994/1939) notes, exemplifies figuration as a 'plurality of reciprocally oriented and dependent individuals' where the dance of figuration is independent of the particular dancing individual but not individuals *per se* (p. 214). This suggests an intimate association between the dynamics of interdependencies and of the dynamics of the individual that 'operates' within them.

As the above passages hint, society, conceived as a figuration, is dynamic. It needs to be grasped through a focus on inter-relations: crucially, these are marked by power (understood as a 'structural characteristic of … all human relationships'; Elias, 1978, p. 74). That is, power is not a 'thing' but a relationship and it is the balance of power as it swings first in one direction then in another that lies at the heart of changing figurations. In light of this third principle, the fourth holds that societies change and, as such, need to be analysed diachronically as emerging from historically extended social processes. Elias's (1994/1939) classic study *The Civilizing Process* is exemplary in this regard. Finally, Elias recognized that sociology is part of the society it studies, and thus sociologists are liable to be deeply 'involved' in what they are studying. Part of the job of the sociologist is to distance or detach themselves from their object of study in order better – more objectively – to illuminate it (even so, as ever, for Elias, there was a to-ing and fro-ing between these positions of involvement and detachment).

b. Elias and ANT

This is the skimpiest of outlines of Elias's perspective. However, for our purposes there is enough here to begin to understand why figurational sociology might be seen to share similar concerns with ANT. Here we turn to Tim Newton's (2002) analysis of what it might mean to change organizations so that they are more likely to act in environmentally responsible ways – that is, to 'green' them. Newton draws on Callon and Elias to mount a critique of 'ecocentricism' as it manifests especially in organizational studies' tendency toward a normative, corporate model of culture change. Within organizational studies, advocates of ecocentricism thus call for wholesale change within organizations in which 'all organizational members [will become] culturally green, and possibly ecocentric, agents' (p. 528). Following Elias, Newton argues that such top-down interventions are likely to yield unintended consequences. Given the interdependencies of individuals, 'over the long term it is difficult for any one individual or group to determine history, because their intentions and actions are always likely to be moderated by others on whom they depend ... there is unlikely to be any simple relation between a particular "strategy" and a particular "outcome" ' (p. 529). This is because, as we have seen, a plurality of individuals, with all their interweaving plans and intentions, yield outcomes planned and intended by none of them. On this view, an ecocentric management plan is unlikely to go to plan.

   Newton suggests that Elias and ANT share a common view of agency not least because both are oriented toward interdependency and to an agent that is 'networked'. The upshot is a need to understand the interdependencies that undergird how the particular organizational orders are created and sustained. Newton writes:

> In relation to Elias, we need to analyze the geometry and strength of the interdependencies that surround particular industries. In Callon's terms, we need to examine how human and nonhuman networks align, converge, and become standardized around processes that encourage environmental degradation. (p. 531)

So, Elias provides the tools for tracing how unintended consequences emerge from the varying interweavings of individuals, not least when there are

'asymmetries within interdependency networks' (e.g. one part of an organization charged with the promotion of greening might be unable to exert sufficient pressure on another, higher status part – see Newton, 2002, p. 532).
Callon adds to this by pointing to the modes by which actors within a network converge (see Chapter 3), for example through (hard won) standardization of internal organizational practices (e.g. greening of work procedures),
or through forms of disentanglement from other networks invested in non-
green processes (e.g. suppliers, markets). Taken together then, Elias and ANT
can be mined for concepts that illuminate, in this case, green network formation, but clearly this applies no less to other networks.

However, bringing together ANT and Elias is fraught because of two major
divergences, according to Newton (2001). The first difference reflects Elias's
insistence on asymmetries within interdependency networks – there are inequalities between actors such that some are able to force others. As we have
seen, for ANT (as for Elias) power is not possessed but relational – an individual can only 'do' power because they have translated and enrolled
(persuaded, even) others. Crucially, for ANT, an actor is but one, and they must
enrol other actors so that through these faithful, enrolled others they can distribute rewards, apply sanctions, or exact punishment. For ANT, then, how a
more forceful actor arose is of key analytic interest, and if this rise of an actor
is not directly addressed, this is primarily a pragmatic issue rather than matter
of principle. As such, one might assume, for the purposes of a given, circum-
scribed analytic project (say, of the Pasteurization of France), that a singular
actor (such as Pasteur) is more or less 'forceful' (or docile); however, there is
nothing in this stance that excludes such an actor from being subjected to an
actor-network analysis (see Chapter 3) that investigates how it comes to be in
such a position.

The second disparity reflects ANT's seemingly preferential focus on nonhumans whose networked-ness is subject to far more detailed analysis than that of
the relevant humans. This apparent lack of concern with human actors is particularly acute insofar as there is little ANT consideration of how individuals, as
seemingly independent agents, have emerged historically. This is clearly important because how networks operate rests, in part, on the routine and entrenched
attribution of responsibility, capacities, agency, etc. to individuals. Now one
might point out that some ANT studies have indeed focused on the emergence
of particular sorts of human actors (e.g. the GPs in Singleton's study of the
Cervical Smear Programme), and indeed of humans-in-relation-to-nonhumans
(e.g. Latour's positing of the citizen-gun). Moreover, it is also possible to argue
that to place emphasis on 'figurational contexts' that reproduce longstanding
perceptions of the individual (including their agency, subjectivity, emotionality,
etc.) is to neglect ANT's (ethnomethodologically-tinged) view that such contexts
are themselves 'made' and 'remade'. To put this another way, 'contexting' is a
proactive process, and needs to be studied in its specificity (Asdal and Moser,
2012) if we are to grasp how the 'individual' is at once reproduced and more
or less subtly altered. So, while the long-term figurational contexts routinely

re-enact 'the individual (and its qualities)', the particularities of 'an individual' needs to be studied as it is played out through shorter-term, concrete emergent (heterogeneous) relations.

In the current context (sic), however, we can identify a methodological quandary in this contrast between figurational sociology and ANT. On the one hand, there are analytic gains to be made by focusing on long-term figurational contexts that illuminate the entrenched character of interdependencies or associations. Such longer-term analysis shows how such interdependencies are affected by, and affect, particular versions of individual human agency that run through shorter-term networks. On the other hand, there are analytic gains to be made by focusing on how 'contexts' – that is, networks – are made in their shorter-term specificity along with the individuals who emerge from, and contribute to, them. In some cases, the workings of these shorter-term networks (and their individuals) might leave untouched longer-term figurational processes: the same type of individual agent might be reproduced. In other cases, however, these shorter networks may reconfigure or refract those longer-term figurational processes, subtly, or dramatically, impacting on the character of the human individual. In what follows, I briefly explore some of these issues through a particular example – that of car driving.

Michael (2000) drew on both Elias and ANT in an exploration of the phenomenon of 'road rage' – the ostensible loss of temper and violent outbursts (including killing) by drivers who felt they had been insulted or impeded in some way by other drivers (and sometimes by cyclists or pedestrians). In particular, Michael attempts to draw out the role of car technology in the apparent 'de-civilization' witnessed in road rage. The notion of 'de-civilization' reflects Elias's classic work in *The Civilizing Process* (Elias, 1994/1939; see also Mennell, 1989). Here, he traced the increasing 'self-control' that arose in medieval Court Society: 'Certain forms of behaviour are placed under prohibition, not because they are unhealthy but because they lead to an offensive sight and disagreeable associations; shame at offering such a spectacle, originally absent, and fear of arousing such associations are gradually spread from the standard setting circles by numerous authorities and institutions' (p. 104). Through media such as handbooks on appropriate comportment and conduct, behaviours were modified not least amongst the bourgeoisie who hoped to transform their interdependencies to become part of the Court. Over time this emotional control was reinforced as the interdependencies that made up society are extended, especially with the establishment of a stable state with its claims to exclusivity of the means of physical vengeance (Spierenberg, 1984).

One element of this change in behaviour (and corresponding emotions such as revulsion) is related to the use of such (nowadays mundane) technologies as the knife, the fork and the serviette. For Elias, the use of these items reflected a 'civilizing' of emotions insofar as the volatility of conduct was brought under self-control. In a later essay, Elias (1995) describes a link between what he calls 'technicization' and civilization: lifeless materials turned into technology can further civilizational processes. As Mennell

(1995, p. 2) puts it in relation to the car: 'the flow of cars and pedestrians in all directions is very dense. There are road signs, traffic lights and police to control the traffic. This external control, however, is founded on the assumption that every individual is regulating his or her own behaviours exactly in accordance with the flow of traffic. Constant vigilance, foresight and self-control are needed, whether a person is driving or on foot.' As we would expect, for Elias things are not quite so simple. Insofar as technologies can expose people to others (transport technology brings people into contact with other people), social differentiation can take place, interdependencies can remain unrealized, and de-civilization – violence – can manifest.

Whether moving in a civilizational or de-civilizational direction, it is the state of social interdependencies that is key for Elias (fewer interdependencies, more 'enclaves', can lead to less civilization). For ANT, however, technology is also central. In the case of the car, this embodies a range of contrary 'scripts' (see Chapter 3) that at once mediate interdependency (e.g. the signalling systems of cars) and individualization (e.g. Urry, 2004). This individualization, enacted prominently through a cockpit design oriented to the individual driver, and the assumed safety afforded by the metal cocoon of the car, arguably gives freer rein to such emotions as pleasure, excitement, aggression even. Obviously, these scripts are interwoven with many other elements such as traffic regulations, car advertising, safety campaigns, surveillance systems and popular commentary (see Michael, 2001). Nevertheless, the point is that in its design, the car can be understood to be instrumental in affording contrasting driving behaviours that *simultaneously* 'civilize' and 'de-civilize'. In terms of our previous discussion, this example suggests that while a longer-term figurational context might indeed imply a civilizational directionality to driving, in the specificity of the particular car's design (along with various other factors), we can detect a concurrent de-civilizational moment. Conversely, the car can also work against Eliasian de-civilizational pressures (e.g. differentiation born of increased social contact) because it is equipped to enable the smooth enactment of interdependency (e.g. signalling systems). In summary, ANT's focus on the complex and contrary affordances of technologies can nuance longer-term interdependencies, and indeed, invite us to ask: 'just how long-term are these figurations, indeed?'

In this section, we have focused on a number of common interests across ANT and Elias's figurational sociology – not least the ways in which the inter-weaving, inter-relationalities and interdependencies amongst actors dynamically affect the figuration of societies. In some ways, Elias's insistence on the unplanned-ness of these figurations prefigures the criticism levelled at 'classical' ANT; namely, that it failed to pay sufficient attention to multiple competing elements that make up, and problematize, networks (see Chapter 4). By the same token, ANT's focus on the planning of networks by key actors can stand as a corrective to Elias's over-emphasis on the unplanned trajectories by which civilization unfolds. As Tim Dant (2006) has cautioned, we need to take note of the planning that, in the case of driving, goes into the legal and regulatory framing of car use, as well as cars' sociomaterial design. In any case, the contrast between long-term figurations and short-term networks suggests the need for further exploration of the relation between networks which have varying durabilities (or manifest different rates of change) and yet are nested one within the other, or at least are inter-related.

Conclusion

This chapter has attempted to situate ANT in relation to three well-known social theoretical traditions. Obviously, this is too large a task to squeeze into a single chapter. After all, these social theories are, like ANT, anything but static. We have tried to deal with these parallel fluidities by discussing studies that have directly drawn on (a version of) ANT in (a version of) practice, structuration or figurational sociologies. In the process, we have attempted to identify some of the possible benefits and shortcomings of such attempts at application and intersection, if not synthesis or rapprochement. These inter-digitations of ANT and practice, structuration or figurational sociologies might well be worth revisiting – notions such as habitus, position–practice, long-term figurations all have the potential to expand the horizons of ANT. In the next chapter, we extend further the 'reach' of ANT by following it as it enters into a number of different disciplinary domains.

6

ON SOME DISCIPLINARY TRANSLATIONS OF ANT

Introduction

In Chapter 1, the relation between ANT and various other disciplines briefly received comment. It was suggested that ANT has gone beyond the borders of its 'home' discipline of science and technology studies to impact on a number of areas including political science, geography, social psychology and anthropology. Given that each discipline is itself a fractious site with competing intellectual traditions and diverse empirical interests, the reception that ANT has received has been varied, to say the least. In this chapter, I set out to illustrate some of the more sympathetic appropriations of ANT by other disciplines. As ever, I cannot claim to be comprehensive but aim to provide indications of how ANT might be productively put to use in a number of disciplines.

Now given the range of disciplines which have entertained ANT, I need to justify why I have chosen the ones I have. The first thing to note is, without getting into the complicated issue of what counts as a discipline (e.g. Whitley, 2000; Abbott, 2001), the areas I have chosen are not always 'strictly speaking' disciplines. Thus I will discuss some of the ways that ANT has entered into (bits of) contemporary social theory (understood as a theorization of the broad framework through which we might understand society and social processes). Social theory might be said to be a specialism of sociology, yet at the same time it often spans disciplines (feeding off and into science and technology studies, geography or anthropology, say). I also discuss how ANT underpins recent developments in 'economic sociology'; however, as we shall see, this 'economic sociology' also shapes cultural studies approaches to production and consumption. Even where I do directly address seemingly identifiable disciplines, issues arise. For instance, geography turns out to be hugely amorphous encompassing such disparate fields as the conceptualization of space and species, the experience of mountain climbing, and the negotiation of environmental problems. I will have to be selective within disciplines too.

To the question 'why look at ANT in these particular fields?', the answers reflect the specificities of those fields. With regard to social theory, it seems to me important to see how ANT has affected how social scientists think about thinking about 'the social' and 'social processes' in general (as opposed to the more empirically oriented appropriations of ANT by scholars interested in Bourdieusian, figurationist and structurationist social theories – see Chapter 5). When it comes to the new 'economic sociology', here we see how certain sensibilities of ANT have been adapted for the study of new substantive areas (e.g. markets), and how ANT has come to influence fields which have a shared interest in those substantive areas (e.g. cultural studies). Like the 'new economic sociology', 'management and organization studies' shares scholars with ANT (e.g. John Law) and is a field in which versions of ANT have been developed and refined. Finally, geography has been chosen because (it seems to me) this is where some of the most exciting and inventive work in post-ANT is currently being conducted.

In what follows I begin with a discussion of how ANT has entered directly into the writing of two social theorists, John Urry and Nigel Thrift. These scholars have been hugely influential in articulating new approaches to social dynamics, and ANT has played no small part in shaping their approaches. We then consider ANT's role in the 'new economic sociology' and the wholesale rethinking of the 'economic'. We also examine an example of how ANT, through the 'new economic sociology', bleeds into cultural studies. In the next section, we trace some of the many manifestations of ANT in management and organization studies. While an effort is made to chart ANT's influence, the main focus is on the work of Czarniawska, who has both shown how ANT can inform the analysis of organizations, and responded creatively to its limitations. Finally, we address ANT's uptake in geography, highlighting especially Murdoch's early unpacking of ANT's potential for geography, and Whatmore's use of ANT in her account of the *'more-than-human'*.

ANT and Some Recent Social Theory

I have chosen two social theorists whose works seem to me to have been particularly influenced by ANT: John Urry and Nigel Thrift. While Urry is a sociologist by discipline, and Thrift a geographer, both illustrate the sorts of uses to which ANT can be put to change how we think about the analysis of society, the social and social processes.

a. Urry and Mobilities

In an impressive series of books, John Urry (e.g. 2000, 2003, 2007 also Law and Urry, 2004) has developed a way of thinking about society that stresses the mobilities that constitute it. If sociology has primarily equated society with the nation state, Urry argues that we need to move beyond this focus 'upon individual societies and upon the generic characteristics of such societies' (2000, p. 1) such as the rights and duties of national citizenship. In particular, he points to the central role of technologies and technological systems that, in straddling national borders, and serving in the global flows of ideas, persons, currency, goods and so on, reconfigure space and time and thereby render the idea of individual societies problematic. As he puts it: 'Social relations are never only fixed or located in place but are to very varying degrees constituted through "circulating entities". ... There are many such circulating entities that bring about relationality within and between societies at multiple and varied distances' (Urry, 2007, p. 46).

This is not to say that notions of the individual 'society' no longer have any use: they can be deployed by national authorities as a means of resisting global flows and reasserting a particular version of nationhood. Conversely, 'society' can also be linked to the 'demand for rights of citizenship and for the institutions of civil society' (2000, p. 162) that ironically draw on those very global technological flows that complicate notions of citizenship and civil society. For instance, the internet has been central to the cross-national circulation of discourses about global citizenship and human rights that go on to contribute to the mobilization of nationalist movements. Nevertheless, despite (or perhaps because of) these complexities, Urry derives from the inter-relation of global flows that 'criss-cross societal borders in strikingly new temporal-spatial patterns ... the possibility of a major new agenda for sociology. This is an agenda of mobility' (2000, p. 2).

In developing 'a mobilities agenda', the role of technology is clearly paramount insofar as it permeates and reconfigures the social. Here Urry draws on ANT's account of the hybridity of the social: 'the human and the material intersect in various combinations and networks' (2000, p. 78). When it comes to studying the complexity of societies, again there needs to be 'analyses of the interdependent material-social, or "inhuman" worlds' (2003, p. 18). Moreover, agency is not the preserve of human actors, but 'is achieved in the forming and reforming of chains of networks of humans and nonhumans' (2000, p. 78). Here what we have is a 'profound relationality' which draws on ANT, but also a range of other traditions, notably post-structuralism.

At once, this hybridity is composed of, and the mediator of, the flows that are the object of Urry's mobile sociology. Urry is interested in both the patterns that such flows take, and their extent or 'globalization'. Here ANT again comes in useful insofar as it provides metaphors for thinking about such patterns, their stability and their 'globalization' (not least as contrasted to 'the local'). Thus, Urry draws on Mol and Law's (1994; Law and Mol, 2001 – see Chapters 3 and 4) discussion of a number of models of spatialization (the making of space). First, there are regions – such as individual societies – with their 'clear and distinct boundaries'. Second, there are networks that 'stretch across diverse regions' and are traversed by stable entities such as immutable mobiles (see Chapter 3). Third, there are fluids – namely, those entities that change in the process of their movement – that 'slowly transmute as they move within and across space' (Urry, 2003, p. 41).

Clearly, Urry (2003) wants to get away from the sociological privileging of 'society', and thus sociology's evident dependence on the metaphor of region. 'Network' and 'fluid' seem to be far more useful metaphors if sociology is to come to grips with the sorts of mobilities that Urry detects. Accordingly, he differentiates between 'Globally Integrated Networks' (GINs) and 'Global Fluids' (GFs). Thus 'GINS consist of complex, enduring and predictable networked connections between peoples, objects and technologies stretching across multiple and distant spaces and times' (pp. 56–7). Examples of GINS include Coca-Cola, Microsoft or American Express. However, despite their seeming inflexibility, these are sometimes able to bend, that is to say, they can adapt to 'local' circumstances. Which brings us to GFs. These take 'uneven, emergent and unpredictable shapes' and while they may travel along more structured networks, or scapes, they can escape them in various ways. More concretely, these fluids 'result from people acting upon the basis of local information but where these local actions are, through countless iterations, captured, moved, represented, marketed and generalized within multiple global waves, often impacting upon hugely distant people and places' (p. 60). GFs take many forms and Urry usefully points to a number of instantiations: travelling peoples making up turbulent migration patterns; the internet with its horizontal, promiscuously interconnecting structures; even the global brand that circulates like a virus at once retaining a core identity while proliferating its meanings and associations. Of course, these fluids do not operate in isolation from one other: 'they pass into, through, over and under, each other' (2003, p. 73). This raises the possibility of yet another metaphor, '*fire*' (Law and Singleton, 2005; see Chapter 4), to capture the complex topologies of these spaces that are 'oscillatory, flickering, both here and there, both inside and outside' (Urry, 2003, p. 74) and, we might stress, both present and absent.

Arguably there is a certain ambivalence in Urry's approach to globalization. On the one hand he is interested in delineating large-scale processes and systems. Thus he wants to draw on complexity science in order to 'illuminate the global as a system or series of systems' (2003, p. 7). While the terminology of GINs and GFs suggests a concern with local processes by which the global emerges (a staple of complexity theory), this still hints at 'lifting out' of the global from the local. On the other hand, Urry is clearly aware of the global as a local performance – something that needs to be 'made'. Thus he cites approvingly Latour's quote that there is no macro or micro (or local and global) – these are both the local effects of linking up to entities that are in the process of circulation (2003, p. 123). Indeed, we can quote Law (2004b) and say: 'the global is situated, specific and materially constructed in the practices that make each specificity ... it is specific to each location, and if it is bigger or smaller, it is because it is *made* bigger or smaller at this site or that' (p. 24). Here, then, the local seems to be afforded a precedence over the global: this stands at odds with Urry's complex abstraction of the global.

Another issue with Urry's project concerns the performance of the global by social scientists themselves. As noted, Urry has been critical of sociology's limited perspective on the social and society, and he has drawn on a number of metaphors to expand sociology's analytic toolkit. He is of course aware of the performativity of such a toolkit and its associated methods: that is to say, 'they have effects; they make differences; they enact realities; and they can help to bring into being what they also discover' (Law and Urry, 2004, p. 393). One way of dealing with this is to propose 'complexity theory' as a potential source of metaphors and theories to engage the realities of the twenty-first century. A contrasting route, taken by Law (2004a), is to develop a 'messy methodology' which enables not only the exploration of how social scientists perform 'realities', but are, in return, performed by those 'realities', not least a reality in which the vocabulary of complexity theory circulates (see below). This is a point developed by our next social theorist, Nigel Thrift.

b. Thrift – Toward the Non-Representational

Over a range of writings in the last 20 years or so, Thrift has developed an influential account of the complex changes in contemporary society and how we might complexly approach this complexity. Especially, in the course of three books – *Spatial Formations* (1996), *Knowing Capitalism* (2005) and *Non-Representational Theory* (2008) – Thrift has 'been engaged in an attempt to develop … non-representational theory' (2008, p. 1). In brief, non-representational theory can be understood as a revaluing of academic practice that counters the pre-eminence of theory, a revision of our conception of the world to take in the 'inhuman' and the 'construction of new matterings' (2008, p. 22), and all this with a focus on the embodied, precognitive or affective dimension of humans. Here we see the interdigitation of ontology (the world is full of objects with which we are embroiled) and epistemology (the ways we come to 'know' the world are affected by the fact that we are bodies in interaction with objects).

Thrift, like Urry, is concerned with mobility and draws on 'the leitmotif of movement in its many forms' (2008, p. 5). However, for Thrift 'movement' also serves to emphasize other things. Thus 'movement' can be found in the relations of academic discourse and practice to the rapid changes that characterize other social domains. On this score, he effectively applies ANT to academe itself to show how the rise of complexity metaphors in social science might be linked to 'actor networks … that have translated the metaphors of complexity to their purposes and then circulated them in these mutated forms'. On this score, he identifies three networks – science, management and New Age – as being of particular importance. In making these connections, Thrift tacitly suggests that there is a need to be wary of facile translations of such notions as 'complexity' across networks. Yet, he also sees in such movement 'a sign of something of wider cultural interest and most especially a greater sense of openness and possibility concerning the future' (2005, p. 68). This links to another connotation of movement, namely, the dynamics of 'openness' or processuality in which the world constantly (and 'inventively') unfolds.

In common with Urry, Thrift draws on ANT in order to afford the nonhuman a greater prominence in social theory (e.g. 1996, p. 40). This is echoed in a later insistence on the importance of human–nonhuman hybrids: 'there is every reason to believe that we are surrounded by innumerable hybrids' (2008, p. 19) that constitute 'a world made incarnate by a co-shaping which is neither an intrinsic property of the human being nor of the artefact' (p. 50). What Thrift is telling us is that human agents and subjects emerge (in part at least) from their embroilments with nonhumans, in their hybridity. This is no less the case for larger 'social' entities such as the city which can be 'understood [as] a set of constantly evolving systems or networks ... which intermix categories like the biological, technical, social, economic, and so on' (Amin and Thrift, 2002, p. 78).

At the same time, Thrift cautions us that we cannot necessarily know these hybrids: we are 'surrounded by an ocean of hybrids whose nature we do not know or at best imperfectly understand because we bleed into them in so many odd ways [such that] all sorts of things just seem to show up because we are unable to trace their genealogy or all the forces that trigger how they participate in an event' (2008, p. 19). This also serves as a warning against the tendency of some ANT analysts to 'frame actor-networks as discrete entities pulling in various bits of the world into them as and when it suits their purposes' (2005, p. 57). His broader point is that we need creatively to engage with the complex movements and barely intelligible heterogeneous imbroglios that comprise the world.

Having noted this, Thrift is keen not to 'lose' wholly the sense of human distinctiveness. While, in keeping with ANT, he stresses the relational character of the human, he also identifies the human as unique insofar as it possesses 'capacities of expression, powers of invention, of fabulation, which cannot be gainsaid, in favour of a kind of flattened cohabitation of all things' (2008, p. 111). For Thrift, this is important in that he wants to address how humans are especially equipped imaginatively to project complex worlds and creatively to posit how such worlds unfold toward the not-as-yet.

Here, we come to another of Thrift's criticisms of ANT: it is too 'static' in its accounting: it is 'much more able to describe steely accumulation than lightning strikes, sustained longings and strategies rather than sharp movements that may also pierce our dreams' (2008, p. 110). Relatedly, in ANT there is 'only an attenuated notion of the event, of the fleeting contexts and predicaments that produce potential' (p. 111). Instead, events 'have to be seen as genuinely open to at least some dimensions, and notwithstanding the extraordinary power of many social systems' (p. 174), alternatives, resistances, interruption, surprise and failure abound (see Chapter 7). Such 'event-thinking' has two implications for Thrift's project. The first concerns epistemology. How can we know the world that is characterized by openness and surprise, when we ourselves as knowers are a part of that world and similarly subject to openness and surprise? Under these basic ontological circumstances 'epistemological privilege is impossible' (2005, p. 26) and we can at best only practice some sort of 'modest theory'. The second implication concerns method. What sorts of methodological approaches are adequate to a social world understood in terms of events? Thrift (2008, p. 12) suggests more playful, artistic, experimental methods as means to 'seeing what will happen' and of enabling 'the event to sing to you (as "social researcher")'. We elaborate on this in Chapter 7.

ANT and 'New Economic Sociology'

a. Callon and the 'New Economic Sociology'

In 1999, Michel Callon posed a question in relation to the wider applicability of actor-network theory: 'is ANT of any use to us in understanding markets? And if so, in what ways will it have to be modified?' (Callon, 1999, p. 183). For Callon, this question was partly concerned with addressing the perceived weaknesses of ANT's treatment of the actor. As we have seen, ANT underspecifies the actor: it is treated as radically underdetermined (or rather it emerges in relation to the specificities of particular networks). In the context of economic sociology, two models of the human actor are counterposed: the rational, calculative, self-interested *homo economicus* of economics and the socially embedded, socially determined *homo sociologicus* of sociology. As Callon (1998a) notes, despite their differences, both of these rely on a self-enclosed actor – *homo clausus* – possessed of pre-existing and stable capacities (also see Elias, 1998; Chapter 5). Building on the path-breaking work of Granovetter (1973, 1985), Callon argues that a network account in which the actor and network are sides of the same coin (the actor is a network and a network is comprised of actors) allows us better to grasp the 'adaptability' of actors to the uncertainties and dynamics of markets. Thus, in the case of traders, Callon (1998a) writes: 'The problem of the trader is that of being at any moment able ... to identify those agents whose decisions will have an effect on the one he intends to make or who, inversely, will react to his own decisions. In order to not be caught unawares, he must be capable of following the connections, the unexpected links, without however being submerged in the mass of relations and events' (p. 25).

So here we have an actor that must remain acutely open to the rapid changes 'around' it if it is to function 'at the heart of the stock market'. Against *homo clausus*, then, Callon juxtaposes *homo apertus* – an open, responsive, emergent actor who must nevertheless act as *homo clausus* pursuing her own interests, realizing her particular capacities: 'How is it possible to become *homo clausus* when survival requires one to be *homo apertus*?' (1998a, p. 25). To be sure, this contrast is particularly acute in the case of speculative trading on the stock market. Nevertheless, the same question applies to any market transaction.

How do we explain the emergence of 'agents which are generally individual, calculating humans, foreign to one another, and engaged in the negotiation of contracts … [out of] a proliferation of relations' (Callon, 1999, p. 186)? This is a question that echoes key concerns within ANT: how do specific associations come to be forged, and how are discrete actors emergent in this process?

In order to answer his question, Callon develops a series of concepts that allow us to trace the ways in which the morass of relations is reduced as economic transactions, along with their constitutive calculations, are conducted. Key here are the notions of *disentanglement, framing* and *overflowing*. Framing indicates the 'clear and precise boundary [that] must be drawn between the relations which the agents will take into account and which will serve in their calculations, on the one hand, and the multitude of relations which will be ignored by the calculations as such, on the other' (Callon, 1999, pp. 186–7). Working with economics' idea of externalities, Callon (1998a, p. 17) sees framing as a general term to describe the means by which agents are rendered defined, distinct and dissociated. This framing process applies no less to merchandise and financial goods which are themselves extricated from a tangle of associations. In this way a market supporting transactions amongst individual agents and goods becomes possible.

The idea of framing clearly has echoes of 'classical' ANT: an association is forged between actors in which certain elements of their respective identities are privileged, while others are sidelined (through the processes of interessement, problematization and so on). In the case of markets, framing takes place in numerous ways: it 'does not just depend on this commitment by the actors themselves; it is rooted in the outside world, in various physical and organizational devices' (Callon, 1998b, p. 249). In the case of a contract, presupposed are the existence 'of courts of law … a body of legal texts defining, for example, the content and scope of property rights … solicitors entrusted with recording the state of knowledge held by each of the contracting parties' (p. 254). Callon is particularly interested in the way that 'economics', understood as a repertoire of concrete tools for accounting or marketing, is part of the process of framing. On this score too, we can again detect echoes of the ANT argument that sociology, by virtue of its focus on an exclusively social society, has enacted social relations in a very particular way.

Callon goes on to complicate this picture. Both the calculative tools that serve in the processes of framing, and the processes of framing themselves, are never complete. To frame is to draw on tools that bring with them new associations, and which can become modified over the course of their application: 'Any framing produces overflowing, and any procedure of disentanglement produces new attachments' (1998a, p. 38). Thus Callon (1999, p. 188) proposes 'the term "overflowing" to denote this impossibility of total framing'. This seems like an important nuancing of the 'classical' ANT perspective: the means of rendering associations between actors carry with them other associations (or overflows) that can serve as potential routes to the problematization of those means (see Chapter 4).

Callon's ANT-tinged reworking of economic sociology has inspired a range of elaborations (e.g. Callon et al., 2002, 2007; MacKenzie et al., 2007) as well as attracting numerous critiques (e.g. Miller, 2002). For present purposes I want to focus on the idea of a market 'device' (or thing). This concept usefully extends the coupling of framing and overflowing to address the ways in which connections are made across a variety of areas or spheres – the economy, politics, society, technology while at the same time engaging with what is distinctively economic about these relations. In some ways, the idea of device simply picks up Callon's (1999, p. 193) point that there is a 'variety of possible configurations of actions and actors', and expands on the observation that the processes of economic calculation (or framing) also serve to both subdue and precipitate problematization and contestation (and thus politics – see Barry and Slater, 2002).

According to Muniesa et al. (2007, p. 2) a 'market device' is, put simply, anything that can 'intervene in the construction of markets'. Such market devices can be considered to have agency as long as agency, as with ANT, is understood to be 'distributed' through an 'assemblage' (or agencement). A market device is active in rendering 'things, behaviours and processes economic' (p. 3) but such 'economization' is historical and contingent, though it can be durable too. These economizing market devices take many forms. At the more 'abstract' end of the scale 'pricing techniques, accounting methods, monitoring instruments, trading protocols and benchmarking procedures ... enter into the construction of economic agencement' (p. 4). At the more 'concrete' end, there are such devices as supermarket design (marketing, arrangement and packaging of goods – see Cochoy, 2007) and market research (e.g. the focus group – see Lezaun, 2007). Insofar as these devices 'economize', they can be said to be framing certain relations, actions and objects as 'economic'. Yet, as we noted above, such framing can bring with it entanglements or overflows which can be said to be, amongst other things, 'political'. For instance, the packaging that renders an organic salad mix 'economic' can also overflow and draw connections to the political (for example, gender politics of body shape, or the labour politics of mass production – see Guthman, 2003).

b. The Plastic Bottle as Device

An excellent analysis of the complexity of a market device as it overflows the economic to bring in the cultural, the civic, the ecological and the political can be found in Hawkins et al.'s (2015) *Plastic Water*. This book, which straddles cultural studies, new economic sociology and science and technology studies, concerns the ways in which markets for branded bottled water have emerged to the point that bottled water has become an unexceptional part of everyday life. These authors are interested in how certain devices have successfully framed water as 'economic' in particular ways (e.g. as a form of portable property that is a valued source of routinized self-hydration). However, Hawkins and her colleagues are also interested in the ways in which bottled water has been 'framed' politically as a controversial object. This can take the form of both explicit concerns about the plastic waste generated by associated water consumption practices, and more tacit worries about the impacts on the reputation of civic infrastructures for collecting, cleaning and distributing water.

In particular, Hawkins et al. focus on specific devices, such as the plastic (polyethylene terephthalate or PET) bottle, understood in terms of an assemblage that encompasses the enterprise of relevant corporations and related capital flows (e.g. investment in innovations in plastics manufacture), but also the impact of numerous mundane objects, calculations and practices (e.g. the presence or absence of state-funded water supply systems). Amongst this nexus of relations, the PET bottle was a key market device. Given its lightness, transparency and mould-ability, the PET bottle was key to framing market associations between producers, consumers and water. However, as noted above, this has to be understood in relation to other 'devices' related to, for instance, health (anxieties around 'adequate hydration') and the supposed risks posed by other sorts of water supply systems.

In sum, Hawkins et al. are concerned with the processes by which a market (in this case, for bottled water) is constituted through a specific distribution – an assemblage – of sociomaterial processes that makes certain forms of consumption possible. However, while we might say that the PET bottle is a specific market device that is central to the emergence of a particular, highly complex and heterogeneous, economic assemblage, it is nevertheless a fluid entity (in the sense discussed in Chapter 3). It is thus many things, varying dramatically in what 'it is' as 'it' moves across different settings (or assemblages). So, in addition to a drinks container for ready 'hydration', it is also, for instance, a major pollutant, a waste management problem, or the object of recycling by economically desperate communities. In each of these cases, the PET bottle is contestable.

Let's unpack this a little by following one particular contestation in which the PET bottle is not only a container of health-giving water but also an object that evokes controversy, protest and boycott. Here, what was previously in Callon's terminology called 'overflowing' can be understood as 'multiplicity'. Rather than focus on the ways in which the economic framing of the PET bottle necessarily generates overflows (in the immediate case, the externalities of environmental impact), Hawkins et al. outline the ways in which the PET bottle is enmeshed and enacted through a number of overlapping assemblages, each of which render it a different thing or device. To illustrate crudely, the PET bottle that is a convenient package of health-giving water can be contrasted to the PET bottle that is a wasteful use of resources and a major global pollutant. Drawing on Annemarie Mol's work (2002; see Chapter 7), Hawkins et al. neatly trace the PET bottle's 'ontological multiplicity', and the related ontological politics. One form the politics took involved trying to shift drinking habits so that people use long-lasting bottles and fill these from public water fountains. However, this is not to say there is a level playing field amongst these ontologies. As they argue, some ontologies (and their assemblages) predominate: established corporate assemblages (that manufacture bottled water) are likely to be somewhat more potent than local environmentalist assemblages, though as Hawkins et al. show, such hierarchies can be overturned.

Management and Organizational Studies

Management and organizational studies (MOS) entails a dense constellation of perspectives and topics. For present purposes I want simply to give a flavour of the variety of ways in which ANT has been variously adopted, translated and critiqued by scholars working under the broad umbrella of MOS. As mentioned above, there are key figures who have contributed both to ANT and MOS, notably John Law, Bob Cooper and John Hassard (e.g. Cooper and Law, 1995; see below) and the relationship between MOS and ANT has been a complicated one. Some authors engage in a straightforward application of ANT (e.g. to the writing of business histories; see Ponzoni and Boersma, 2011) or assimilate ANT more or less unadulterated into a larger project (e.g. the development of a critical organizational historiography; see Durepos and Mills, 2012). By comparison, others take a more circumspect view, critically drawing on ANT and/or supplementing it with other theoretical perspectives.

At the more critical end of MOS, Whittle and Spicer (2008) suggest that many devotees of ANT within MOS have failed to cultivate the 'healthy scepticism' that marks much ANT writing and thus have neglected many of its shortcomings. For example they argue that ANT's privileging of the technological results in a reduction of 'organizations to the effects of the essential properties of the non-human world, [thus] ANT hinders our ability to examine the stabilization of an organization as a constructed achievement' (p. 615). The implication is that ANT is not especially useful for the critique of how organizations take, sustain and alter their shape. ANT fails properly to address the role of humans, and relatedly the possibilities of resistance, in these processes of organization. This cautionary tale about the adoption of ANT in MOS is echoed in other work. For example, Hull (1999) draws on the work of Gillian Rose to introduce a desired critical element into ANT, one that, for instance, takes into account both the openness of, and the constraints upon, conduct (specifically as related to knowledge management). Bloomfield and Vurdubakis (1999) suggest that (post-)ANT's problematic relation to its 'outside' or 'other' (see Chapter 4) parallels the practical issues faced by organizations. Organization must socially respond to 'others', not least those strange hybrids (odd admixtures of previously distinct organizational elements) that arise out of processes of change (e.g. working from home erodes the private/public and leisure/work distinctions). Alcadipani and Hassard (2010) similarly take up insights from post-ANT (or what they call 'ANT and After'), notably arguments about the performativity of research (how research constitutes its objects of study) and ontological multiplicity and politics (how a 'thing' such as diabetes turns out to be multiple within and across organizations and thus subject to politics through which this multiplicity is managed). Alcadipani and Hassard suggest that these developments have major implications for 'a reflexive politics of organizing' within MOS and, more particularly, 'Critical Management Studies'.

a. Translations of ANT

In trying to navigate through this nexus of partial appropriations and tactical adaptations, we can draw on an overview of ANT's take-up within MOS by MOS scholars themselves. So, in what follows, I will closely follow Toennesen et al.'s (2006) suggestive account of the varieties of translation of ANT into MOS. In conducting a systematic survey of the MOS literature, Toennesen et al. identify two broad scales against which ANT-related MOS research could be situated. On the one hand, MOS research papers focus on ANT either as a method (for the analysis of organizational and management processes) or as a theory (for reconceptualizing organizational and management processes), though this distinction is not always so clear-cut. On the other hand, the MOS literature makes practical use of ANT terminology as a helpful analytic resource as against engaging 'profoundly' with ANT to question the epistemological and ontological underpinnings of MOS's theory and methods. Within this general framework, Toennesen et al. go on to locate four translational strategies which they call ' simulating', 'emulating', 'reasoning' and 'crafting'.

'Simulating' involves taking up certain elements of ANT and applying them in essentially instrumental ways. While the analytic aim does not include contributing to ANT itself, this does not mean that (the applied bits of) ANT cannot be adapted through a combination with other perspectives (e.g. Foucauldian). So, Dent (2003) examines the shifting relations between doctors and managers within an organizational environment in which hospitals are threatened with closure and managers are attempting to subject medical work to 'rationalization'. For instance, as part of the reconfiguration of the hospital, management aimed to ensure that doctors became more obviously accountable for their actions. This involved an enrolment of doctors into new positions in which they were 'responsibilized' into managerial functions as part of the hospital reorganization. Of the various factors that Dent identifies as playing a part in this remaking of the hospital network, rhetoric was crucial. Thus the management's rhetorical emphasis on hospital 'closure' (as opposed to 'rationalization') facilitated a greater alignment of doctor and management interests, and thus a greater willingness on the part of doctors to adapt their professional roles to the emerging hospital network.

'Emulating' refers to work which draws on ANT as read through the lens of an alternative analytic approach. For instance, Mutch (2002) appreciates how ANT raises the profile of technologies in MOS (especially with regard to implementation of information systems) but, drawing on another version of structuration theory (namely, that of Margaret Archer), is critical of its analytical flatness in which both human actors and society are seen to be emergent from heterogeneous processes. For Mutch this fails to address the specificity of humans, not least their 'embodied, emotional nature' (p. 487). Nevertheless, attending to the role of technologies can assist in understanding how 'society' emerges, but only if technologies are, for instance, properly understood to operate in ways contingent upon their human users. With this reframing of ANT, Mutch grants it a minor corrective role within a social realist perspective on organization.

'Reasoning' refers to translational strategies which entail a more sustained engagement with ANT in order to interrogate and potentially modify the assumptions beneath particular MOS approaches. Here, ANT's function is to provide an alternative to existing ways of theorizing and conceptualizing organizations and organizing. Stephen Fox (2000) draws on ANT (along with certain elements from Foucault's work) to rethink organizational learning (understood through communities of practice theory; see Wenger, 1998). This reconceptualization proceeds down a number of avenues. For instance, he uses ANT to avoid the recourse to macro/micro dichotomies that is evidenced in such common notions as 'organizational culture'. Relatedly, he draws on ANT's translational model of power, and its insistence on technology's role in the constitution of social relations. In this way, Fox sketches an alternative approach that does not presume the 'organization' as the unit of analysis. Instead, ANT helps reorient analysis to the relations of power by which organizational learning takes place – relations that should be understood in terms of how 'masters enrol and mobilize apprentices and other masters and materials, knowledge and practice, how they become an obligatory point of passage' (p. 864). In the terminology of communities of practice theory, this means looking less at how learning spreads through an organization by changing an overarching 'organizational culture', and more at the ways in which communities of practice go about 'growing'. Broadly speaking, these are communities based on shared expertise and common work interests (Wenger, 1998) and do not necessarily respect the ostensible borders of an organization. Thus while they can be located within the 'formal' organization (e.g. a company), they can also extend beyond it. For example, on the basis of shared skills and orientations, a community of practice might encompass both an internal human resource department and an external head-hunter consultancy firm. In other words, the focus is on how specific communities accomplish what seems to be 'organizational learning' by spreading their influence through the processes of 'translation, enrolment and mobilization' (Fox, 2000, p. 864), even if, ironically, that organization's formal borders are breached.

The final translational strategy is 'crafting'. Accordingly, ANT is refashioned in ways that make it more practically relevant to MOS. Where the strategy of 'reasoning' entails the conceptual adaptation of ANT, crafting tends to pursue ANT's methodological implications for MOS. The work of Barbara Czarniawska (2004) is used to illustrate crafting, but she clearly falls into the reasoning category too. Her work has involved a sustained engagement with ANT (e.g. Czarniawska and Hernes, 2005; Czarniawska, 2008; Pippan and Czarniawska, 2010) through which she has developed her own '*action nets*' perspective. The rest of this section focuses on this particular approach as a way of illustrating the fruitful alignment of ANT and MOS concerns.

b. Czarniawska and Action Nets

Czarniawska (e.g. 2008), partly drawing on SSK and ANT, takes a broadly constructionist approach to the social study of organizations. As such she expounds a performative account according to which organization arises out of the social perceptions, interpretations and practices of actors. There are a number of corollaries to this definition. First, actors are engaged in a continuing process of constructing organizations: actors' practices with regard to organizations, and their interpretations of their own and others' practices, are central to this process. Second, given that there are many different sorts of actors with varying perceptions and practices, there are divergent constructions of organizations. Third, no MOS analyst has a privileged overview of this process of construction in organizations – at best they can compare the varying accounts of, and practices concerning, the organization. Finally, the aim of MOS is to document these accounts and practices.

All this reflects Czarniawska's emphasis on the 'processuality' of organization – the continuous effort that goes into making an organization. In other words, MOS should reorient itself to 'organizing' rather than 'organization'. On this score she approvingly cites Law's (1994) call for a 'sociology of verbs'. Of course, Czarniawska does not deny the existence of 'organizations' as more or less stable entities, but she wants to see these as 'temporary reifications, because organizing never ceases' (Czarniawska, 2004, p. 780). To get at this contrast between the process of organizing and the impression of organizational solidity she develops the notion of 'action net'.

Czarniawska (2004) sees 'action nets' as a modest intervention that at root aims to minimize 'that which is taken for granted prior to analysis', which means that, contrary to more traditional treatments of organizations, to conduct an action net analysis is to trace how both 'actors and organizations are the products rather than the sources of organizing' (p. 780). Action nets have much in common with actor-networks – most crucially they both concern processes of translation (see Chapter 3). However, we might say that action nets analysis operates with a more 'dispersed' and 'mutualist' version of translation, especially from the perspective of 'classical' ANT. Czarniawska argues that the latter has concentrated on the translation processes enacted by a few key actors (e.g. Pasteur, Electricité de France) in order to build an actor-network that might act, eventually, as a singular macro actor (such as an organization). ANT thus does 'not focus on organizing processes that do not construct macro actors'. This is the terrain to which the action nets approach lays claim: the 'focus of attention is different ... organizing may or may not lead to a construction of macro actors, depending on the degree to which connections between actions are stabilized and whether or not there is a spokesperson to represent such an actor-network' (2008, p. 21). So, in studying city management, Czarniawska followed the connections amongst actors, connections which traversed the borders of an 'organization' to include, in the case of a city's public marketing, links from 'advertisement production, to finance, to street administration, to publicity regulation, etc' (2004, pp. 782–3). These points of connection can take various forms – some are more 'formal' (e.g. contracts), some more directional (hierarchical, relations of subordination), some more informal (relations of friendship, or empathy). With this variety of connections comes a variety of translations, and it is an advantage of action nets that they are open to all forms and combinations of translation.

One implication of this view of translation is that it becomes difficult to specify any overarching macro actor. Or rather, one needs to empirically engage with actors' own specification of macro actors (including where that actor is the MOS analyst). For Czarniawska key to this process is narrative. In the same way that Czarniawska (2008, pp. 32–49) herself as a researcher organizes her collection of data (e.g. fragmented observations and recordings of talk) along a timeline to produce a retrospective narrative, so too the actors in an action net narrate what they do and what is done to them. Again these narrations take different forms depending on where one sits in an action net: for some actors chronological reports are their main formal narrative tool; for others, such as company directors, it is full-blown stories that are 'properly emplotted and with a point' (p. 36). Actors are thus constantly crafting and deploying their more or less polished narratives in the course of their everyday lives within action nets: they are no different from social scientific analysts weaving together the many fragmentary events and conversations into narratives in order to make sense of them. Czarniawska (2008) mentions several ways of analysing narratives, though crucially these narratives are present in 'small talk in the corridors [as much as in] official decisions' (p. 40). Some talk will draw in more supporters, and finding the right spokesperson (e.g. a company director) can add considerably to a narrative's longevity and reach. It is also important to attend to talk about talk which can reshape the original point of a narrative.

Czarniawska's (2008) concern with narrative does not mean she is uninterested in other elements of action nets. As with ANT, she is keenly aware of the complex roles of technologies in organizing, but stresses that they are simultaneously symbolic, political and practical. As she notes, a hammer can symbolize the dignity of labour, impose a particular relation of power and/or bang in a nail. The analyst's role is to 'capture such transformations of what appears to be the same object, explain how such transformations are possible, and describe their consequences' (pp. 51–2). She is also interested in how organizing is affected by the standards that are inscribed in technologies (and their use). For instance, standards that determine what counts as optimal lighting and heating in offices (Shove, 2003) will shape how organizing takes place, not least because people adapt their comportments accordingly. As Czarniawska points out, these standards are not necessarily available to all organizational actors, though they can sometimes be contested by other actors, for instance the environmental movement (who might influence actors within an organization, such as environmental officers – though see Chapter 5).

Methodologically, action nets follow a modified version of Latour's (1987) injunction to 'follow the actor' (see Chapter 3): 'follow the actant' advises Czarniawska. This means pursue as many points of connection as possible (not just those of the primary actor). Thus to take 'entire action nets as the object of study ... unveils a more comprehensive picture of how organizations are formed, stabilized, dissolved or relocated' (2004, p. 783). Needless to say, this is no easy task. While Czarniawska (2004) recommends forms of participant observation (and observant participation), including shadowing particular actors, and conducting narrative interviews, she retains a powerful sense of the partiality and contingency of all these methods. By balancing immersion in and distance from an action net, action net analysis can at least yield alternative and suggestive narratives.

(Elements of) Geography

ANT has long featured in geographical thought (e.g. Bosco, 2006) to the extent that it is fair to say that some of the most innovative work in post-ANT is found amongst geographers. Geographers have pushed post-ANT in a number of novel directions, elaborating on notions of assemblage or topology in relation to such geographical topics as 'scale' (Marston et al., 2005; Collinge, 2006), the 'urban' (Farias and Bender, 2010; Brenner et al., 2011; Farias, 2011), and 'social-spatial change' (Anderson et al., 2012). Others have drawn on ANT to inspire methodological innovation in geography, for instance in relation to the matter of 'mess' (Ruming, 2009), or the process of cosmopolitical engagement with the relevant actors in nature conservation initiatives (Hinchliffe et al., 2005; Hinchliffe, 2007). We shall return to a number of these concerns in the next chapter where we discuss in more detail aspects of ANT's complex legacy. For present purposes, I consider an early 'appropriation' of ANT to rethink spatiality. I then address an ANT-tinged concept that has been particularly influential, namely the 'more-than-human' (Whatmore, 2002). The relation of species to space, and the role of technologies in the specific experience of landscape through climbing are used further to illustrate this concept.

a. ANT and Spatiality

Jonathan Murdoch was at the forefront of introducing ANT to geographers. In a series of influential papers in the 1990s (e.g. 1997a, 1997b, 1998), he provided a memorable exposition and application of ANT, asking such questions as: how does ANT's symmetry impact on geographical analysis and critique? and how does ANT's commitment to heterogeneity reshape geographical formulations of the local and the global? Thus, he shows how the emphasis on technological actors has a major implication for thinking about spatiality. He notes how, from the perspective of ANT, interaction 'is never (for humans, at least) purely local; it is constituted, construed and configured by distant actions. The key to understanding this … is the role played by resources in stabilizing and maintaining past actions in ways which allow them to bear upon the localized present' (1997a, p. 329). Of course the 'resources' referred to here are the materials and technologies which have been inscribed with particular properties and have been set to work at a distance – framing, defining and configuring the interactions between and amongst the humans and nonhumans elsewhere. One upshot is that actors themselves are emergent from these interactions, and the heterogeneous associations that make up a network (relations which might well be agonistic) are what eventually delineate who or what is ascribed agency (and, indeed, power). For Murdoch, what is geographically interesting in all this is that space (and time) need to be seen as effects of networks mediated by nonhuman resources which, because they act at a distance affecting heterogeneous relations, 'make' space: they bind 'space into social, natural and technical processes' (p. 332). Moreover, because these nonhumans can render associations durable, they also make these associations 'historical', of a particular time.

It is this distinctive attention to nonhumans that Murdoch sees as being one of ANT's most valuable contributions to geographical thinking. So while various geographers have used network-like motifs – Murdoch, for example points to Doreen Massey's (e.g. 1991) influential model of 'power geometries' – they tended, like most social scientists of the time, to privilege the human and the social. In any case, he goes on to suggest there are two main types of spatiality that can be found in ANT studies: spaces of prescription and spaces of negotiation. Thus, in the emergence of networks, a particular locale (such as a centre of calculation like a laboratory) can mobilize various elements (nonhumans, immutable mobiles) to shape (problematize, translate) actors and in so doing associate them to the central locale in specific ways. In some cases these 'links and relations become stabilized … and, therefore, predictable' (Murdoch, 1998, p. 362), and the centre can 'speak' for the whole network (which now effectively acts as a singular actor). These are networks in which norms, as prescribed by the centre and inscribed in certain texts and technologies, are stable, circulate without much modification, and thus impose 'fairly rigid and predictable forms of behaviour'. In contrast to these 'spaces of prescription', there are networks where the associations between elements are 'provisional and divergent, where norms are hard to establish and standards are frequently compromised' (p. 362). These are spaces marked by negotiation and shifting associations amongst elements. Such 'spaces of negotiation' will be 'fluid, interactional and unstable' (p. 362). Of course, Murdoch does not see these two types of space as a dichotomy but as analytical devices that afford purchase on the complex spatialities that ANT brings into view.

However, this raises the issue of who or what enables negotiability. Murdoch presents various arguments that the capacity to 'negotiate' is exclusively human. As Murdoch puts it, one implication is that ANT's commitment to a symmetrical analysis may well fail us when what we wish to address is human actors' ambivalence toward, or marginal connection to, a network (here he draws on the works of Singleton and Star – see Chapter 4). Yet, as Murdoch notes, even 'humans' who display ambivalence or marginality can nevertheless be seen as effects of a network (or multiple networks), as emergent from complex chains of translations. There seems to be an oscillation in Murdoch's geographical framing of ANT between a vision of the human as effect of networks, and a sense of the uniqueness of the human.

b. The More-than-Human

One concept that might 'accommodate' this oscillation is Sarah Whatmore's (2002) 'more-than-human'. In her *Hybrid Geographies*, she sets out her own 'heterogeneous conception of social life' (p. 4) in relation to a number of broad perspectives. So along with an engagement with approaches to biophilosophy, corporeality and everyday practices of knowledge, she also draws on science and technology studies, in particular ANT and the work of Donna Haraway. What this provides is a nexus of themes through which to think the nonhuman in relation to a distributed conception of agency. First, there is a shift from regarding associations as intentional to seeing them as affective, not least in the sense that experience as well as materiality needs to be addressed when talking about nonhuman animals. These are 'creatures "saturated with being" but ... which sit uneasily with the extended casting of social agency figured by ANT in the guise of "quasi-objects" ... or material artefacts' (p. 36). In other words, nonhuman animals need to be differentiated from other sorts of nonhumans (such as technologies) and amongst each other, because the ways in which they are affected by elements within their 'networks' will vary according to their specific capacities (e.g. different sense organs). Second, ANT alerts us to the process of becoming in that the differences between humans and nonhumans shift, allowing for 'a more fluid sense of the spatiality and temporality of hybridity' (p. 161). In other words, Whatmore sees in ANT a resource for mapping the complex ways in which hybridities morph. The particular character of a hybrid is not settled once and for all; it is liable to shift and change depending on what new associations are entered into, what old associations are severed, and what associations become partial or ambiguous. Third, and relatedly, such morphing takes place not within an externally fixed 'geometry' of space and time, but entwined with a topology in which spatiality and temporality are themselves emergent (see also Whatmore and Thorne, 2000). Thus, as hybridities emerge, they combine elements seemingly distant in time (e.g. ancient and modern representations) and space (e.g. scientific or laboratory and everyday or lay practices). As such, it becomes problematic to assume, or impose, external parameters or frameworks of time and space. To do so would be to hamper the analysis of the ways in which the spatially and temporally close and far combine in unexpected ways. In addition to these benefits, Whatmore also values ANT's sensitivity to the ways in which nonhumans can 'kick back' or resist. On this score (and this inflects with recent literature on the 'vitality' – or 'thing power' – of nonhumans, e.g. Bennett, 2010), all nonhumans are 'lively' – though this liveliness is specific to the type of nonhuman. In light of all this, Whatmore supplements ANT by extending the assemblages of associations beyond scientific or technical realms to take in other knowledge practices such as those found in law, governance and everyday life, but also the specific contingencies of nonhuman agency.

Whatmore's nuanced analytic of the more-than-human world – and especially its capacity to explore multiple hybridities – can be illustrated by her case study of the elephant. She traces the elephant's embroilment in two networks each concerned with its conservation. In the first, elephants are mediated by textual and electronic traces that document the lineages and breeding capacities of animals that, as part of zoological collections, are meant to ensure the survival of the species. In the second, elephants emerge through the practices of scientists, volunteers, donors, etc. that come together to form 'an international programme of "science-based conservation research" projects' (Whatmore and Thorne, 2000, p. 38). Whereas the former is associated with 'tales of foresight' and the future survival of species by virtue of their structured captivity, the latter entails 'tales of authenticity' where the elephant is performed, scientifically and popularly, as wildlife in its native habitat. For each of these networks and 'modes of ordering' (Law, 1994), Whatmore identifies three concurrent enactments of elephants: as 'virtual bodies' digitally circulating as data or portraits; as 'bodies in place' affected by the exigencies of zoos or nature reserves; and as 'living spaces' in which the animals are shaped as experiential subjects adapted to one space (e.g. the zoo) rather than another (e.g. their native habitat). Here, then, we see how the elephant becomes, assuming multiple forms through a heterogeneous panoply of practices (e.g. transformed into data, constrained and enabled as a body, and formulated as an experiencing subject).

Now this hybridity of the elephant reminds us that humans too are enmeshed in a more-than-human world. Geographers have explored this human hybridity in some detail in a number of settings. For instance, in some cases, relatively simple technologies serve as a means for exploring how the more-than-human constitutes particular sorts of spatialities. Thus, Barratt (2011, 2012) studies new spaces of climbing that come to be constituted through existing and emergent technologies. In that these technologies (e.g. climbing shoes, bouldering mats, the cam) are enmeshed in accounts of risk and authenticity, they serve in simultaneously shaping the capacities of the body, the affordances of the rock face or crag, and the experience of the climb. At the other end of the scale, comparatively advanced technologies such as Global Positioning Systems (GPS) affect the relationships between humans and 'the landscape' (e.g. Lorimer and Lund, 2003; Michael, 2009b). In these cases, GPS can simultaneously 'expand' the spatial possibilities offered by landscape (e.g. one more or less always knows where one is, so one can move more quickly and safely) and 'reduce ' a landscape's affordances (e.g. GPS-mediated security means that there is less opportunity for the skilful performance of landscape as a risky space of survival). In sum, the 'more-than-human' is a selective adaptation of elements of ANT that illuminates spatiality as fluid and multiple, complex and contested, connected and differentiated.

Conclusion

This chapter has charted a few of the ways in which ANT has been involved in a two-way exchange with disciplines other than science and technology studies. If these disciplines have absorbed much, or parts, of ANT's analytic sensibility, they have worked back upon ANT, developing new concepts (e.g. actor nets, the more-than-human) better suited to their specific empirical domains and conceptual concerns, but also expanding the horizons of ANT. However, against this sunny scenario of mutual advance, we should reflect on the point that these disciplinary engagements with ANT are highly selective: there are traditions in each of these disciplines that remain antagonistic toward an ANT sensibility (to the extent that they even acknowledge its relevance). So, lest this chapter gives the impression that ANT is welcomed with open arms – or even a cautious nod of the head – in other disciplines, we should acknowledge that, taken in the round, the reception that ANT generally receives is, at best, a fragmented and ambivalent one. This is hardly surprising given its still controversial standing even within its home disciplines (see Chapter 4). Having noted all this, recent ANT has begun to propose ways in which dialogues across otherwise disparate and uncommunicative practices might be opened up and sustained. We turn to this key post-ANT theme, amongst several others, in the next chapter where we begin to examine some of ANT's latterday incarnations.

7

ON SOME POST-ANTs

Introduction

Over the course of the last three chapters, we have documented a few of the ways in which ANT has been transported, translated and traduced as it has been applied to various case studies, criticized on numerous grounds, and combined with diverse approaches. Out of the more or less cogent early articulations of ANT we have glimpsed the complex unfolding of a nexus of practices, concerns, accounts that can loosely be brought under the umbrella term 'post-ANT'. At the same time, Latour (2013) has latterly argued that something of ANT is retained: for all the current heterogeneity that comprises post-ANT, a little 'essence' of ANT remains, even if it manifests itself as something different every time it appears. In the present chapter, however, it is the proliferations of post-ANT that concern us.

The take-up of ANT, as we have seen above, has been wide-ranging and in some ways profound. Even where ANT is not directly, or is sparingly, referenced, its influence can be detected. This is particularly the case in those approaches in which the material and the nonhuman have come to be seen as constituent elements of the social, and in which there is a shift from a focus on 'epistemology' (crudely, how is it that we can know something?) to ontology (crudely, what things can exist, or in post-ANT terms, how are things enacted?). On this score, ANT has been integral to the so-called 'ontological turn' or 'material turn' in science and technology studies and, beyond that, in sociology, anthropology and geography. Now, while each of these 'turns' is much contested, 'classical' ANT not only informs, but is also, to borrow Pickering's (1995) phrase, mangled by them, emerging with novel questions and reshaped by new framings. Similarly, ANT has been caught up in evolving philosophical movements, not least that of 'speculative realism' which is concerned with how we might address a world that is constantly in process, opening out toward the 'virtual' or unfolding in relation to the 'not-as-yet'. Again ANT has been a resource in these speculative discussions, but has also turned into something 'other' in the process, for instance, becoming methodologically attuned to the messiness of a 'world of becoming'.

In brief, ANT has been adopted and adapted in very many ways and it would be foolhardy to claim that justice can be done to all the uses to which it has been put or to all the translations it has undergone. So, once more, I have to make my apologies and reiterate the proviso that here I can address only a sample of these post-ANT developments, which inevitably reflect my own trajectories and translations (for an alternative account of post-ANT, see Gad and Bruun Jensen, 2010).

So, the post-ANTs that I discuss in the following traverse a motley but interconnected array of concerns. To begin, there is the issue of politics – post-ANT has arguably become more 'activist' insofar as it aims to develop new ways of thinking about how politics might be conducted. This folds into ANT's typical disclosure of how knowledges – *'matters of fact'* – are produced, circulated and entrenched, but also how these can be reworked as 'matters of concern'. This latter term brings into relief the construction or composition of different matters of facts, and thus their contestability. In our later discussions of such authors as Latour, Stengers, Mol and Puig de la Bellacasa, we encounter a number of ways in which divergent matters of fact and their composition might be productively 'managed'. Now, underpinning many of these accounts is a more or less shared ontological understanding of the world as a 'world of becoming', a world in process, unfolding toward the 'not-as-yet'. This model of the world has particular implications for how we might go about researching it, not least because we as researchers are bound up in this process of unfolding. One implication is that we treat social scientific research practice as an 'event' through which its objects of study are enacted, rendered 'real'. Another implication is that, given that researchers are themselves being affected by the realities they enact, then perhaps a more speculative ethos for doing research is in order, one which researcher, researched and research topic co-emerge.

In what follows, we engage these post-ANT themes in the following way. We initially present an extended overview of the ways in which ANT has 'become political' insofar as it has examined the sorts of conditions under which diverse, antagonistic actors, assemblages and matters of fact emerge yet might be brought together. Key to this has been post-ANT's advocacy of particular sorts of forums into which the presence of otherwise marginal or excluded actors can be incorporated (Latour's Dingpolitics, Stengers' cosmopolitics, Callon's hybrid forums). But we also trace some post-ANT accounts of the *de facto* politics that mark specific settings in which divergent actors go about practically managing their differences and potential antagonisms (Mol's hospital, Born and Barry's art–science collaborations). Finally we trace this 'becoming political' as it applies to post-ANT methodology: *research events* entail the interactions of disparate researcher and participant worlds, interactions that are inevitably political. We therefore also address methodology: Law's concept of *'method assemblage'* is central here, as is more recent thinking on method in terms of *speculation*.

Concern, Composition and the Common World

In his *Politics of Nature*, Latour (2004a) attempts to reimagine the nature of a politics that can appropriately respond to the impending ecological catastrophes that hang over us. Accordingly, within this new politics, nature will have to acquire some sort of 'voice' or, as Latour puts it in his opening discussion, 'new beings that have previously found themselves underrepresented or badly represented' (p. 9) will need to be brought into a renewed political process. Ironically, such representation requires that nature itself must be abandoned. This is because, to put it simply, nature has been the preserve of Science – with a capital 'S' and in the singular to distinguish it from the complexities and contingencies of the sciences (small 's' and plural). It is Science that speaks definitively on nature's behalf, and as such it 'render[s] ordinary political life impotent through the threat of an incontestable nature' (p. 10). On this basis, Latour develops, in this book and other writings, a rethinking of what it means to do an 'ecological politics' (or politics *per se,* for that matter) where the privileged position of Science (or any privileged 'Way of Knowing', for that matter) has been revised.

However, this revision does not mean a simple critique of Science. In Latour's (2004b) article, 'Why has critique run out of steam?', he describes how his reservations about critique are partly motivated by the need to provide a better account of how to engage with 'reality'. Critique operates through a debunking of 'matters of fact' (not least those that are delineated by Science) – showing how they are contingent on the particular circumstances out of which they arose. The problem is that critique itself is no less subject to the same sort of debunking, this time with regard to the 'matters of facts', and the 'particular circumstances' that underpin that critique. By comparison, Latour wants us to engage with the multiplicity that makes up reality or what he sometimes calls the *pluriverse* (Latour, 2004a, 2005a) or *multinaturalism* (Latour, 2011). There are many different ways in which reality manifests itself, and each of these entails the bringing together, the *composition* or concrescence, of diverse heterogeneous elements (Whitehead, 1978/1929; Latour, 1999). If critique rests on mobilizing a particular reality which is itself, ironically, open to critique, perhaps it is more productive to suggest that there are multiple realities (each with their own contingency, given that each can be subject to critique) which can be put into some sort of 'dialogue'. Given that these realities are always emergent through particular circumstances and conditions, no longer should they be understood in the terms of 'matters of fact'. Rather for Latour these are really 'matters of concern' insofar as each is constitutively open to critique, interrogation or unravelling by virtue of its contingency in particular circumstances and conditions. Latour writes:

> The mistake we made, the mistake I made, was to believe that there was
> no efficient way to criticize matters of fact except by moving *away* from
> them and directing one's attention *toward* the conditions that made them

possible. But this meant accepting much too uncritically what matters of
fact were. ... Critique has not been critical enough in spite of all its sore-
scratching. Reality is not defined by matters of fact. Matters of fact are
not all that is given in experience. Matters of fact are only very partial
and, I would argue, very polemical, very political renderings of matters of
concern and only a subset of what could also be called *states of affairs*.
(2004b, pp. 231–2)

In other words, Latour is suggesting that 'matters of fact' are just one particular and potent way of thinking about 'things'. What the idea of 'matters of
concern' does is point toward the ways in which 'things' are gathered or
assembled together, that is composed out of a multitude of elements, practices,
'interests' and so on. (Latour [2010b] also speaks of this contrast in terms of
reals or facts versus constructions or fetishes that together combine as 'factiches'.)
The aim is not to 'do critique' by disassembling these elements, but to acknowledge, and indeed celebrate, the concern that goes into the process of assembling
'things', that is, that renders matters of fact. As Latour goes on to say: 'The critic
is not the one who debunks, but the one who assembles. The critic is not the one
who lifts the rugs from under the feet of the naïve believers, but the one who
offers the participants arenas in which to gather. The critic is ... the one for whom,
if something is constructed, then it means it is fragile and thus in great need of
care and caution' (2004b, p. 246).

   The idea of an 'arena in which to gather' ties in with Latour's (2005b)
interest in 'the various shapes of the *assemblies* that can make sense of all
those *assemblages*' (p. 14). As such, in engaging with matters of concern it
is necessary to engage with the sorts of gatherings (of humans and nonhumans) through which to address the gatherings that constitute matters of
fact. Latour has discussed this in terms of Dingpolitik which is, amongst
other things, an assembly in which: politics is conducted not simply by
humans but includes the many concerns with which they are entangled (not
least their embroilments with nonhumans – in other words, the participants
in such an assembly are themselves assemblages); matters of facts are translated in terms of their complex relationalities, as matters of concern; there
is an open 'invitation' to contribute to an assembly that is extended to all
those assemblages that have a claim, whether or not those assemblages are
'proper' (for instance, in possession of certain expert or professional skills);
the process of assembling matters of concern is not derailed by a powerful
desire for unity amongst participants, or waylaid by an anxiety that there is
too much disunity.

   Latour (2010a) has further developed this view of Dingpolitik (or what
he also calls the 'Parliament of Things') through a discussion of '*compositionism*'. This is another term that again references how both assemblies and
assemblages are put together, assembled. Compositionism likewise contrasts
to critique: 'what performs critique cannot also compose' (p. 475). Instead
of debunking through critique, of exposing the fact that something has been

constructed, compositionism urges us to accept that everything is composed. The issue now becomes one of asking 'what is *well* and what is *badly* constructed (or composed)' (p. 478)? Or to reframe this in terms of matters of concern – how well is this or that matter of concern put together? But in pursuing these questions, in composing these matters of concern, there is a need to proceed carefully, for the assemblages that come together in a composed assembly might enact themselves in very different ways, they might well 'speak' in terms unfamiliar to one another (speak is placed in inverted commas to denote that, as Latour insists, the interactions between assemblages are not simply linguistic). Under these circumstances, to compose means incorporating all the 'meanings of the word, including to compose with, that is to compromise, to care, to move slowly, with caution and precaution' (p. 487). Out of this careful assembling and composing Latour hopes that there will emerge a 'common world', one that stands in contrast to the pre-established 'common world' of, say, Science.

We can note one final term from Latour's evolving 'political ecological' vocabulary, that of '*propositions*'. For Latour (2004a, p. 247) the proposition – which he derives from Whitehead (e.g. 1978/1929) – denotes 'an association of humans and nonhumans' before it becomes settled, instituted or durable. It is, in other words, an assemblage whose composition is still in process, that is yet to be fully articulated not least insofar as it seeks articulation with other propositions within an assembly in pursuit of a common world. Proposition also connotes a certain uncertainty and an openness to new associations that are more complicated and extended (2004a, p. 83). As Latour has put it elsewhere, propositions are 'occasions given to different entities to enter into contact. These occasions for interaction allow the entities to modify their definitions over the course of an event' (1999, p. 141), an event such as an assembly. Propositions also throw something else into relief, namely, that everything is potentially subject to change: the grounds of the common world, the issues at stake within the assembly are themselves subject to rearticulation. We shall return to these issues when we discuss Stengers' parallel notion of cosmopolitics.

Here we can make two additional observations. First, Latour's articulation of the processes by which a common world is composed is meant to be 'unthreatening' to those who have much to lose, such as scientists. Rather than debunk them, Latour's is a 'diplomatic' effort to acknowledge and value the sciences' contributions in a collective process of working out what issues are at stake, while also acknowledging and valuing the contributions of others who are less formally accredited. As noted above, the aim of Latour's schema is to avoid the impasses of critique in order to enable the productivities of composition and collectivity. The second observation is that Latour places particular value on the multiplication and extension of associations within and across assemblages (or propositions). It is out of this complication that a good common world can emerge. This normative dimension is especially clear in his (2004c) discussion of the body for which a 'good life' entails the proliferation of associations with other bodies and entities, that is, the enhancements of the capacities to affect and be affected. As Michael and Rosengarten (2012b) point out, this is not always a good thing: one body's (read assemblage's or assembly's) expansion can be another's contraction; to forge new connections to others, might mean that the connections of others are severed (or undermined, or reinforced in unwanted ways). In other words, compositionism invariably excludes as well as includes. This 'matter of concern' is taken up below when we address Law's (2004a) account of social scientific methodology. In brief, if empirical research entails the making of new associations between researchers and participants, this potentially entails a prospective contraction of the latter's associations elsewhere.

Performativity and Politics

In the Introduction to this chapter, it was suggested that post-ANT can be attached to what has been called the 'ontological turn', not least in science and technology studies. This term evokes a refocusing of empirical and analytic attention away from how representations are crafted (for example, how scientific facts are 'socially constructed') toward how 'reality' is made or enacted. As Sismondo (2015) remarks, STS has long been interested in 'ontology' and ANT has been at the forefront of such an interest. However, what the post-ANT accounts do is place ontology in relation to practice, acknowledge the multiplicity of these practices and their performance of particular realities, and address the politics by which such ontologies (or realities) interact with one another. As such, this post-ANT (re)turn to ontology is paralleled by Latour's recent *'political ecology'* where multiple realities or ontologies are portrayed as diverse propositions.

a. Ontological Multiplicity

A foundational argument for the 'ontological' approach in post-ANT is that it does not assume a singular reality on which there are variable perspectives. Rather, as Mol (1999) puts it, there is a shift to a notion of reality that is 'done and enacted rather than observed. Rather than being seen by a diversity of watching eyes while itself remaining untouched in the centre, reality is manipulated by means of various tools in the course of a diversity of practices' (p. 77). As Mol goes on to say, this means that the activities that perform an object do not reveal one or other characteristic of a pre-existing object. In her example of cutting, viewing with ultrasound, or weighing, each activity enacts a different object: it is not that this same body is fleshy, opaque or heavy – rather this is a fleshy body, now it is an opaque body, now a heavy body: 'They are multiple forms of reality itself'. This can be more formally understood in terms of primary and secondary qualities. Accordingly, primary qualities denote the substance of an entity, and secondary qualities the characteristics that are laid 'on top' of this substance not least through the vagaries of human perception (see, for instance, Whitehead, 1978/1929, 1967/1933; Halewood, 2011; Latour, 2011). However, if we attend to the specificity of the performance of an entity, then we find that we never encounter the essential (or abstracted) entity. For example, we never see 'the car' that happens to be red or rusted or broken but always the particular car ('this red car', 'this rusted car', 'this broken car'). And even when we do think we encounter an essential (or abstracted) entity, it has always had to be enacted as such. If we were to imagine 'the car' it turns out to be this engineer's or that designer's, or, perhaps more likely, a particular philosopher's, abstraction of a car (e.g. Law and Singleton, 2000; Michael, 2012b).

One of the implications of this is, to reiterate, that reality is multiple. As Mol (1999) puts it, 'if reality is done, if it is historically, culturally and materially located, then it is multiple' (p. 75). In one key example, Mol shows that what anaemia 'is' varies in keeping with the practices that perform it – clinical, statistical or pathophysiological. In Mol's (2002) now classic study *The Body Multiple*, she traces in detail how atherosclerosis is enacted in different spaces within a hospital (the waiting room, the consulting room, the pathology lab, etc.). Under the pathologist's microscope atherosclerosis is something very different from the atherosclerosis that is rendered through a doctor's touching of a patient's leg. Indeed, this difference can be further dramatized when we recognize that they can be mutually exclusive: the former requires an amputated leg, the latter an intact patient able to communicate. It goes without saying that such divergent enactments depend on very different arrays of objects and technologies (but also on some that are held in common – e.g. chairs and lights).

A word of clarification is in order here. So far the terms '*perform*' and '*enact*' (or performance and *enactment*) have been used interchangeably. While some authors are quite happy with this (e.g. Law, 2011), Mol is clear that she prefers enact and enactment, not least because perform and performance have some undesirable connotations. For instance, they might suggest, following Goffman's (1959) dramaturgical model, that there is a 'backstage' where 'real reality is hiding' (Mol, 2002, p. 32), or that an activity is difficult and can be successfully or unsuccessfully accomplished, or that there are 'performative' effects such that what is done in the 'here and now' has impacts beyond that 'here and now'. Enactment, by comparison, neither implies a 'performer' nor a 'real reality' behind or beyond the here and now. Thus, it is 'in practices [that] objects are enacted [which] … leaves the actors vague. It also suggests that in the act, and only then and there, something is – being enacted' (Mol, 2002, p. 33). Law (2011) reinforces the view that practices do not implicate a performer as such; rather they should be understood as 'assemblages' in which bodies, discourses, technologies, objects, and so on are brought together to perform or enact a particular reality (in the above cases, particular versions of anaemia or atherosclerosis). Later, it will be suggested that 'eventuate' is perhaps preferable to both 'enact' and 'perform', but for what immediately follows these will continue to be used interchangeably.

So, if reality is multiple, how do the various versions interact? For Mol (1999) versions of anaemia can sometimes simply coexist, or sometimes collaborate, or sometimes be co-dependent, or sometimes clash. Similarly, the different enactments of atherosclerosis that arise within a particular hospital can be coordinated to generate a single disease, as, say when vascular surgeons consult and collaborate with pathologists, or they can remain distinct and separate as in the cases of the haematology laboratory and vascular surgery department. These discrete versions of atherosclerosis are not necessarily a source of tension or anxiety – as Mol (2002, p. 87) comments, 'there is not always a necessity to search for common ground'.

This 'turn to ontology' is clearly allied to a model of reality as multiple: as such, a multiplicity of practices is generative of a multiplicity of realities which more or less tightly cohere. This 'more or less coherence' can be understood in terms of what Law (2011) calls non-coherence which he places in contradistinction to incoherence with its normative connotations that the goal is coherence. For Law, 'coherence is simply an aspiration. In practice, practices are always more or less non-coherent. They work by enacting different versions of reality and more or less successfully holding these together' (p. 175). As we saw above, non-coherence is especially well illustrated by 'the' hypoglycaemic body (Mol and Law, 2004). In dealing with their hypoglycaemia people engage in 'pertinent' practices such as measuring blood sugar levels, avoiding particular foods, negotiating care with their friends and relatives. But they also practise 'impertinent' things such as drinking a little too much, or indulging a sweet tooth. These 'divergent' enactments of the body might not be 'coherent' but it does not matter as long as the non-coherent body does not fragment, fall apart.

The obvious question that follows is: through what practices are practices 'held together'? In Mol's case study of the enactments of atherosclerosis within a particular hospital, she points to a number of 'coordination' practices – the ontological politics – that manage these ontological differences. For instance, she notes cases where one reality wins out over another, though it is not always pre-given which reality that will be. Thus, it might appear that, under a regime where therapy depends on laboratory findings, the practices of 'subjective complaints' are always subordinated to the practices of 'objective laboratory tests'. While this might be the norm, it turns out that things can be more pliable and on occasion lab measurements are discarded (especially if some of their contingencies are taken into account and the lab measurements' reliability is thrown into doubt). Mol also reports on cases where a 'composite' reality emerges. For example, the enactment of the object 'atherosclerosis that requires invasive treatment' (2002, p. 70) entails not only objective diagnostic tests but also a series of other 'social' considerations such as the patient's home circumstances or the extent of recovery time after surgery. In sum, in addressing the hanging together or otherwise of multiple realities, we need also to consider the sorts of coordination practices that are possible ('hierarchy' or 'composite' in the above illustrations).

Needless to say, Mol's analysis reflects the specificities of her case study – the practices she describes take place within a particular hospital. These practices are relatively 'close' to each other – to enact atherosclerosis as a 'treatable object', materials and texts must circulate in a timely way amongst various relevant practitioners. By comparison, Brosnan and Michael (2014) suggest that 'coordination' can take place through what we might call a 'prospective reality', such as the promise of future collaboration. In their account of a university-based research group in which there was very limited 'common ground' between laboratory and clinical researchers, it was their enactment of the future that was key to 'holding together' the group. In particular, their enactment of the research group leader as someone who straddled laboratory and clinic was also an enactment of the prospect of future collaboration. (As an aside we might register the ways in which this is a reality-in-waiting that parallels the not-quite-realities documented by Law and Lien [2013] in their discussion of salmon farming, and various types of salmon that never managed to get properly enacted.) The broader point here is that practices enact many different sorts of realities that enable the coordination, or at least the management, of different realities and their practices.

b. Interdisciplinarity

Another way of thinking about this inter-relation of different realities or ontologies is in terms of interdisciplinarity. For our purposes, interdisciplinarity can be minimally defined as the collaboration of experts from different specialisms. We make no attempt to differentiate interdisciplinarity from other terms such as transdisciplinarity or cross-disciplinarity, nor to specify what the specialisms might be, nor to delineate the character of the collaboration. This is because here we are primarily interested in the empirical ways in which the differences in discipline-based practices are managed (as opposed to providing recommendations for how disciplines – and their interactions – should best be organized). The work of Andrew Barry and his colleagues has been particularly insightful in this respect (Barry et al., 2008; Barry and Born, 2013), not least because they are interested – like Latour, Mol and Law – in the sorts of realities that enter into, and emerge through, these interactions.

Barry et al. (2008) conducted research into the collaborations across disciplines that fell into, on the one hand, natural sciences or engineering and, on the other, social sciences or arts. In common with the views outlined above, they argue that interdisciplinarity should be regarded in terms that capture both the processes of 'coordination' (and sometimes 'synthesis') as they play out across contributing disciplines, but also the tensions between disciplinary and interdisciplinary practices. Interdisciplinarity is as much marked by agonism and antagonism as by cooperation and collaboration. With this in mind, and through their investigation of collaborations across disparate disciplines, Barry et al. develop a classification of three conceptually distinct, though empirically entwined, logics that shape collaboration.

In the logic of accountability exposure to artistic or social scientific practice might serve to make scientists more aware of, and responsive to, public
or stakeholder concerns and priorities. Barry et al. partly exemplify this logic
with the work of Callon et al. (2001) on *hybrid forums*; these are discussed
in more detail below. The logic of innovation is marked by the role of social
science as a means to identifying potential users, desires or markets for technoscientific innovations. For example, anthropologists might feed findings
about emerging user preferences into the processes of design, engineering or
information and communications technology innovation. Finally, in the logic
of ontology the different disciplines work together to generate a new ontology in which both the research object of concern, and the relations of
research, are transformed.

This logic of ontology is elegantly illustrated in Born and Barry's (2010)
discussion of the PigeonBlog. This 'public experiment' involved collaboration
between an artist, Beatriz da Costa, and air quality control scientists. Instead
of the usual static processes of measuring air quality (sensors fixed to street
posts across the city), da Costa attached to homing pigeons GPS-linked sensors
which could transmit 'real-time location-based pollution data and imaging to
an online mapping and blogging site' (p. 113). The website on which the
PigeonBlog data were displayed also contained educational material which
linked into, and aimed to raise, the profile of air quality as a public issue, and
to encourage contributions from the public (including the gathering of air quality data). As Born and Barry discuss, this amounts to 'a reconceptualization of
air quality as an object of measurement ... [a] different kind of public knowledge of air quality ... [and a] reconfiguring [of] the objects both of art and of
scientific research' (pp. 114–15). If PigeonBlog indicates the emergence of new
objects and relations typical of the logic of ontology, we can nevertheless detect
the play of the logics of accountability and innovation in, respectively, the
increased presence and status of the public, and scientific innovation in
response to emerging public concerns.

This latter observation suggests that seemingly singular practices (or projects such as PigeonBlog) can themselves enact – simultaneously – multiple
realities, or what Law (2011) has called 'collateral realities'. This is because
practices entail a multitude of implicit elements. So while the explicit ontological politics of atherosclerosis might entail managing the differences
between clinical and laboratory practices (winning over, composite), there are
implicit practices at play too. For instance, we can point to the dress code or
professional comportment or language (terminologically expert or otherwise)
shared across the different practitioners. While these practices are seemingly
incidental, they are nevertheless crucial to the coordination of other more
explicit practices. It is these 'background' practices that usually escape notice
that allow for the smooth interaction – Law says 'choreography' – amongst
ostensibly distinct practices to take place (e.g. clinical and laboratory – and
scientific and artistic, in the case of PigeonBlog – practices can be coordinated

because the practitioners share a language, a comportment, a code through which they implicitly recognize their commonalities). On one level this allows ontological politics to proceed, on another it silences politics because a particular unquestioned common reality is tacitly assumed and enacted. In the present case of treating atherosclerosis, we might say, for convenience's sake, that it is something like the collateral reality of the expert/public or practitioner/patient division that is being discreetly performed. Law's point is, as well as the explicit enactments of realities (and their coordination), these tacit performances of collateral realities also need to be addressed. After all, it is these that are liable to remain unnoticed and thus uncontested.

In this section, we have discussed how reality is enacted through practices, how these different realities butt up against each other and how yet other practices manage this diversity and disparity. We have also seen how some of these realities are rather less accessible than others, not least because they emerge out of the tacit dimensions of practice. Of course all this applies no less to academic – including post-ANT – practices. The realities being enacted by post-ANT practitioners are ones in which the multiplicity of reality can be put on display, and the practices by which particular – more *and* less explicit – realities are established can be empirically explored. In contrast, some post-ANT authors have begun to develop 'framings' for how to enable the 'coordination' of divergent practices. Thus, rather than document how a 'common ground' is made present – or not – in the enactment of multiple realities, is it possible to set out some parameters or practices by which such a 'common ground' might be established? That is to say, how might post-ANT contribute to the development of processes or procedures through which distinct ontologies might be brought together in ways that are productive?

Cosmopolitics

In the foregoing we have seen two post-ANT enactments of, let us call it, a 'politics of reality'. On the one hand, there is Latour's 'normative', or rather diplomatic, invitation to engage in the practical negotiation of multiple realities. On the other, there is Mol's and Law's accounts of how multiple realities emerge and are managed (or 'mismanaged') in and through practice. The former aspires to articulate the conditions under which disparate realities may be assembled with a view to addressing the common emergence of urgent 'problems' (the most obvious problem is, *prima facie*, the threat of global environmental catastrophe). By contrast, the latter charts the ways in which actual 'problems' such as atherosclerosis, anaemia, or farm animal welfare (Law, 2011) turn out to be multiple realities whose enactments can be empirically traced as they coordinate, coexist, or tacitly yield other realities. In this section, we begin to examine another attempt to articulate some of the conditions of an ecological politics – or a cosmopolitics – and begin to ask how this might inform our thinking about ontological politics.

a. Stengers

Latour's perspective is much indebted to the writings of the philosopher Isabelle Stengers. Both share an interest in Whitehead, and both have explored – in often intersecting ways – how different practices (and the realities they perform) might be brought into practical dialogue with one another (while making sure that they remain open about the character of that 'practical dialogue'). In Stengers' (e.g. 2005a, 2010a) vocabulary, the term 'cosmopolitics' has been especially influential (not least for Latour), though Stengers herself has been circumspect about its usefulness (e.g. 2005b), on occasion preferring the term '*ecology of practices*'. As with Latour's 'ecological politics', for Stengers, cosmopolitics is concerned with composing the 'good common world' – that is what the 'cosmos' of cosmopolitics denotes, after all. Cosmopolitics is thus concerned with bringing together the disparate practitioners and practices that can contribute to the making – the emergence – of the issue at stake. And again, as with Latour, this common world is uncertain, an 'unknown constituted by these multiple, divergent worlds, [composed of] the articulations of which they could eventually be capable' (Stengers, 2005a, p. 995). Now, a key priority for Stengers is 'precisely to slow down the construction of this common world, to create a space for hesitation regarding what it means to say "good" ' (p. 995).

One way in which the making the common world might be slowed down is by attending to what she calls the 'idiot'. This is a conceptual figure that denotes those who refuse to enter the process of cosmopolitics: 'the idiot can neither reply nor discuss the issue ... [the idiot] does not know ... the idiot demands that we slow down, that we don't consider ourselves authorized to believe we possess the meaning of what we know' (p. 995). The task of the analyst – and indeed the practitioner within the process of cosmopolitics – is to 'bestow efficacy upon the murmurings of the idiot, the "there is something more important" that is so easy to forget because it "cannot be taken into account", because the idiot neither objects nor proposes anything that "counts"' (p. 1001). Put succinctly, the idiot, as the one who refuses cosmopolitics, is crucial to the very operation of cosmopolitics because it serves to remind the practitioners that their particular practices and perspectives have implications and impacts beyond what is immediately apparent.

We can take as an initial, and brief, example of this Callon and Rabeharisoa's (2004) reflections on what it meant for them as researchers to be faced with a 'participant' – Gino – who, as a sufferer of limb-girdle muscular dystrophy, refused to take on the relevant genetic knowledge, to get involved in the complex advocacy networks that represented him, or to participate 'properly' in an interview. Callon and Rabeharisoa take the interview situation to be akin to something like an experimental public arena (which for our purposes can stand in as a cosmopolitical event). By refusing to enter into it in order to state his 'position' or 'view', Gino poses a nexus of challenges to what is assumed by this arena: he resists a certain 'geneticization' of his identity (as a genetic carrier of limb-girdle muscular dystrophy); indeed 'he chooses other forms of human-ity', and a different 'form of morality and reason' (p. 6). The main point here is that Gino's muteness affords a 'slowing down' of the experimental public arena that is the interview, a circumspection about its value, and thus an 'insight into the limits and conditions of sociological inquiry' (p. 24).

If the idiot enables a certain hesitation in the cosmopolitical process it is because it stands outside of it. Yet hesitation is central to cosmopolitics irre-spective of the idiot's impact. If cosmopolitics is to proceed hesitantly, other mechanisms – Stengers refers to art, artifice and staging – must also be in play. Thus while expert accounts are taken as relevant they must be staged in ways that give voice to those – minorities, for instance (Stengers, 2005b) – that might be disadvantaged or thwarted by the decisions that are based on expert testi-mony. Cosmopolitics thus operates with a staging that puts participants 'into equality' but not 'equivalence': there are no common criteria, standards or measures by which the practices and realities of protagonists can be compared: protagonists have to be present in 'a mode that makes the decision as decision as difficult as possible, that precludes any shortcut or simplification, any dif-ferentiation *a priori* between that which counts and that which does not' (Stengers, 2005a, p. 1003).

But how is this equality to be rendered? Let us take a step back. We noted at outset that a pivotal element in cosmopolitics and political ecology is the pres-ence of the nonhuman. For Stengers (e.g. 2010a, 2010b), the nonhuman must be understood in relation to the practices that enact it. Practices, insofar as they entail forms of 'experimentation' that access the nonhuman, are heterogeneous. That is to say, practitioners' enactments of the nonhumans are not 'social con-structions' but involve – as we have seen throughout this book – associations between practitioners and a panoply of heterogeneous elements (human, non-human, sociotechnical, etc.). Drawing on Latour (1999), Stengers refers to this process as a sort of knot (Stengers, 2010b, pp. 14ff.) – or what above was called a 'composition'. The point is that such a knot incorporates 'nonhuman interven-tions' that are accessed by practitioners. Nonhumans (such as a disease entity, or an at-risk species) thus make themselves 'felt' in these knots, through the practices of the practitioners who, in working with them, both exercise particu-lar professional standards, and flexibly, practically engage with those nonhumans. Along the way, practitioners differentiate between what can be regarded as a 'fact' (true) or an 'artefact' (untrue) in relation to a nonhuman. However, for Stengers, practices further connote a 'hesitation' about following the profes-sional standards that inform practitioners' activities (and this applies to any relevant knowledge-producing activity, as much to witchcraft as to science). So while practitioners can be spokespersons for 'their' particular nonhumans within a cosmopolitical event, they are, on the one hand, 'obligated' to those nonhumans insofar as 'accurately' representing them according to their own professional standards, and, on the other, 'hesitant' insofar as these standards that allow them to represent the nonhumans are contingent. To put this another way, any representation is propositional (see above) in that it reflects the possibility that a nonhuman remains open to new associations, to becoming something different, and thus betraying their spokespersons (recall the three biologists of St Brieuc Bay betrayed by their scallops – see Chapter 3). And, it goes without saying, practitioners might also be undermined by their human allies who can unexpectedly abandon them (say collaborators who once supported their version of the 'nonhuman' in question).

In any case, we could understand cosmopolitics as an artful, indeed experimental, event in which practitioners' obligation and hesitancy opens out onto different forms of practice that might mutually 'resonate' with the practices of other practitioners (Stengers, 2010b). It is in this commonly shared obligation and hesitancy that the equality mentioned above might be said to be grounded: everyone is committed to and circumspect about their nonhuman and their practices. On top of this, any such experimental or artful cosmopolitical event that aims to enable resonance across disparate practices cannot stand above or beyond those practices, for such an event is similarly composed of practices, this time political ones. As Stengers insists, it is necessary to guard against imposing particular 'universal' models (say, where spokespersons are singular agents replete with pre-given interests) of how such a resonance might proceed. The nature of interactions that make up the cosmopolitical event must itself be open. There is, in effect, an equality about the form that equality takes. Taken in the round, what cosmopolitics promises is the possibility of change in which the practices of others become 'available' in open ways, thus enabling practitioners' own practices potentially to shift. Note that there is no guarantee of consensus here, though there is the prospect of alignment amongst practices.

b. Hybrid Forums

There have been various attempts at developing cosmopolitical experiments (e.g. Hinchliffe et al., 2005; Hinchliffe, 2007; Whatmore, 2013) and we shall address some of these below when we turn to the speculative dimensions of cosmopolitics. For now, as a partial example of how cosmopolitics might play out in practice, we can draw on Callon's (e.g. Callon et al., 2001) discussion of 'hybrid forums'. To reiterate, these are arenas in which a range of divergent actors can gather to negotiate openly particular technical issues. Thus those who have a stake in the issue might be drawn from a variety of backgrounds – science, technology, politics, law, the public – and the discussions that constitute the issue can span numerous topics and approaches – legal, ethical, biological, medical, chemical, political, economic, even experiential.

Central to the hybrid forum is a dual shift in the form of politics (which echoes the account of ecological politics and cosmopolitics presented above). On the one hand, laypeople – ordinary citizens – can participate in, and contribute to, those technical discussions which had previously been the preserve of specialists and experts. Along the way, as we have noted, the 'technicity' of those technical discussions is expanded to incorporate a multitude of heterogeneous concerns and queries. The divide between lay persons and their usual representatives or delegates begins to dissipate: professional politicians lose their privileged role of providing the voice for ordinary citizens, and of determining the 'appropriate' shape of the forum, that is the 'composition of the collective'. In other words, the 'identity of the groups making up the collective [of the hybrid forum] and the very composition of the collective are left open for debate' (Callon et al., 2001, p. 128). Under such conditions of openness, groups are enabled to find their voice and to express their identity, but also begin to listen to other groups thereby negotiating and articulating their identity anew in an emergent process of composing the collective (and a common world). One implication is that it is not possible to specify at the outset what these forums will look like – it will depend on the peculiarities of the issues at stake and the actors who wish to contribute: indeed, as Stengers insists, such arenas need to be 'experimental'.

Nevertheless, Callon et al. attempt to set out a number of criteria against which to assess the operation of hybrid forums, crucially in relation to the extent to which lay groups are enabled to contribute. As such, they devise three 'organizational criteria': 'intensity' refers to, for instance, how early on in a forum's process laypeople are involved; 'openness' indexes, amongst other features, the variety and difference amongst groups who enter the forum; and 'quality' invokes, for example, the extent to which a group is able to articulate, support and defend its arguments. They also present 'implementation criteria' which concern the capacity of a hybrid forum to realize the sorts of negotiation (and transformative) processes described above: is access to the debate equal for all the groups concerned? are the procedures which structure negotiations and debate transparent and clear? Callon et al. apply these criteria to a range of hybrid forum-like mechanisms that have been developed over the last 30 years or so: citizen juries, various forms of focus groups, consensus conferences.

Other scholars, situated within the field of 'the Public Engagement with Science and Technology', have also developed standards by which to judge whether participatory or engagement events facilitate the voicing of the lay public's accounts, let alone the 'composition of a collective', or the emergence of a 'common world' (e.g. Chilvers, 2008). Unsurprisingly, these forums are often, in one way or another, found wanting. For example, to enter into a hybrid forum or a cosmopolitical event is in actuality to diminish one's political capacities because any voice that is available is restricted, and any negotiation unfolds through a limited set of identities. In other words 'in actuality' these voices and identities can serve to detract from what some consider to be more radical forms of public actor (e.g. Elam and Bertilsson, 2003; Welsh and Wynne, 2013; Chilvers and Kearnes, 2016). However, from the post-ANT perspectives on cosmopolitics and political ecology, such an actor's radicalism is arguably grounded in the practices of critique – that is, in claiming that others' accounts are mistaken, contingent, artefactual. And this returns us to the point with which we opened this discussion: critique is part of the problem not part of the solution, precisely because it denies the contingency of its own 'matters of fact', those that ground its problematization of others' 'matters of fact'.

Yet, even where the contingency of knowledges is apparent – where scientists are 'post-sovereign' in that they no longer monopolize the account of nature – there can still be little possibility of the transformations that mark Stengers' cosmopolitical proposal and Latour's political ecology. Consider Anders Blok's (2011) analysis of the controversy over whaling. Accordingly, whales are multiple: they emerge as multinatures in conflict. Thus, on the one side they are enacted as 'abundant, Japanese, and fish-predating' (p. 74) by Japanese spokespersons and, on the other, as 'endangered, rights-bearing, and complex' (p. 69) by Euro-American spokespersons. Each of these enactments is 'post-sovereign' but there seems to be no chance of fashioning a common world: the irreconcilability of these enactments reflects the disparate extended assemblages – that span 'the spheres of science, politics, industry, NGOs, as well as "ordinary" citizens' (p. 64) – into which these enactments are tied. Blok characterizes this controversy over whaling as one of 'agonistic cosmopolitics', and while it might be read as a 'failure' insofar as there is no common world in sight for the foreseeable future, lessons can nevertheless be learnt from it if there is to be movement toward 'a more constructive cosmopolitics' (p. 74).

In light of this apparent inertia, perhaps a different tack is called for. At one point Stengers talks of taking 'care of the event', in which the possibilities of cosmopolitics is a matter of artifice (as we have discussed above). This also translates as what she calls a 'care of the possible' (Stengers and Bordeleau, 2011): cosmopolitics is as much a matter of speculation, of affirming 'the possible … actively resist[ing] the plausible and the probable targeted by approaches that claim to be neutral' (Stengers, 2010a, p. 57). The next section turns to the issue of care. In particular, 'matters of care' are brought to the fore in order to explore recent discussions about the constitutive (and speculative role) of care in ontological politics.

'Matters of Care'

Over recent years, 'care' has become a topic of considerable interest in science and technology studies (e.g. Mol et al., 2010; Kerr and Garforth, 2016). A key text in this respect is Annemarie Mol's (2008b) *The Logic of Care*, in which she counterposes the 'logic of choice', which ostensibly predominates in medical practice, to the 'logic of care'. Put simply, the former entails the enactment of the patient as an individual, empowered, responsible citizen engaged in informed calculation in order to decide amongst pre-existing, discrete options. As Mol beautifully shows, this logic finds itself in difficulties when it is confronted with bodies that are not able to make choices, with practices in which responsibility circulates between patient and practitioner, and with situations in which treatment is a matter of practical attunement rather than overt calculation. The notion of a 'logic of care' aims to capture these complex, interactive and recursive practices not in order to dismiss outright the logic of choice but to modulate it. In several ways, Mol's analysis echoes previous writings on standardization and audit in which the messiness, multiplicity and mutuality (or collaborative-ness) of work (in hospitals, in commercial organizations, in universities) is reclassified into discrete activities through systems of categorization that are used to evaluate that work (e.g. Power, 1999; Bowker and Star, 1999). Mol's 'logic of care' serves positively to reassert the messiness, multiplicity and mutuality of medical work, or what she calls 'shared doctoring' (as opposed to the 'managing' of the 'logic of choice'). In 'doctoring' we find a potent evocation of cosmopolitics, not least because it is a shared process. Accordingly, 'Shared doctoring requires that everyone concerned should take each other's contributions seriously and at the same time attune to what bodies, machines, foodstuffs and other relevant entities are doing. Those who share doctoring must respect each other's experiences, while engaging in inventive, careful experiments … they must change whatever it takes, including themselves. Shared doctoring requires us taking nothing for granted or as given' (Mol, 2008b, p. 65).

Now, Mol's approach is a resolutely empirical one: she is not especially interested in providing definitions of care, nor in hitching her use of 'practice' to claims for a 'practice turn' in sociology (e.g. Schatzki et al., 2001), or to recent formalizations of practice (e.g. Shove et al., 2012). She and her colleagues are, however, concerned to map and compare – carefully – the different forms of care as they are practised across a variety of domains such as health and farming (see Mol et al., 2010, 2011). Here too we can detect a cosmopolitical sensibility: one cannot step outside of care to study care for to study the practices of care, one must attend to how one practises care in such studies.

If Mol's approach to care is primarily empirical, Puig de la Bellacasa (2011, 2012) provides a reconceptualization in which she expands Latour's 'matters of concern' into 'matters of care'. Puig de la Bellacasa wants to draw from 'matters of concern' an 'emphasis on care [that] signifies … an affective state, a material vital doing, and an ethico-political obligation' (2011, p. 90). Thus, for the process of cosmopolitics, to pursue 'matters of care' is to affect and be affected by the thing at stake within a controversy or debate (the sports utility vehicle, or SUV, is used as an example). Crucially, this thing is itself emergent in relation to both one's own practices (what Puig de la Bellacasa calls material vital doings) but also to those of others, others who might be adversaries within a particular controversy or debate. As such, to care for a thing means also taking into account all those others who have also cared for it, whatever their standpoint. So, while one might care for the environmental impacts of the SUV, one must nevertheless also care for alternative carings of the SUV (as, say, a marker of status).

In other words, one needs to 'take care in caring', as it were. The ethico-political element of 'matters of care' – in part derived from feminist standpoint theory – adds a recursive dimension to caring. As such, to care also means to ask such questions as 'who is doing the caring?', 'who is being harmed or excluded by this caring?', and 'what are the observer's (researcher's) own cares?' (Puig de la Bellacasa, 2011, see pp. 91–2). And further, to engage with 'matters of care' is to be wary of care's limitations and pitfalls: it should not be used to exploit, to belittle or to moralize – or to serve as a proxy for critique as problematized by Latour ('if only you cared more or cared better!'). Rather, to care is to be attuned to connectedness which, Puig de la Bellacasa notes, can nevertheless incorporate 'critique'. However, here critique needs to be understood not so much as detachment (in the sense of, for instance, cutting the links between critic and criticized and thus inducing conflict between them), but rather as reattachment (in the sense of generating new caring relations). That is to say, a critical relation does not necessarily exhaust the relations that bind antagonists. If critique severs one type of relation, care can generate another (as can many other things, such as a shared sense of humour, a co-commitment to third parties, or curiosity in another's practice – all of these might be brought under the auspices of 'care'). In any case, care juxtaposed to critique in this way implies a 'transformative ethos' – a positive openness to the possibility of change.

The further implication, and we saw this in Mol's work, is that care cannot be easily pinned down (see also Martin et al., 2015). This is because care invokes a sensibility toward how things unfold or become. So, drawing on Haraway's (e.g. 2008) work on companion species, Puig de la Bellacasa suggests that care can take the form of practices through which there is a commitment to 'knowledge and curiosity about the other' (2011, p. 98; also 2012). Crucially, this opens up the possibility of mutual becoming, or co-transformation: here, to 'care for' the other means also to change in relation to the other, to adapt oneself in light of the other – whether that be a human as in Mol's case studies, the bodily recalcitrance of animals such as dogs (Haraway, 2008) or salmon (Law and Lien, 2013), or the complexities of soil (Puig de la Bellacasa, 2015). This is further complicated by the recursive qualities of care. The researcher observing interactions between practitioners and patients, trainers and dogs, scientists and soil, also cares specifically for their 'objects of study'. If the 'objects of study' are 'becoming', so too is the 'one who studies' (whether that be natural scientist or social scientist) by virtue of studying 'carefully'. What then is sayable, when the sayer and the said are in a state of unfolding? Arguably, it is 'speculation' that is best suited to accommodating these process of co-emergence. This is addressed in the next section where developments in post-ANT methodology take centre stage.

Doing Methodology

In the preceding sections of this chapter, an overarching motif has been that of 'reality as multiple'. Signalled by such terms as multinatures, pluriverses and ontological multiplicity (and politics), the world is seen to be made up of divergent ontologies. In the case of Latour and Stengers, what is at stake is the (multiple realities of) bringing together these multiple realities in ways that can address the problems we currently face (however these turn out). For Mol,

Callon and Law it is the tracing of the practices that enable interaction, coordination, even merger (or, sometimes, polarization) of multiple realities that is of key concern. This is a far cry from 'classical' ANT with its focus on the emergence of singular networks.

Perhaps foremost amongst these shifts is the sense that, if the world is comprised of multiple interacting ontologies, sometimes these can settle into stable patterns, and sometimes they can combine, (non-)cohere, redivide, or polarize in unforeseen ways. That is to say, as John Law (2004a; see also Deleuze and Guattari, 1988) argues, reality needs to be understood as multiple (many ontologies), relational (these ontologies relate to each other through a variety of processes) and emergent (the patterns of these relations are fluid and generative of new ontologies). In brief, reality should be conceived in terms of what William Connolly (2011) has called a 'world of becoming'. Now this generates all manner of issues for the doing of empirical research, though probably the most dramatic of these can be distilled in the question, posed by Adkins and Lury (2009: see also Back and Puwar, 2012; Lury and Wakeford, 2012): 'What is the Empirical?' When reality is in such flux, and we researchers are part of that reality, how do we access it, when 'we' might ourselves be part of that flux?

a. Method Assemblage

Law (2004a) sets out a potent argument for rethinking the empirical engagement with reality not through the standard categories of 'method' or 'methodology' but in terms of what he calls a 'method assemblage'. Accordingly, the shifting and multiple realities of which we are a part as researchers will interact in a variety of ways with the shifting and multiple realities that we wish to study. These interactions are not straightforward – they cannot be contained by the technical tools of the social sciences (e.g. questionnaires, focus groups, ethnography) for several reasons.

First, these interactions operate on many levels – not only through 'representation' (registering and depicting the objects of study) but also affectively through multiple senses. Thus, we as researchers are affected by 'our' participants, but in ways that are not always immediately apparent, not least because they work on many levels (e.g. through senses such as smell or touch) which are difficult to translate into an academic, analytic, or indeed any, account (see Massumi, 2002; cf. Wetherell, 2012). One upshot of this is that post-ANT needs to develop multisensory (or multimodal) methods which can better address the range of senses that people use in their social activities (in everyday life, in professional work, or in social scientific research). Here, there are lines to be drawn to a recent 'turn to affect' in the social sciences (e.g. Clough, 2009; Latimer and Miele, 2013), and to ongoing innovations in multisensory methods (e.g. Pink, 2012; Dicks, 2014).

Second, our practices as researchers are *performative*. A method assemblage (and that includes theory and analysis as well as empirical technique) enacts 'its object of study' and as such it constructs a particular version because its engagement with reality is always partial. Bits of the world are inevitably missed out, obfuscated, *othered* or necessarily neglected in order to render relations with the world under scrutiny, and to derive an account of 'that' world. Law has put it thus: to 'apply' a method assemblage involves the 'crafting of a bundle of ramifying relations that generates presence, manifest absence, and Otherness' (Law, 2004a, p. 45). To make something present is to sideline something else: an obvious example from 'classical' ANT is that the focus on the successful building of a network absented those moments of ambivalence or marginality that also fed into the process of network-building. *Otherness*, by comparison, points to those types of absence that are not made manifest – that are routine, or insignificant or repressed (p. 85): a network hangs together because of such routine but unacknowledged elements as furniture and electricity supply, or 'uninteresting' dynamics as friendship and love. In any case, to do empirical work – to 'apply' a method, even a method assemblage – is unavoidably to draw boundaries between presence, manifest absence and Otherness. One benefit of thinking and doing in terms of a method assemblage is that we are at least now in a position to 'imagine more flexible boundaries, and different forms of presence and absence' (p. 85). That is to say, we can begin to query the typical patterns of presence, manifest absence and Otherness that arise in the doing of research.

In addition to the foregoing, we can draw out a third dimension to the idea of method assemblage. A method assemblage and its 'implementation' is itself not immune from the vagaries of a 'world of becoming'. After all, we as researchers are part of a world that is constitutively multiple, relational and emergent. So, to engage with our 'empirical objects' is to enact them, but to engage is also to be enacted. As researchers we are, to some degree or other, also performed through our method assemblage as it interacts with other assemblages such as those inhabited by the 'object of study'. This can be clarified through the notion of the 'research event' (Michael, 2012a).

b. Research Event

Grounding our argument in Mariam Fraser's (2010) analysis of the event (she traverses Latour, Whitehead and Deleuze), we suggest that 'events' can be grasped in two broadly different ways. Events can be understood as 'compositional' (see above), comprised of heterogeneous elements (e.g. human and nonhuman, micro and macro, conscious and unconscious, and so on) that combine together. In this process of combination, the constitutive elements can retain their identities – in other words, they can be-together, cohabit within the event of their combination. Alternatively, the elements brought together within an event co-become in the process of their combination. They mutually affect one another, and their identities are transformed in the process. One way of putting this is that these entities are '*eventuate*d': rather than think in terms of enactment or performance (both of which can connote a directional relation between enactor and enacted), the focus on the event allows us to think in terms of how entities (and, to reiterate, that includes humans and nonhumans) co-emerge out of the event.

In the case of the 'research event' these two formulations of the event have rather different implications. In the 'co-being' research event, the researcher remains essentially unaffected by their engagement with their object of study. In the 'co-becoming' research event, both researcher and researched are mutually changed, as they are eventuated they are no longer necessarily researcher and researched, and indeed the research event might no longer be a research event as such. If that is the case, what then is the 'researcher' witness to and involved in?

It should be obvious that there are resonances between the 'co-becoming research event' and cosmopolitics as discussed above. In both cases the parties or elements that come together are co-transformed and in the process what their coming together 'is' shifts so that what has happened and what emerges are not altogether clear. Or rather, there arises the opportunity to ask 'more interesting questions' of (the eventuation of) the 'research event', and to engage in what Fraser calls 'inventive problem-making'. That is to say, can the research question that initially frames the research event be transformed, and opened up to new, unforeseen problematics?

To illustrate, we briefly draw on Horst and Michael's (2011) discussion of a science communication installation – 'Landscape of Expectations'. This was designed to engage with the Danish public's views on recent biotechnological developments and their governance. Set up in a shopping mall close to Copenhagen, the installation contained a number of information panels as well as exercises by which visitors could register their views on the risks, benefits and politics of emerging biotechnology (e.g. stem cell research). Horst and Michael identify a key moment in the installation's eventuation when a group of teenage girls were observed to 'misbehave'. To one of the questions presented in the installation ('what are you most worried about?'), one girl responded 'my biggest fear is that all shopping centres in the world close'. Reading this as a 'co-being research event', one could say that, at least for this group of girls, the research event failed. But in saying this, the installation retains its identity as an engagement device (albeit a problematic one), and the girls can be safely attributed the identity of something like 'recalcitrant teenagers'. Apprehended as a 'co-becoming research event', we might construe the following: the girls were eventuated as a group who creatively appropriated the installation as a means of affirming their peer group dynamics; the installation was eventuated as a structure that distracted from the everyday activities of shopping; and the 'research event' of engagement eventuated as an intervention that enacted the 'seriousness' of science and politics that encroached on the 'pleasures' of leisure and consumption. In all this, to echo Puig de la Bellacasa, care was taken not to dismiss the teenage girls or over-value the installation. In any case, an 'inventive problem' that emerged served to problematize the parameters of 'science communication and engagement'. This applied not only to the specificities of the installation itself, but also, more broadly, to disciplinary conceptualizations of the relations between science and the public. In sum, in taking into account the multiple and heterogeneous components that entered into a particular science communication and engagement event, and treating these components 'carefully', we move away from a vision of science communication and engagement as the conveyance of information, or as the facilitation of dialogue. Instead we can propose that something very different has eventuated, say, a challenge to, and a reworking of, the assumptions behind the 'seriousness' of biotechnology's governance.

Notice that the account of the 'Landscape of Expectations' installation is laced with a certain diffidence. We are not saying this is a definitive understanding of what happened – we are pointing to a potential interpretation of the 'teenage girls' event. Or rather, we are hinting that the 'co-becoming research event' is an interesting way of thinking about how we do research. Instead of denying or dismissing certain eventuations because they are 'mere possibilities', perhaps we should pursue them. Insofar as this version of the research event presupposes 'a world of becoming', it opens up the prospect of positively grasping how the world is becoming, unfolding toward the possible and the not-yet (see Stengers, 2010a). In the case of the installation, we speculate on the eventuation of the girls, the researchers and the research problem. In the process we open up new possibilities for what science communication and engagement might become. Another way of putting this is to situate the 'Landscape of Expectations' as a sort of accidental methodological tool that allowed us to speculate on the not-yet of science communication and engagement. In what follows, we turn to how post-ANT might *proactively* enact speculative research events.

Speculation

What has (hopefully) taken shape over the course of the preceding discussions is a vision of the world as something in process, open, emergent. The elements that make up the world are in flux – they combine and differentiate, stabilize and destabilize. In the view of Deleuze and Guattari (1988), who have had considerable influence – directly or indirectly – on post-ANTs, the world entails both territorialization and deterritorialization. If the former denotes the stable orderings or patternings of relations and objects, the latter points to the ways in which those orderings and patternings are disrupted and rendered fluid, and where objects and relations begin to take new, sometimes unexpected, configurations. To do post-ANT research in relation to this conception of reality (of which we, to repeat, are a part) is to engage with the empirical world that is at once eventuated, escapes that eventuation, and reciprocally eventuates us (as potentially something other than 'researchers') and our research event (as potentially something other than 'research'). Any method that is responsive to these conditions is a method in pursuit of the unattainable to paraphrase Parisi's (2012) comments on speculation: it aims to somehow access the stuff of the world (including itself) that is still taking shape.

While it is possible to attach our suggestions around speculative method to what has been called the 'speculative turn' in philosophy and beyond (e.g. Bryant et al., 2011), we are more interested in the practices of speculation, rather than it situating within the history of philosophy. So let us begin by asking how we nurture openness to this 'world of becoming'. For William Connolly (2011), this could involve what he has called an 'exquisite sensitivity to the world' – a capacity to be affected by and to register its shifts and changes. This is, to say the least, an ambitious suggestion not least because the response to this flux might be less an engagement with it, than a denial, or a reversion to standard categories (which was certainly the researchers' initial response to the 'recalcitrant schoolgirl' eventuation of the 'Landscape of Expectations' installation). Similarly, Jerak-Zuiderent (2015) urges us to resist reading the 'fleetingly subtle' interruptions that occur in interview situations (laughter, expressions of fear) in standardized ways (to critique, in her case study, Dutch healthcare indicators and their implementation). Rather, she exhorts, we should cultivate the capacity to be disconcerted by these enactments so that we can reimagine what is unrealized or emergent within the field of 'Dutch healthcare indicator implementation': it opens up a space for asking alternative questions and for doing things differently – for, to requote Mariam Fraser (2010), 'inventive problem-making'.

Both Connolly and Jerak-Zuiderent aim to encourage certain sensibilities in the researcher so that they can speculatively engage with the social world. However, there are also more 'experimental' tactics available. In particular, we can use techniques which directly enact – provoke even – the potentialities of particular realities. Thus, 'speculative design' (e.g. Gaver et al., 2008; Michael and Gaver, 2009; Boehner et al., 2012) aims to develop, design, build and give to users artefacts that, through their playfulness, opacity, ambiguity, novelty, a-functionality, allow for the exploration of what design can do both socially and technically. As Michael (2012a, 2012b) has argued, speculative design lends itself to pursing the potentialities of social life more generally.

Consider the 'energy babble' (Gaver et al., 2015). Very simply, this is an artefact that was developed and designed through several forms of engagement with 'energy communities' (groups involved in reducing their energy consumption). Scraping information about energy demand, energy policy, energy innovations from the internet, and registering inputs from energy community users, the energy babble emitted a stream of commentary that was more or less comprehensible (texts were, for instance, translated into several languages before returning to English). Placed in users' homes (and sometimes in communal settings), the babble seemed to relay information energy demand reduction but didn't quite. While not exactly gibberish, the statements that were broadcast one after the other by the babble never quite made sense. In the process, the babble potentially opened up a space in which the standard meanings – or territorializations – of such things as energy, information and community became unsettled, or deterritorialized. Of course, there was recourse amongst participants to the usual categories – for instance, some people were disappointed that the babble failed to relay what they saw as useable information. But there were also other more 'interesting' responses that hinted at the emergence of inventive problems. For instance, many participants were delighted by the strange but suggestively retro look of the babble, and several enjoyed the babble's constant flow of not-quite-sensible talk. This gestures toward – or rather, allows us to speculate about – how a new 'inventive problem' might be posed: for instance, can we rethink the problems of 'energy demand reduction' in terms of an 'aesthetics of information circulation' (as exemplified in the energy babble's material design and aural operation). To reiterate, this is not to derive a definitive 'inventive problem' but to open up the possibility for such novel, and potentially productive, problematizations.

Of course, there is much more to be said about the energy babble (as well as other experiments in speculative method that draw on a number of artistic traditions – see, for example, Michael et al., 2015). However, all these have their limitations and we would not want to value one over any other. Suffice it to say, that we have seen here how post-ANT continues to be translated into, and by, new fields, and enriched by their practical orientations and sensibilities. At the same time, we see how post-ANT's own practical orientations and sensibilities can inform how practitioners in other fields might think about their own practical orientations and sensibilities. Here too, there is co-becoming between post-ANTs and other traditions of enquiry.

Conclusion

In this chapter we have explored a number of recent and emerging – and interconnected – developments in post-ANT. In some ways, the picture of post-ANT painted here is rather too coherent. After all, we have processed through a relatively neat sequence of themes: the unpicking of critique to yield multiple 'matters of concern' (or practices or ontologies); the means by which multiple practices are practically coordinated in various domains (for example, hospitals, interdisciplinary collaborations, or social scientific method assemblages); the advocacy of 'means' for the practical coordination of different practices despite seemingly intractable divisions (cosmopolitics, hybrid forums); the shaping of such means through 'careful' practices or 'speculative' technique. There is, in other words, much that has been left out of this account of post-ANT. In the next chapter we survey a selection of still other routes post-ANT has taken.

8

CONCLUSIONS: SOME PROSPECTS AND SOME PRACTICAL ORIENTATIONS

Introduction

In this concluding chapter, there is a brief review of the book. Into this are folded a number of regrets about some of the many byways that might have been taken. As we shall see, there were several themes, histories and empirical fields that could have been addressed but were not, or not fully enough. I also indulge in a little, albeit unsystematic, 'horizon scanning' – where is post-ANT heading? What new empirical fields will capture post-ANT scholars' attention? What conceptual trends will influence ANT, and what theoretical innovations will add to its vocabulary and analytic sensibilities? Inevitably, this is an 'enactment' – as much a hopeful 'performance' as a predictive 'overview'. The book ends with a tentative and heuristic summary of the sorts of sensibilities and practical orientations that someone interested in drawing on ANT and its various legacies might find useful.

One Overview and Eight Regrets

In Chapter 1, we began with an introduction to the main characteristics of ANT and post-ANT, but insisted that the main thing it had to offer was not a recipe for 'doing ANT' (though see below) but a sensibility along with a number of ways of approaching the practice of empirical and analytic work. This book, it was hoped, would thus serve as a resource for further exploration of the key texts that have anchored 'classical' ANT, and the many debates that have nuanced ANT and contributed to the proliferation of post-ANTs.

Chapter 2 situated ANT along a number of intellectual trajectories – for instance, Sociology of Scientific Knowledge, the works of Serres and Whitehead, ethnomethodology. Some lineages were referred to rather less (e.g. Tarde and Greimas) and some (Regret No. 1) were missing altogether, for instance, the dialogue with two important sociological approaches to the analysis of technology, namely the technological system perspective of Thomas Hughes (Hughes, 1983) and the social construction of technology or SCOT (e.g. Pinch and Bijker, 1984; Bijker, 1995). In Chapter 3, a general overview of 'classical' ANT was presented, and a panoply of ANT's 'core' conceptual terms was introduced: inscription devices, actors, networks, interessement, obligatory passage point, immutable mobiles, enrolment, etc., etc. Again (Regret No. 2) there were certain texts and directions that were not followed up – Latour's *Aramis* (1996a) or the 'Irreductions' section of *The Pasteurization of France* (1988a) for instance, or Law's (2002b) *Aircraft Stories*. This does not only indicate the 'incompleteness' of the present account of 'classical' ANT, but also how 'classical' ANT is itself a particular 'fiction'.

In Chapter 4, some of the early and by and large 'sympathetic' critiques of ANT were discussed. Here we saw the emergence of a number of critical concerns: ANT was too managerial and its model of the world too agonistic; ANT was not especially well equipped to capture the constitutive roles of culture or ambivalence or multiplicity in the durability and changeability of networks; and ANT was 'too encompassing' when there might be social processes that cannot be accommodated within its schema. There was also an extended discussion of various debates around ANT's treatment of agency (as distributed and ascribed) and, in particular, its supposed tendency to invest nonhumans – 'natural' and 'technological' – with agency. Of course, (Regret No. 3), there were several critiques that couldn't be elaborated. For instance, there is much to draw out regarding the critical impact on ANT of Haraway's work (e.g. 1991) or of feminist science studies more generally. ANT might also have been situated within debates about the compromised political and policy roles of constructionist – social or heterogeneous – approaches to science and technology. If both 'facts' and 'errors' are constructions, how can sociologists of science and technology champion or support particular disempowered groups and their versions of a contested state of affairs? After all, critical claims about community pesticide poisoning or local accounts of environmental damage are themselves 'mere' constructions (e.g. Scott et al., 1990; Richards and Ashmore, 1996; also Fuller, 2005).

In Chapter 5, we moved on to situate ANT in relation to a number of sociologically important attempts to theorize the relation between microsocial processes and wider social formations. Only the bare minimum could be said about the frameworks developed by Bourdieu, Elias and Giddens and not much at all about how they have been subsequently extended and elaborated. The comparison with ANT was handled pragmatically through an examination of case studies which had attempted to deploy elements of ANT (usually, its capacity to integrate technology into 'social analysis'). The cost of this (Regret No. 4) was that conceptual similarities and differences could not be more extensively discussed. However, more tellingly, these reflect my own (Anglophone) limitations. For instance, there was no reference to French new pragmatism (e.g. Boltanski and Thévenot, 2006) whose entwinement with post-ANT seems to be gathering pace (e.g. Blok, 2013; Latour, 2013), nor to the influential work of Niklas Luhmann (2012). On top of this neglect, there are more middle-range theoretical perspectives that might have been usefully contrasted with ANT: we have already made passing reference to practice theories and the practice turn (Chapter 7); we have singularly failed to make mention of social network analysis (e.g. Freeman, 2006).

Chapter 6 addressed a few of the ways in which ANT has been taken up by 'other disciplines' – more social theory, economic sociology, geography, management and organization studies. Perhaps somewhere there is a study which has systematically mapped ANT's more or less successful infiltration across a fuller range of disciplines, with an account of why it has taken hold in some disciplines but not so much in others (Regret No. 5). For instance, why is it that ANT has been recently making substantive inroads into design research (e.g. Yaneva, 2009; Gaver et al., 2015; Storni et al., 2015; Ardevol et al., 2016)? Interesting though this might be, what seems more intriguing is how, in its travels across different disciplinary terrains, ANT has been translated and transmuted. Certainly one of the functions of Chapter 6 was to explore how scholars from a variety of disciplinary backgrounds could feed into, and supplement, ANT's analytic vocabulary (e.g. action nets, the more-than-human).

Chapter 7 was dedicated to a charting of some of the ways in which ANT has proliferated into a number of intersecting post-ANTs. While we took note of post-ANT's partial connections to recent 'turns' in the social sciences (ontological, practice, affect, material, object, speculative), we paid rather more attention to a series of emerging practical foci around, for instance, method, performativity, multiplicity, co-becoming, concern and care that together suggested a rethinking of the political role of post-ANT, but also a reformulation of politics itself. Once again (Regret No. 6), more could have been done to locate post-ANTs in relation to the various turns mentioned. For instance Latour has been a key interlocutor of Graham Harman's, a leading scholar in the turn toward speculative realism (e.g. Harman, 2009); and several post-ANT treatments of agency and the emergence of subject/object divides are indebted to the works of Karen Barad (e.g. Barad, 2007).

On top of all this, there are certain features of the post-ANT landscape that have featured barely at all (Regret No. 7). Some of these are empirical – for instance, the relation of post-ANT to the impact of digital technologies on the making, understanding and study of the social; some are thematic – the way in which post-ANT might illuminate 'experience' especially in a world faced with rising levels of forms of dementia; some are conceptual – new or evolving metaphors for thinking through relations (in terms of atmospheres or topology, for instance); and some are methodological (for instance, the use of 'experimental' methods derived from such disciplines as the arts and computer science). Ideally, we would like to redress some – though by no stretch of the imagination all – of these shortcomings in this chapter. In reality, there will be a rather superficial encounter with these post-ANT-related concerns. In the end, this is a partial listing – rather than a cartographic survey – of yet more recent developments in post-ANT.

Importantly, in what follows, I do not seek to disambiguate the methodological from the conceptual and theoretical from the empirical and substantive. Any particular version of post-ANT emerges through the peculiar combination of conceptual, methodological and empirical/substantive concerns. In this respect, post-ANTs are no different from their 'objects of study' – they too are 'composed' (to draw again on Latour) of heterogeneous elements (which might include bits of other post-ANTs). So, in the next section, I loosely derive – that is, enact – a number of post-ANT assemblages as a way of alerting readers to some of the emergent possibilities of post-ANT. My purpose here is to convey a sense of the excitement in, and enthusiasm for, the future prospects of post-ANTs, and to invite readers to pursue these yourselves.

However, lest we forget, such excitement and enthusiasm are not shared by everybody. Beyond the confines of the post-ANT 'community', or rather, 'assemblage', there are many scholars who are intensely hostile toward, even dismissive of, ANT and its offshoots. I have not especially engaged with these critiques, preferring to explore select examples where ANT has been critically adapted and deployed (see Chapters 5 and 6), rather than simply sidelined. Typically, these critiques will deride ANT's eschewal of critique and mainstream social scientific categories, or derogate its preference for description and its focus on microprocesses, or despair at its supposed *de facto* collusion with contemporary neoliberal politics. Even so, some of these critiques are worth engaging with in more detail (Regret No. 8). For instance, Pellizzoni (2015), while generally scathing about ANT, can be read 'carefully' as opening up potential links between the works of Agamben (on impotentiality), Adorno (on negative dialectics) and ANT. The point is that even such antagonistic commentaries can be treated 'cosmopolitically' and 'carefully' – in the end, they might, despite themselves, lead ANT toward yet 'more inventive problems'.

Composing Some More Post-ANTs

In what follows, I present five broad 'fields' that post-ANT is having a hand in shaping. As mentioned, these 'fields' straddle emergent empirical topics, conceptual innovations and methodological inventions. In discussing, variously, nonhuman animals, disasters, experience, publics and the digital the aim is less to chart the contemporary unfolding of post-ANT than simply to display the continuing potential of ANT to inspire contemporary scholarship.

a. Nonhuman Animals, Humans, Agencies

Nonhuman animals have become a 'topic' of increasing interest in the human-ities and social sciences. Even so, given their ubiquity (e.g. as companions, as quasi-objects of knowledge and consumption, as vectors of disease and impu-rity), it seems strange that animals are a relative newcomer to the social sciences (see Hobson-West, 2007; Pegg, 2009). We have encountered a few animals in this book, scallops being the most prominent and a prime exemplar of the nonhuman actor within a 'classical' actor-network (see Chapter 3). However, as the brief list above hints, 'nonhuman animals' is barely a sufficient category to capture the multiplicity of ways in which they associate with humans. Nevertheless, here we can point to a few of the possible avenues down which nonhuman animals might lead post-ANT.

As we have seen, a key issue regarding ANT's analysis of nonhumans is that of agency. For some, ANT-like analyses of nonhuman animals entail too ready an attribution of 'agency' (understood as 'having an effect', see Carter and Charles, 2013): accordingly, a much more nuanced notion of agency is needed if some version of this is going to be applied to animals. However, for others, it is ANT's openness to the possibility of agency (loosely defined though this might be – see Chapter 4) that sensitizes analysis to the multiple forms that 'agency' might take amongst nonhumans and humans alike (Sayes, 2014).

With this latter point in mind, recent explorations of the 'agency' (loosely defined) of nonhuman animals have tapped into their impacts on humans, especially how they enter into relations of emergence or becoming in which humans (and nonhumans too) change together. Haraway (2008) thus speaks of 'becoming-with' her companion dog through, for instance, training for competition. Gisler and Michael (2011) propose a 'becoming because of' the horseshoe crab whose blood is used for the detection of gram-negative bac-teria: its blood has thus saved countless lives (which have had the opportunity to 'become' as a consequence). Latimer (2013) argues for a 'being alongside' in which the differences between humans and nonhumans are preserved (though partial, connections occur). Latimer and Miele (2013) further hint at a 'becoming differently' in which nonhuman animals and humans diverge from how they are normally depicted or enacted (for instance, the objectifica-tion of laboratory animals leads to their becoming more 'human' insofar as they are susceptible to that most human of conditions, namely, boredom; and human scientists become more animal-like insofar as they become 'captivated by their environment' – see Davies, 2012; also Despret, 2004, 2008). Crucial to all these discussions is how the animal's becoming cannot be dissociated from the assemblages in which it is immersed (see also Whatmore, 2002). However, what is also implied is the multiplicity of ways in which animals affect becoming amongst humans and their relations, from the shifts in a per-son's 'identity' or comportment (as we have seen), through the unfolding of an environmental or biomedical disaster (e.g. Rodríguez-Giralt et al., 2014), and on to the emergence of particular forms of modernity (e.g. Nimmo, 2010).

It seems like this is a particular area that is likely to continue growing as post-ANT scholars explore more and more species in more and more settings, not least in response to the impact of certain sociomaterial practices that have, ironically, exacerbated the likelihood of certain disasters.

b. Disasters, Topologies, Ironies

As mentioned above, animals have played a part in a variety of recent 'disasters', most obviously in the spread of zoonotic diseases. Post-ANT has been instrumental in thinking about how 'disasters' might be understood. John Law (2006), for instance, has noted that certain protective legislative measures have ironically generated unforeseen disaster risks. As he traces, the requirement for in-house inspectors at abattoirs to protect against the spread of BSE, or mad cow disease, has meant that animals have had to be transported to slaughter over longer distances because there were fewer abattoirs that could afford to employ an inspector. The result was that when there was a local outbreak of foot and mouth disease, this could move far more widely across the United Kingdom, spread along the now extended transport to slaughter routes. In a similar vein, Hinchliffe et al. (2012) have documented, to put it simply, how various strategies designed to keep disease out of poultry factory farms operate with a model of an inside that is safe, versus an outside that is dangerous. As they show, the inside/outside is a point of contact, and in that life needs movement in order to survive (bacteria, bodies, foodstuffs, waste must all move or be moved at some point), then such boundaries are always liable to be breached, however stringent the surveillance or sanitation procedures. Once breached, the conditions of the inside can incubate disease (as, for example, bacteria can spread rapidly amongst factory-farmed chickens whose immune systems are stressed).

The simple point is that the ironies by which these measures (which can be variously understood as preparedness, pre-emption or precaution – see Anderson, 2010) serve in the 'making' of disasters deserve extended analysis. For instance, against the linearities of borderlines (where exclusion is enforced), we would benefit both analytically and practically, according to Hinchliffe et al., by thinking in terms of the topologies of borderlands. It is here that we will likely find the unlikely routes by which infections can travel, and disasters can take form. What topology does is sensitize us to these complexities. It would seem that, despite the references to topology throughout this book, it is a concept which can further illuminate the sorts of processes that concern post-ANT scholarship. This is especially the case if it is elaborated in relation to treatments of topology in other fields, such as cultural studies (e.g. Lash and Lury, 2007), or linked to notions that might do similar work such as Tim Ingold's (2011) 'meshwork' which, in Rodríguez-Giralt et al.'s (2014, p. 46) phrasing, 'offers a far more dynamic figuration and opens up the possibility to disasters as messy processes permanently enacting new actors, actions and scales'.

c. Experience, Knowledge, Distribution

In our discussion of nonhuman animals above, we emphasized their role in affecting humans, and in enabling particular sorts of co-becoming. What was missing from that brief account, and what has been relegated to a rather minor theme throughout this book, is the matter of 'experience'. Nonhuman animals as parts of networks or assemblages clearly have some sort of impact on the 'experience' of human actors (and vice versa, of course), however that is defined. We see this especially in observations of direct interactions with animals, such as technicians handling laboratory rats or mice (e.g. Birke et al., 2007) or geriatric ward patients responding to the presence of a West Highland terrier (Symons, 2009). However, this portrays experience as too bounded – located within a body as opposed to distributed across a nexus of heterogeneous relations. Certainly that is how 'experience' has been understood within the ANT-allied work of Antoine Hennion, who has explored how the experiences of 'music lovers' emerge out of a nexus that might include technologies, festivals, drugs, clothing and social relations (e.g. Gomart and Hennion, 1998; Hennion, 2001).

This line of work has been continued more recently by, amongst others, Annemarie Mol, who has examined the experiences (and subjectivities) of eating. Thus, to eat with the fingers is to experience food in multilayered ways that take in such elements as developing manual dexterity and sensation, professional and linguistic expertise, and histories of colonialism and migration (Mann et al., 2011). If experience is distributed, so too is subjectivity. This should come as no surprise given its 'circulation' and 'distribution' amongst (quasi-)objects (see Chapter 2). Moreover, Mol (e.g. 2008a) has begun to unravel further the complex specificities of this distribution of the 'subject'. She asks, given that the food we eat – she focuses on the apple – sustains us, does it not also form part of our subjectivity? More tellingly, she suggests that we need to think 'through' eating in order to shake up the Western philosophical tradition with its key motif of the lone heroic thinker. Instead of thinking, can philosophy be enacted through eating (and related metaphors such as swallowing and digesting)?

This can be linked to another set of concerns around the doing of research through practice, or what is increasingly called practice-based or practice-led research (e.g. McNamara, 2012; also see Chapter 7). Here, corporeal and semiotic engagements with materials of various sorts entail a similar distribution or circulation of subjectivities and experience. How do such practices as designing and building artefacts, or making artworks, yield knowledge about the world? Again, some of this has been touched upon amongst post-ANT scholars. For instance, Latour (2008; see also Callon, 2004) has proposed that designers – especially through their drawing skills – develop techniques whereby they 'draw things together' as 'matters of concern'. Latour (Latour and Weibel, 2002) has also been involved in the curation of exhibitions which have pursued what he has called 'iconoclash' (in comparison to 'iconoclasm').

Here, the contingency and constructedness of artistic, religious and scientific imagery are laid bare and juxtaposed (but, crucially, not debunked).

There is another implication to this move toward different sorts of practice (that contrast to the 'scientific' or the 'analytic'). Such practices must take place somewhere, and recent work is beginning to attend to these somewhat neglected sites and spaces where practice-based knowledge may be generated, notably the 'studio'. Drawing on examples from Farias and Wilkie's (2016) volume, *Studio Studies*, we might ask how such practices as struggling to get a prototype to work in a design studio, sweating in the process of blowing glass in a workshop, or getting aggressive in the process of testing an online game are generative of 'knowledge', or even suggestive of new ways of thinking about knowledge *per se*. In sum, and no doubt too grandly, perhaps post-ANT can explore, and multiply, new ways of grasping the world through the panoply of human experience as complexly mediated by, for example, the digestive tract, the sweat glands, tired and inept fingers, or an aggravated nervous system.

Finally, we need to turn to studies of the 'limits' that can attach to experience. In particular, people who suffer from dementia can, as Schillmeier (2014) has movingly shown, occupy what he calls a network of Angst. Within this, the common, pre-supposed associations that underpin a network – associations into the past and into the future – are severed because of the way episodes of dementia operate. The dementing person thus finds their 'spatio-temporal networks [cut] into messy, fractious, stubborn, and highly individualized configurations' (p. 87). The result is that the demented person is fundamentally lost amongst objects and persons that they cannot remember, and which, from the demented person's perspective, cannot remember them. In this scenario of tragic dislocation we see what sort of capacities for experience need to be in place for networks, assemblages, fluids to be possible, let alone durable. Conversely, this also raises the issue of how dementia is both 'made' and 'accommodated'. Of course there are highly medicalized ways in which such conditions are treated and institutionalized that enact dementia in very particular ways. Yet, there might also be means by which post-ANT can contribute to alternative enactments of dementia. For Schillmeier, this means finding ways of caring (which also reflect on the very conditions of care), and implementing a cosmopolitics that treats seriously and caringly the demented person's reality (see Chapter 7).

d. Publics, Issues, Devices

The 'public' has long featured in ANT and post-ANT accounts. Whether as an actor to be enrolled (as in Callon's early case studies – see Chapter 3) or as a part of hybrid forums (in Callon's later work – see Chapter 7), there has been sporadic focus on the role of publics in particular networks or assemblages. However, within Science and Technology Studies, it is the fields of 'Public Understanding of Science' (PUS) and 'Public Engagement with Science and Technology' (PEST) where publics have received the most sustained attention.

Within these large and contentious fields, publics have been variously conceptualized in terms of: individuals deficient in scientific knowledge; communities in possession of lay expert (or folk) knowledges; scientific citizens whose views should be collected and inputted into the science policy-making process (see Bucchi and Neresini, 2008). However, several authors have drawn on aspects of post-ANT to show how, for example, publics are themselves heterogeneous and emergent and need to be understood as – ethno-epistemic – assemblages (Irwin and Michael, 2003). Moreover, insofar as publics have been invited to participate in engagement events (that is, forms of focus group, consensus conferences, citizens' juries, etc.), they are being enacted in a number of different ways that potentially dilute their political potential (e.g. Lezaun and Soneryd, 2007; Michael, 2009a; Felt and Fochler, 2010).

Put succinctly, the enterprise of PEST is characterized by procedural processes by which the public voice can be incorporated into institutional decision-making on scientific and innovation issues (e.g. Marres, 2012; and Chapter 7). For all the many criticisms of PEST, a core concern remains how best to develop mechanisms that enable public views (on such controversial issues as nanotechnology, genetically modified organisms or synthetic biology) to feature more prominently and with greater heft in state (and increasingly corporate) discussions about risk, policy and strategy. By contrast, Marres (2007) has stressed the need to address those publics that escape this institutional or 'official' demarcation of what count as politically controversial issues, and explore how such publics articulate the issues that most concern them. For Marres, drawing on the American pragmatist tradition, it is with the articulation of the issue that the public takes shape (though, this will clearly interleaf with the enactment of publics and issues by other actors, governmental and non-governmental).

Now, one novel dimension of this approach is that, like other post-ANT approaches, it does not make assumptions about what contributes to the articulation of issues and the emergence of publics. As such, materials, devices, technologies, objects can all be involved, and it is only through empirical scrutiny that the analyst can determine what makes an 'issue public', as it were (see Marres and Lezaun, 2011). As mentioned, the heterogeneous composition of publics has been noted before (e.g. Irwin and Michael, 2003), but in Marres' and others' hands we begin to see how the role of stuff, from everyday objects to digital media technologies, can serve in not only the publicity of issues, but also in questioning the nature of 'the political' itself. For instance, how do such objects as plastic bottles (Hawkins, 2011) serve as public (as well as market – see Chapter 6) devices, operating in ways that organize particular types of political participation? In other words, we need to understand publics as materially implicated: their embroilments with specific technologies, devices, etc. shape the sorts of politics they can follow. If those technologies and devices are taken away, then those publics and their issues would be very different. Against the usual emphasis on human political actors, this is a version of politics that is 'distinctively and irreducibly material' (Marres and Lezaun, 2011, p. 497). The focus on such 'political materials' also, as Marres and Lezaun note, enables a degree of experimentation in the types of politics and participation that develop. So, to the extent that devices attached to a particular concern proliferate (e.g. multiple domestic carbon-accounting devices – see Marres, 2011), or because of the multiple versions or ontologies of a seemingly singular object (such as the plastic water bottle – see Hawkins, 2011; Hawkins et al., 2015), there is the possibility here to examine how publics exploit the multiplicity of technologies in order potentially to innovate participatory forms. Put simply, the complexity and multiplicity of technologies and objects open up possibilities for publics to frame issues and pursue politics in new and inventive ways.

e. Digital, Social, Method

Now, one 'domain' where controversies and public participation take place is online. Across platforms and sites, debates, diatribes and discussions are taking place that are central constituents in social and political processes (in the recent past, it was the 'Arab Spring' that was held up as an example of the political potential of the internet; in the present moment – early 2016 – it is the concern with online processes of 'radicalization' that seem to hold sway). In any case, 'the digital' is a rapidly expanding area of study that addresses how the internet, along with a complex of associated technological and social relations, is implicated in, variously, new forms of political action and reaction, emerging media of surveillance, governance and control, redistributions of expertise (including social scientific expertise), opportunities for the reconfiguration of embodiment, selfhood and social relations (see, for example, Lupton, 2015).

As might be expected, post-ANT has engaged with 'the digital' in several ways. For instance, in relation to the previous section's reflections on post-ANT treatments of publics, there have been discussions on how publics of one sort or another are increasingly able to make use of online data analytic and visualization devices to generate their own depictions of society (or particular bits of it). One implication is that what had been the preserve of professional social scientists is becoming available to anyone: with minimal skills, it is possible to draw on many online data sets to generate a distinctive 'amateur' account about this or that social process or phenomenon (Savage and Burrows, 2007). Of course, as we have noted at a number of points, this is not necessarily a worry for post-ANT: after all social scientific accounts have always comprised just one competing version of society. For other authors, it is important to trace how publics use 'the digital' in its specificity: how does a particular web-based technology sit within an ecology of communication practices, yet contribute something novel (e.g. Horst and Miller, 2006). For instance, the GPS-enabled smart-phone, when placed in relation to other communicative technologies (e.g. the map, the guide book) can tell us a lot about how publics are enacted and enact themselves (as urban, as unskilled, as more or less 'authentic', etc. – see Chapter 7; Michael, 2009b).

With the rise of the issue of 'big data' and its roles in, for instance, profiling and the processes of marketing, or surveillance and the government of people and things, post-ANT has also begun to grapple with people's everyday grasp of the meanings and implications of 'big data' (e.g. Michael and Lupton, 2016). As Michael and Lupton note, such studies are methodologically and conceptually challenging as in the very process of conducting a study, the study itself can enter into a big data set, and thus become a part of its own 'object of study'. As participants interact within a research event they might well be simultaneously engaged in continuous online activity, thereby contributing accounts about the research event (on big data) to big data sets. This sort of recursion suggests that new methods are needed that can address the ways in which research events unfold.

Be that as it may, what should be apparent from the foregoing remarks is that in grappling with 'the digital', this needs to be situated in relation to an array of sociomaterial processes. Even in its supposedly most rarified form, such as the algorithm (the set of instructions that need to be followed to reach some sort of goal), it might need to be treated in its specificity, as something messy and fluid. As Neyland (2015) argues, algorithms respond to and fold into how people use them.

This applies no less when we turn our attention to post-ANT's approach to digital methods. For Ruppert et al. (2013), social scientists are fast exploring ways of drawing on digital resources to develop accounts of social processes (which includes charting how the 'digital' is a part of the 'social', and vice versa). In particular, social scientists have the opportunity to use 'the digital' to interrogate predominant assumptions about the social. But to do this they must treat the digital in its specificity, as particular devices and data, and ask: 'where and how they happen, who and what they are attached to and the relations they forge, how they get assembled, where they travel, their multiple arrangements and mobilizations, and, of course, their instabilities, durabilities and how they sometimes get disaggregated too' (p. 32).

Let us take the example of issue mapping (e.g. Marres, 2015). For Marres, this is one way of charting the existence of a controversy through the online presence of, and the relations amongst, various statements around 'an issue'. However, this charting needs to be, as with other post-ANT projects, symmetrical in terms of where these statements are made (platforms, websites), who is making them (policy or public actors), and the form they take (tweets, pdfs). The aim of this eclecticism is to map without bias how the issue develops, moves, shifts and jumps. Yet 'digital bias' might be unavoidable because the digital in its specificity might shape an 'issue' in a very particular way. By virtue of, say, the way that certain platforms connect to one another, or that particular platforms can proliferate statements (e.g. via automated 'bots' that mechanically retweet when particular keywords appear – see Wilkie et al., 2015), then 'the digital' can 'make' an issue in rather 'biased' ways. However, for Marres (2015, p. 671), this 'digital bias' is not necessarily an issue in itself – especially if one does not distinguish between the 'public issue' and the 'digital issue'. As she puts it: assuming that 'digital media technologies are leaving their traces in the very form, content, and character of public controversy, then this would surely present an important topic of inquiry for controversy analysis'.

In sum, if 'the digital' allows for a reconfigured form of social scientific investigation of particular phenomena (e.g. issues and controversies, identities and social groupings, governance and surveillance), it is also a part of these phenomena, mediating them in highly specific and not always coherent ways. However, the digital can also play another grander part in post-ANT: it can serve to demonstrate the very viability of (a version of) post-ANT as an alternative to mainstream social scientific frameworks (see Chapter 5). Thus, Latour et al. (2012), drawing on Tarde's framework, have argued that digital databases (for all their shortcomings) allow one to show, through following the links, how seemingly singular actors are networks composed of many association. As a corollary, seemingly larger entities such as organizations can, in similar ways, be shown to be composed of multiple actors. This means that there is no need to posit higher level entities such as organization or state or country, for these are always composed of many individuals (a composition that is necessarily changing, and inevitably affected by the way that links are made manifest through different digital mapping tools). It also implies, there is no need to presume 'individuals' for these too can be shown to emerge from a shifting array of map-able links. So, depending on how one enters into and moves through these databases, one encounters the network-ness of actors, or the actor-fulness of networks. Key here is that these links are more often than not transitory: so while one can track a few shared and repeated attributes (thus deriving – or collecting – a large unit or grouping), those attributes might change as the links shift. There is difference as well as repetition so that what looks like a collected grouping of a particular sort might, over many iterations, change into something markedly other. Nonetheless, if the change is 'gradual enough … [it can] … preserve some continuity' (Latour et al., 2012, p. 610).

In this section we have touched on a (very) few of the ways in which post-ANT has engaged with 'the digital'. This is a hugely fecund area – one still very much in its infancy. However, there is one aspect of the digital that we have not mentioned – what Lupton (2015) calls 'professional digital practice'. Here, academics use digital methods as a means of teaching, publicizing their research, making available certain resources, rendering online profiles, and, crucially, building their own networks. In the present case we can point to Latour's (2013) 'Inquiry into Modes of Existence' project. This is an ambitious attempt to map different 'modes of existence' (understood as the 'inverse' of networks) that characterize modernity. As such, rather than, as in ANT-mode, tracing the heterogeneity and relationality that make up a seemingly 'integrated' entity (that is, the 'network-ness of integrity'), in 'modes of existence mode', one examines the associations that bind entities together in particular, continuing patterns (that is, the 'integrity of networks'). This is clearly a gargantuan project and his book *An Inquiry into Modes of Existence* is merely a starting point. Latour's AIME online platform serves as a means of advancing this project: here contributors were invited to offer their views, ideally enriching, supplementing and adding to Latour's existing list of 'modes of existence'. The broader point is that post-ANT can deploy 'the digital' in building its own post-ANT networks.

In this somewhat breathless ramble through an array of latterday post-ANT developments, we have tried to portray the empirical, conceptual and methodological liveliness that characterizes post-ANT. Hopefully, this is of some use, inspiring, if not directly instructing, the reader. However, there is still a lingering suspicion that the foregoing makes up a dense, inchoate picture that is not a little disorienting. So, to finish, I present a few suggestions on how to navigate through this potential confusion...

How to do Post-ANT

The irony of this last heading will not be lost on the reader. For a start, as Chapter 7 and the preceding sections have indicated, there is no singular post-ANT, but a multitude of post-ANTs that are spinning off in different, though more or less loosely inter-related, directions. In addition, how is it possible to derive a generic 'how to do' list when any particular version of post-ANT emerges through the specific combination of conceptual, methodological and empirical/substantive concerns?

Even if the sorts of analytic and methodological issues that exercise post-ANT scholars are intimately tied with the sites of their empirical research, in what follows we nevertheless try to abstract a preliminary list of the conceptual concerns that characterize post-ANT-in-general. Loosely reflecting the sentiment behind Latour's 'modes of existence', we might ask: what perseveres across the many instantiations of post-ANT? At best we can say that there is a range of sensibilities and practical orientations. So, let us, finally, distil a few interconnected pointers – tentative and heuristic sensibilities and practical orientations – for doing post-ANT:

1. Engage with the 'stuff' (human and nonhuman) that is in front of you, attend to its specificity, follow it in its heterogeneity, multiplicity and complexity, though you will...

2. Be acutely aware that not everything 'relevant' is directly in front of you, or specifiable, or follow-able, and that is partly because...

3. You will recognize that 'you', in your specificity and complexity, are not fully in front of your 'stuff', which means that...

4. You should try to be 'careful' with the stuff you strive to follow as it (and you) differ, perhaps even inhabit different realities or ontologies, as does other stuff you encounter along the way of your study, which suggests...

5. You might want to cultivate a sensitivity toward the different realities you come across and the patterns of their interactions. Sometimes such realities will conflict, sometimes sit in parallel, sometimes merge, sometimes depend on one another's absence. Even so…

6. You will want to develop a keen sense of how you are 'othering' realities that don't fit with the patterns you detect amongst the stuff you are following. The patterns of associations, of relations, of coordination and conflict also need to be treated in their specificity, which implies that…

7. You will take 'care' of the social scientific temptation to 'abstract' from those patterns and see them as effects or exemplifications of higher or deeper processes or phenomena (such as neoliberalism or risk society), not least because the associations that make up these patterns can shift and change. Nevertheless…

8. You will aim to monitor the possibilities that emerge as these patterns unfold. And sometimes, you might even seek ways – experimental, speculative, pragmatic – of enabling new patterns to emerge…

To be sure, these sensibilities and practical orientations have turned out to be rather vague, abstract and incomplete. They are certainly not a set of instructions but rather a sequence of prompts about the 'care' one needs to take in doing post-ANT research. Along with the rest of this book, they might even serve as a sort of modest invitation to the adventure and promise of post-ANTs.

A SELECTIVE GLOSSARY OF ANT AND POST-ANT TERMS

Actant

Derived from the semiotics of Greimas, 'actant' is a term that designates a particular entity – human or nonhuman – which acts within a narrative of network-building. 'Pasteur' is such an actant – a signifier derived from various texts and deployed in the narration of the rise of Pasteurism (Latour, 1988a). Other authors are sceptical of its utility, suggesting that it unnecessarily complicates what are in actuality realistic accounts about a real entity or persons such as Pasteur (Lynch, 1993).

Action Nets

'Action nets' has been proposed by Czarniawska (e.g. 2004) as a supplement to actor-networks that places more stress on the processes of organizing rather than on organizations or actors, and prefers a version of translation that is more dispersed, often spreading beyond the ostensible confines of an organization (or network) and more mutualist (in which actors at all levels of an organization contribute to the process of organizing). On this score, story-telling and story-sharing is of particular importance in the everyday sense-making necessary for organizing.

Actor (macro, micro)

Actor is used in several ways in ANT. It connotes any entity (human or non-human) within a network (hence actor-network). It is opposed to an intermediary, and as such does not simply faithfully transfer information or materials from a sender to a receiver. And it implies a 'primary entity' that makes some sort of major difference in the emergence of a network. Actors are composite entities, comprised of networks. Macro-actors, such as institutions, are really micro-actors (a single actor, or a few actors) who have successfully associated together many other actors, and can serve as spokespersons for the macro-entity.

Actor-network

An actor-network 'emerges' with the successful alignment of an array of heterogeneous elements that, in 'classical' ANT, will 'do the bidding' of the 'primary actor', and in post-ANT more or less loosely hold together. Importantly, the process of alignment is also heterogeneous entailing the circulation of materials and signs that serve in the (partial) enrolment of elements into the relevant (though sometimes ambivalent) roles.

Ambivalence

In some networks, actors can take on ambivalent roles – both integrated into a network and antagonistic toward it. Contra the 'classical' view of actor-networks, despite this chronic ambiguity, a network can remain durable, and even thrive.

Amodernity

According to Latour (1993a), modernity is characterized by the ostensible separation – or purification – of the human and nonhuman. However, humans have always already been embroiled with nonhumans. We are thus located in an amodernity in which humanity is necessarily marked by hybridity. The proliferation of noteworthy hybrids through modern technoscience has sensitized us to our amodern constitutive hybridity.

Assemblage

Though not a worthy translation of the French 'agencement', assemblage is a patterned array of connections and composed of all manner of heterogeneous elements. These arrays can be 'territorialized' into sets of structured (or root-like) patterns and/or deterritorialized into promiscuous or fluid (rhizomic) patterns.

Associations

Associations are the links or connections that are made between actors. In 'classical' ANT associations are engendered when one actor interposes itself between other actors, translating their interests, severing other associations, and aligning those actors with itself.

Black Box

A black box contains that which no longer needs to be considered. All that is of interest is the input and the output. If input and output reliably link, then the work that has gone into making the black box loses relevance. Anything that operates as black-boxed is thus resistant to problematization and can therefore be used for making associations and building networks.

Boundary Objects

Boundary objects straddle different networks (or social worlds). They are sufficiently stable and robust to retain their identity, while sufficiently adaptable and plastic to be understood and used in divergent ways by those inhabiting different networks (or worlds). The result is that collaboration across networks is possible, without threat to the participating network members.

Centres of Calculation

These are sites wherein technoscientists bring together and combine many heterogeneous components – experimental materials and technologies, particular analytic and calculative skills, various inscription devices. The work that goes on in centres of calculation yields 'immutable mobiles' that can be sent back into the world, and used to generate problematizations, translate interests, and further network-building.

Composition, Compositionism

Composition refers to the gathering and combination of heterogeneous actors and entities to produce a new entity, a particular reality. Compositionism references the view that all such realities are thus constructed. Rather than see this as a problem, the recognition that everything is composed (including the assumptions on the basis of which one critiques) means that politics should proceed less by critique, and more through a gathering of the different compositions. Such gatherings are composed too, so it is not possible to model these separately from those who bring their compositions to that gathering.

Construction

Like composition, construction indexes the ways in which realities are constituted through the bringing together and combination of heterogeneous elements. The construction of the reality known as a 'scientific fact' embraces both the 'social' and the 'technical'.

Convergence

Network elements that might otherwise be divergent can be brought together in various ways to afford that network durability. Convergence is usually a matter of a strict alignment of elements which might lead to the 'irreversibility' of a network (e.g. through standard setting, or potent enrolment). However, convergence can also take looser forms (e.g. through ambivalence, or boundary objects) in which durability is grounded in more pliable associations.

Cosmopolitics (also political ecology, ecology of practices)

Cosmopolitics is concerned with bringing together the disparate practitioners and practices that can contribute to the making – the emergence – of the issue at stake. This is a hesitant process in which final positions must be guarded against. Practitioners can be both 'loyal' to the objects of which they speak, but also recognize that these objects are composed, not least through their disciplinary commitments and skills. This all means, on the one hand, that one cannot presuppose what counts as 'nature' in cosmopolitics (the point of 'political ecology'), and on the other, that one cannot presuppose the nature of the bringing together of practices and practitioners (the point of an 'ecology of practices').

Description

Description is the preferred form of 'analysis' for ANT. Rather than seeking explanations (that draw on social theories about structuration, or practice, or neoliberalism, or risk society), ANT analysts seek to describe what they observe in close or 'thick' detail. In this way they can reveal the local mechanisms by which associations are realized, and networks built.

Disentanglement

This term addresses the ways that framing a market exchange simultaneously breaks up entanglements or associations. Thus the object of an exchange is disentangled from previous owners. However, such disentanglement also generates new attachments (e.g. to the legal system).

Displacement

Displacement indicates the many means by which technoscientists, in the building of their networks, go about directing information, people, materials and resources. In order to enrol others, various ways of rendering associations need to be put into play: organizing public events, meeting with important actors, circulating publicity, all serve in the process of enrolment.

Durability

Durability denotes the continuation of a network through a variety of means, notably the movement of intermediaries continuously and faithfully repeating a given message and in the process replicating, normalizing and perhaps standardizing roles, associations and their distribution.

Enactment, Enact

Enactment and enact fulfil similar functions to performance and perform. Both reference the ways in which discourses, practices, technologies, bodies act in ways to construct and distribute a particular reality. For Mol (2002) the advantage of enactment and enact is that they do connote a central 'performer' or a reality behind the performance.

Enrol, Enrolment

At base, these terms index the successful placing into designated roles of given entities. By translating the interests of these entities, these entities are dissociated from previous relations and placed into new desired associations so that they can perform appropriately within a network.

Event, Eventuate

Event is a complex and contested term is used here to indicate that when elements come together within a specific occasion, they can mutually change or eventuate – co-become – in ways that redefine the event in unexpected ways. This means that the event is not easily identifiable – indeed, it needs to be treated in terms of potentiality, that is, the possibilities that it eventuates.

Fire, Fire Objects

The shifting patterns or presence and absence in the composition of certain objects mean that they manifest in dramatically different ways from one location to another. Rather than the more or less smooth transitions of fluids, these 'fire objects' move as in a bush fire – in fits and starts across locations, sometimes they are creative, sometimes destructive.

Flatness, Flat Ontology

In opposition to those mainstream sociological accounts which look to explanations in terms of factors above, below or beyond actors (e.g. neoliberalism, risk society), ANT works with flatness – or a flat ontology. It is assumed that any large social actor is composed of associations extending out amongst smaller actors. How these associations are accomplished and maintained is always a local matter in which such practices as problematization and translation, etc. are brought to bear.

Fluid, Fluidity

As certain objects move across settings, what they are can change as new associations enter into their making. This transitioning can be thought of in terms of fluidity as the seemingly identical object changes over and over as it moves (much like a fluid).

Framing

Framing refers to the ways in which boundaries are drawn between what is taken into account, and all that is ignored, when actors make calculations (for a financial deal, a contract, or a market exchange). However, framing results in overflowing as the disentanglements involved in framing also generate new entanglements (e.g. to frame something, commitment to certain framing devices is necessary).

Free Association (the tenet of)

Free association refuses any in principle distinctions between the social, natural, or technological. Given the usual hybridity of all actors and entities in a network or assemblage, what 'counts as' social, natural or technological can only be worked out through close empirical study of the particular case study.

Generalized Agnosticism (the principle of)

This principle advocates that the researcher remains impartial as to what or who are involved in any given controversy. The application of the same form of analysis to all human actors – whether the losers or winners of a scientific dispute – is thus extended to all the nonhumans that are present, whatever their position within the controversy.

Generalized Symmetry (the principle of)

In pursuing the analysis of the role of human and nonhuman elements within a network, it is important to apply common analytic tools, not least the use of a neutral terminology that does not distinguish amongst these elements, but rather seeks to trace how they are allocated the status of human or nonhuman.

Heterogeneity, Heterogeneous Engineering

Heterogeneity signifies the ANT commitment to a view of the social world as composed of a variety of elements – humans, natures, technologies. Heterogeneous engineering refers to those actors who in building or engineering their networks have to marshal, enrol and arrange a multiplicity of humans, natures and technologies.

Hybrid

The world is composed of hybrids – mixtures of humans, natures and technologies. Rather than think in terms of humans versus nonhumans, ANT pays attention to the necessary embroilment of these: without books, computer, smart-phone, lighting, projector, desk, etc., etc., one could not function as a 'contemporary scholar'.

Hybrid Collectif

This is another version of actor-networks. Importantly, 'collectif' highlights the problem of network extension. Given that in principle a network can extend indefinitely in terms of number and length of associations, why, where, when and how does one stop bringing more elements into the analysis?

Hybrid Forums

These are arenas occupied by diverse actors who come together to negotiate. What they are negotiating might vary, straddling any field or topic. Key is that the negotiation draws on participants from all relevant walks of life, non-expert as well as expert, amateur as well as accredited. Further, the forum is such that it works against the entrenchment of positions and allows shifts in the identities of the participants.

Immutable Mobile

Usually a text that can, with the aid of certain techniques (notably, the Cartesian coordinate system), combine numerous representations together (figures, graphs, numbers, tables) into simpler and harder representations that resist problematization. Such immutability is allied to mobility – such texts can travel with considerable ease, retaining their meaning as they move, and are able to combine with other texts as and when required.

Infra-reflexivity

Infra-reflexivity is set in opposition to meta-reflexivity (Latour, 1988a). If meta-reflexivity is anxious that representations will be believed despite their social constructed-ness, infra-reflexivity is hopeful that representations are believed precisely because they are (socially) constructed well. The fact is that all representations are constructed, even those that lament or celebrate that fact, and that in their constructed-ness work to enrol their readers into joining the lament or celebration.

Inscription Device

Inscription devices such as bioassays or NMR spectrometers generate inscriptions that are written into papers that become immutable mobiles. Insofar as they are black-boxed, inscription devices produce inscriptions that are not easily problematized. Put another way, inscription devices are arguments transformed into pieces of apparatus.

Interessement

The term 'interessement' captures those practices that an actor employs to impose and stabilize a particular identity on other actors, once that identity has been problematized. First problematize the French public as failing to fulfil their desires for a more ecological France, then 'interesse' them in the identity centred on electric vehicles as the solution to this problem.

Interests

Loosely, interests can be said to refer to the concerns, desires, identities, purposes, etc. which people aim to realize. Within ANT, interests are relational – actors might have interests but these can be fluid and emergent, and, crucially they can be instilled through the processes of problematization, interessement, enrolment, etc.

Intermediary

For Latour (2005a), the 'intermediary' is any entity that faithfully conveys meaning from a sender to a receiver so that an association can be accomplished. It can be contrasted to the figure of the 'mediator'.

Material Semiotics

Material semiotics is the study of how in the making of heterogeneous associations all manner of actors (human and nonhuman) and arrangements (organizations, inequalities) are produced. ANT is a sub-set of material semiotics.

Matters of Care

Matters of care highlights a particular dimension of matters of concern, namely that it is necessary to treat with 'care' those arguments and actors with which one disagrees. That is to say, one must take into careful account the composition of others' enactments, though one must also be careful about this too (does taking care turn to a lack of care under certain circumstances?).

Matters of Concern

Matters of concern points to the gathering or assembling or composing that takes place when producing a matter of fact. Such composing entails a multitude of elements, practices, 'interests', contingencies, and so on. The aim is not to debunk matters of fact, but to show how these are constituted in order to open up the possibility of negotiation amongst them.

Matters of Fact

Matters of fact are matters of concern where the process of composition has been lost or hidden from view. They are partial matters of concern, often put to polemical use.

Mediator

Mediators are unfaithful intermediaries that transfigure, refashion and deform the messages that pass between entities. This does not simply disrupt or destroy associations but can proliferate and complicate them.

Method Assemblage

This term addresses the complex, partial, fluid articulations between the realities of the researcher and the realities of their object of study – realities which are shifting, emergent, messy and multiple. One upshot is that there is much that cannot be included in the explicit account of this articulation (either because it cannot be accessed, or because it is 'othered'). The result is that research, in its 'partiality' and 'selectivity' enacts or performs its object of study.

Modes of Ordering

This term refers to the processes (e.g. the spatial configuration of an organization) and practices (e.g. discourses) that perform orders, that is, patterns of associations (which can be more or less fluid). Modes of ordering has been used to explore the operations of hierarchy and power within organizations

More-than-Human

The 'more-than-human' entails the combination of elements of ANT with other perspectives (such as that of Haraway) in order to illuminate the ways that the human is embroiled within a nexus of nonhumans which should be treated as fluid and multiple, complex and contested, connected and differentiated. Importantly, the more-than-human throws into relief the situated 'experiential' dimensions of nonhumans and how these are partially shaped by the physical constitution and capacities of those entities.

Multinaturalism, Pluriverse

These terms denote the fact that there are multiple realities and multiple natures that reflect the different ways in which diverse heterogeneous elements are brought together and composed.

Obligatory Passage Point, Obligatory Points of Passage

To enrol actors is also to orient them towards particular sites (e.g. centres of calculation) and particular actors (e.g. technoscientists). To realize their new role (or identity) these enrollees must necessarily pass through such obligatory passage points.

Ontological Multiplicity

This concept draws on the argument that reality – or ontology – is enacted. Different enactments (by different specialisms, say) generate a multiplicity of realities. There is thus no real 'reality' that lies behind these enactments, but the complex array of associations drawn into each enactment make different entities. Such multiplicity generates different sorts of 'politics'.

Ontological Politics

The enactment of divergent realities (that together produce ontological multiplicity) can relate to each other in a variety of ways. Sometimes these are overtly political insofar as there is conflict between realities; sometimes they simply coexist; sometimes the politics are more tacit as when they are quietly and practically managed, or hang together non-coherently. Where multiple realities are quietly managed, this rests on 'collateral realities' that allow for communication across divergent realities. This evokes another politics, namely the exclusion of those who do not share in those collateral realities.

Other, Othered, Othering, Otherness

Any form of empirical engagement or analysis entails a process of 'othering' by virtue of emphasizing only certain elements of its object of study. The method assemblage however provides for the acknowledgement of its own partiality, whether that entails excluding others because of the specific contingencies of the empirical engagement and analysis, or because there will always be something that falls beyond the study's wider 'frame of reference'.

Overflowing

The process of framing invariably generates overflowing, as the actors that come together bring with them entanglements that extend beyond their frame, and which can change with the process of framing. Overflowing implies both the impossibility of total framing, but also the possibility that framing produces entanglements through which it comes to be problematized.

Performativity, Perform

This term addresses the ways in which practices produce particular realities or ontologies. How a reality is performed (e.g. the sorts of techniques or arguments that are brought to bear and put into circulation) can also induce others to share this reality.

Power

In ANT power is not a term much used. This is because it detracts from the close analysis of how associations are formed. So, rather than observing power being exercised by one actor 'over' others, ANT traces the local processes of translation, enrolment, etc. which produce and sustain relations. These relations might evoke power, in the sense that they are 'hierarchical', but they can also be subverted at any moment.

Prescription, Proscription

Technologies have 'scripts' integrated into them which affect what can and cannot be done with those technologies. Technologies thus prescribe or proscribe the behaviours or comportments necessary to ensure that they work. These pre- and pro- scriptions can be subverted, not least by reworking what 'working' means for a particular technology.

Problematization

To raise issues about an actor's identity and interests and their realization. By establishing that an actor's 'real' interests are not being met, a technoscientist can enrol that actor to their project through which those interests will indeed be realized.

Proposition

The process of composition generates a state of affairs – an assemblage or assembly, say – that can be open or unsettled. At this juncture, such an assemblage or assembly entails a proposition that 'lures' other associations (or 'proposes' new connections) so that it and its constituent, composed elements might all be modified.

Purification

The ongoing process, characteristic of modernity, in which humans and nonhumans are held to be distinct. Purification works to obscure the actual hybridity of all entities, while also facilitating the unrecognized and unchecked proliferation of hybrids.

Research Event

A 'research event' signals the mutual emergence of researcher and researched through the process of empirical and analytic engagement such that they might no longer be identifiable as researcher and researched, and the research event itself might turn into a totally different sort of event.

Rhizome

The rhizome (synonyms include molecular and smooth) denotes a state of an assemblage in which connections between elements are highly promiscuous – any part of the assemblage can associate with any other part however 'different' or 'distant'.

Scripts

Scripts are the 'instructions' or 'rules' inscribed into technologies that must be followed if those technologies are to 'work'. These often demand (prescribe or proscribe) particular sorts of bodily capacities and comportments.

Sociomateriality, Sociomaterial

In the process of ordering (or disordering) associations between elements in a network or assemblage, entities that straddle the human and the nonhuman, the social and the material, need to be deployed. Thus a scientific paper can go about the process of enrolment because it is sociomaterial, because, at its simplest, it is composed of both paper (nonhuman) and text (human).

Speculation

An approach to research that assumes research events, researchers and researched might all co-become in unforeseeable ways. The aim of research thus becomes one of exploring – speculating on – these possible becomings. In some cases speculation involves close observation of research events and their 'accidental' becomings (e.g. disruptions); in other cases, speculation is based on research events that are designed to facilitate becoming by introducing playfulness or ambiguity into the proceedings.

Spokesperson

The spokesperson is the actor who has situated themselves within a network such that they are able to speak on behalf of all the other relevant entities, ideally without contradiction. To become a spokesperson means enrolling other entities who then ideally act according to their allocated roles.

Technoscience

This term highlights the heterogeneity of science as it goes about constructing its networks through a multiplicity of activities that include shaping a supportive regulatory landscape, securing funding, doing science, cultivating public support, etc., etc.

Translation

To translate is to redefine another's interests or identity by whatever means possible – textual, social, even coercive – so that they do one's bidding, or allow one to speak or act on their behalf (as a spokesperson). Through translation, actors become enrolled into an actor-network.

REFERENCES

Abbott, A. (2001) *The Chaos of Disciplines*. Chicago: The University of Chicago Press.

Adkins, L. and Lury, C. (2009) What is the empirical? *The European Journal of Social Theory*, 12(1), 5–20.

Adorno, T. and Horkheimer, M. (1973) *Dialectic of Enlightenment*. London: Verso.

Akrich, M. (1992) The de-scription of technical objects. In W.E. Bijker and J. Law (eds), *Shaping Technology/Building Society* (pp. 205–24). Cambridge, MA: The MIT Press.

Akrich, M. and Latour, B. (1992) A summary of a convenient vocabulary for the semiotics of human and nonhuman assemblies. In W.E. Bijker and J. Law (eds), *Shaping Technology/Building Society* (pp. 259–63). Cambridge, MA: The MIT Press.

Albert, M. and Kleinman, D. (2011) Bringing Pierre Bourdieu to science and technology studies. *Minerva*, 49(3), 263–73.

Alcadipani, R. and Hassard, J. (2010) Actor-network theory, organizations and critique: towards a politics of organizing. *Organization*, 17(4), 419–35.

Amin, A. and Thrift, N. (2002) *Cities: Reimagining the Urban*. Cambridge: Polity.

Anderson, B. (2010) Preemption, precaution, preparedness: anticipatory action and future geographies. *Progress in Human Geography*, 34(6), 777–98.

Anderson, B., Kearnes, M., McFarlane, C. and Swanton, D. (2012) On assemblages and geography. *Dialogues in Human Geography*, 2(2), 171–89.

Ardevol, E., Pink, S. and Lanzeni, D. (eds) (2016) *Designing Digital Materialities: Knowing, Intervention and Making*. London: Bloomsbury.

Asdal, K. and Moser, I. (2012) Experiments in context and contexting. *Science, Technology, & Human Values*, 37(4), 291–306.

Ashmore, M. (1989) *The Reflexive Thesis*. Chicago: Chicago University Press.

Austin, J.L. (1962) *How to Do Things with Words*. Oxford: Clarendon Press.

Back, L. and Puwar, N. (eds) (2012) *Live Methods*. Oxford and Keele: Wiley and Sociological Review Monographs.

Barad, K. (2007) *Meeting the Universe Halfway*. Durham, NC: Duke University Press.

Barnes, B. (1977) *Interests and the Growth of Knowledge*. London: Routledge and Kegan Paul.

Barnes, B. and Edge, D. (eds) (1982) *Science in Context*. Milton Keynes: Open University Press.

Barnes, B. and Shapin, S. (eds) (1979) *Natural Order*. Beverly Hills: Sage.

Barratt, P. (2011) Vertical worlds: technology, hybridity and the climbing body. *Social & Cultural Geography*, 12(4), 387–412.

Barratt, P. (2012) 'May magic cam': a more-than-representational account of the climbing assemblage. *Area*, 44(1), 46–53.

Barry, A. and Born, G. (eds) (2013) *Interdisciplinarity: Reconfigurations of the Social and Natural Sciences*. London: Routledge.

Barry, A. and Slater, D. (2002) Introduction: the technological economy. *Economy and Society*, 31(2), 175–93.

Barry, A. and Thrift, N. (2007) Gabriel Tarde: imitation, invention and economy. *Economy and Society*, 36(4), 509–25.

Barry, A., Born, G. and Weszkalnys, G. (2008) Logics of interdisciplinarity. *Economy and Society*, 37(1), 20–49.

Bazanger, I. (1998) Pain physicians: all alike, all different. In M. Berg and A. Mol (eds), *Differences in Medicine: Unravelling Practices, Techniques, and Bodies* (pp. 117–43). Durham, NC: Duke University Press.

Beck, U. (1992) *The Risk Society*. London: Sage.

Beck, U. (2000) Risk society revisited: theory politics and research programmes. In B. Adam, U. Beck and J. van Loon (eds), *The Risk Society and Beyond* (pp. 221–9). London: Sage.

Beck, U., Giddens, A. and Lash, S. (1994) *Reflexive Modernization: Politics, Tradition and Aesthetics in the Modern Social Order*. Cambridge: Polity.

Bennett, J. (2010) *Vibrant Matter*. Durham, NC: Duke University Press.

Bennett, T. (2007) Habitus clivé: aesthetics and politics in the work of Pierre Bourdieu. *New Literary History*, 38(1), 201–28.

Bijker, W.E. (1995) *Of Bicycles, Bakelite and Bulbs: Toward a Theory of Sociotechnical Change*. Cambridge, MA: The MIT Press.

Birke L., Arluke, A. and Michael, M. (2007) *The Sacrifice: How Scientific Experiments Transform Animals and People*. West Lafayette, IN: Purdue University Press.

Blok, A. (2011) War of the whales: post-sovereign science and agonistic cosmopolitics in Japanese-global whaling assemblages. *Science, Technology & Human Values*, 36(1), 55–81.

Blok, A. (2013) Pragmatic sociology as political ecology: on the many worths of nature(s). *European Journal of Social Theory*, 16(4), 492–510.

Bloomfield, B. and Vurdubakis, T. (1999) The outer limits: monsters, actor-networks and the writing of displacement. *Organization*, 6(4), 625–47.

Bloor, D. (1976) *Knowledge and Social Imagery*. London: Routledge and Kegan Paul.

Boehner, K., Gaver, W. and Boucher, A. (2012) Probes. In C. Lury and N. Wakeford (eds), *Inventive Methods: The Happening of the Social* (pp. 185–201). London: Routledge.

Boltanski, L. and Thévenot, L. (2006) *On Justification: Economies of Worth*. Princeton, NJ: Princeton University Press.

Born, G. and Barry, A. (2010) Art-science: from public understanding to public experiment. *Journal of Cultural Economy*, 3(1), 103–19.

Bosco, F.J. (2006) Actor-network theory, networks and relational approaches on human geography. In S. Aitken and G. Valentine (eds), *Approaches to Human Geography* (pp. 136–46). London: Sage.

Bourdieu, P. (1984) *Distinction: A Social Critique of the Judgement of Taste.* London: Routledge and Kegan Paul.

Bourdieu, P. (1989) Social space and symbolic violence. *Sociological Theory,* 7(1), 14–25.

Bourdieu, P. (1990) *The Logic of Practice.* Cambridge: Polity.

Bowers, J. and Iwi, K. (1993) The discursive construction of society. *Discourse and Society,* 4(3), 357–93.

Bowker, G.C. and Star, S.L. (1999) *Sorting Things Out: Classification and its Consequences.* Cambridge, MA: The MIT Press.

Brenner, N., Madden, D.J. and Wachsmuth, D. (2011) Assemblage urbanism and the challenges of critical urban theory. *City,* 15(2), 225–40.

Brosnan, C. and Michael, M. (2014) Enacting the 'neuro' in practice: Translational research, adhesion, and the promise of porosity. *Social Studies of Science,* 44(5), 680–700.

Brown, N. and Michael, M. (2003) A sociology of expectations: retrospecting prospects and prospecting retrospects. *Technology Analysis and Strategic Management,* 15(1), 3–18.

Bryant, L., Srnicek, N. and Harman, G. (eds) (2011) *The Speculative Turn: Continental Materialism and Realism.* Melbourne: Re.Press.

Bucchi, M. and Neresini, F. (2008) Science and public participation. In E.J. Hackett, O. Amsterdamska, M. Lynch and J. Wajcman (eds), *The Handbook of Science and Technologies Studies* (pp. 449–72). Cambridge, MA: The MIT Press.

Callon, M. (1986a) Some elements in a sociology of translation: domestication of the scallops and fishermen of St Brieuc Bay. In J. Law (ed.), *Power, Action and Belief* (pp. 196–233). London: Routledge and Kegan Paul.

Callon, M. (1986b) The sociology of an actor-network: the case of the electric vehicle. In M. Callon, J. Law and A. Rip (eds), *Mapping the Dynamics of Science and Technology* (pp. 19–34). London: Macmillan.

Callon, M. (1987) Society in the making: the study of technology as a tool for sociological analysis. In W.E. Bijker, T.P. Hughes and T. Pinch (eds), *Social Construction of Technological Systems* (pp. 83–103). Cambridge, MA: The MIT Press.

Callon, M. (1991) Techno-economic networks and irreversibility. In J. Law (ed.), *A Sociology of Monsters* (pp. 132–61). London: Routledge.

Callon, M. (1998a) Introduction: the embeddedness of economic markets in economics. In M. Callon (ed.), *The Laws of the Markets* (pp. 1–68). Oxford: Blackwell.

Callon, M. (1998b) An essay on framing and overflowing: economic externalities revisited by sociology. In M. Callon (ed.) *The Laws of the Markets* (pp. 244–69). Oxford: Blackwell.

Callon, M. (1999) Actor-network theory: the market test. In J. Law and J. Hassard (eds), *Actor Network Theory and After* (pp. 181–95). Oxford: Blackwell.

Callon, M. (2004) The role of hybrid communities and socio-technical arrangements in participatory design. *Journal for the Centre of Information Studies*, 5(3), 3–10.

Callon, M. (2007) What does it mean to say that economics is performative? In D. MacKenzie, F. Muniesa and L. Siu (eds), *Do Economists Make Markets? On the Performativity of Economics* (pp. 311–57). Princeton, NJ: Princeton University Press.

Callon, M. and Latour, B. (1981) Unscrewing the big Leviathan. In K.D. Knorr Cetina and M. Mulkay (eds), *Advances in Social Theory and Methodology* (pp. 275–303). London: Routledge and Kegan Paul.

Callon, M. and Latour, B. (1992) Don't throw the baby out with the Bath School! A reply to Collins and Yearley. In A. Pickering (ed.), *Science as Practice and Culture* (pp. 343–68). Chicago: University of Chicago Press.

Callon, M. and Law, J. (1982) On interests and their transformation: enrolment and counter-enrolment. *Social Studies of Science*, 12(4), 615–25.

Callon, M. and Law, J. (1995) Agency and the hybrid collectif. *The South Atlantic Quarterly*, 94(2), 481–507.

Callon, M. and Rabeharisoa, V. (2004) Gino's lesson on humanity: genetics, mutual entanglements and the sociologist's role. *Economy and Society*, 33(1), 1–27.

Callon, M., Lascoumbes, P. and Barthe, Y. (2001) *Acting in an Uncertain World: An Essay on Technical Democracy*. Cambridge, MA: The MIT Press.

Callon, M., Méadel, C. and Rabeharisoa, V. (2002) The economy of qualities. *Economy and Society*, 31(2), 194–218.

Callon, M., Millo, Y. and Muniesa, F. (eds) (2007) *Market Devices*. Oxford: Blackwell.

Calvert, J. (2007) Patenting genomic objects: Genes, genomes, function and information. *Science as Culture*, 16(2), 207–23.

Camic, C. (2011) Bourdieu's cleft sociology of science. *Minerva*, 49(3), 275–93.

Carter, B. and Charles, N. (2013) Animals, agency and resistance. *Journal for the Theory of Social Behavior*, 43(3), 322–40.

Chilvers, J. (2008) Deliberating competence: theoretical and practitioner perspectives on effective participatory appraisal practice. *Science, Technology & Human Values*, 33(2), 155–85.

Chilvers, J. and Kearnes, M. (eds) (2016) *Remaking Participation: Science, Democracy and Emergent Publics*. London: Earthscan-Routledge.

Clarke, A.E. (1990) A social worlds research adventure: the case of reproductive science. In S.E. Cozzens and T.F. Gieryn (eds), *Theories of Science in Society* (pp. 15–42). Bloomington: Indiana University Press.

Clarke, A.E. and Fujimara, J.H. (eds) (1992) *The Right Tools for the Job: At Work in Twentieth-Century Life Science*. Princeton, NJ: Princeton University Press.

Clarke, A.E. and Montini, T. (1993) The many faces of RU486: tales of situated knowledges and technological contestation. *Science, Technology & Human Values*, 18(1), 42–78.

Clough, P. (2009) The new empiricism: affect and sociological method. *European Journal of Social Theory*, 12(1), 43–61.

Cochoy, F. (2007) A sociology of market-things: on tending the garden of choices in mass retailing. In M. Callon, Y. Millo and F. Muniesa (eds), *Market Devices* (pp. 109–29). London: Blackwell.

Collin, F. and Budtz Pedersen, D. (2015) The Frankfurt School, science and technology studies, and the humanities. *Social Epistemology*, 29 (1), 44–72.

Collinge, C. (2006) Flat ontology and the deconstruction of scale: a response to Marston, Jones and Woodward. *Transactions of the Institute of British Geographers*, 31(2), 244–51.

Collins, H.M. (1985) *Changing Order*. London: Sage.

Collins, H.M. and Yearley, S. (1992a) Epistemological chicken. In A. Pickering (ed.), *Science as Practice and Culture* (pp. 301–26). Chicago: The University of Chicago Press.

Collins, H.M. and Yearley, S. (1992b) Journey into space. In A. Pickering (ed.), *Science as Practice and Culture* (pp. 369–89). Chicago: The University of Chicago Press.

Connolly, W.E. (2011) *A World of Becoming*. Durham, NC: Duke University Press.

Cooper, R. and Law, J. (1995) Organization: distal and proximal views. In S.B. Bacharach, P. Gagliardi and B. Mundell (eds), *Research in the Sociology of Organizations: Studies of Organizations in the European Tradition* (pp. 275–301). Greenwich, CT: JAI Press.

Cussins, C. (1996) Ontological choreography: Agency through objectification in infertility clinics. *Social Studies of Science*, 26(3), 575–610.

Czarniawska, B. (2004) On time, space, and action nets. *Organization*, 11(6), 773–91.

Czarniawska, B. (2008) *A Theory of Organizing*. Cheltenham: Edward Elgar.

Czarniawska, B. and Hernes, T. (eds) (2005) *Actor-Network Theory and Organizing*. Malmo/Copenhagen: Liber/CBS.

Dant, T. (2006) Material civilizations: things and society. *The British Journal of Sociology*, 57(2), 289–308.

Davies, G. (2012) What is a humanized mouse? Remaking the species and the spaces of translational medicine. *Body & Society*, 18(3–4), 126–55.

de Laet, M. and Mol, A. (2000) The Zimbabwe Bush Pump: mechanics of a fluid technology. *Social Studies of Science*, 30(2), 225–63.

Deleuze, G. and Guattari, F. (1988) *A Thousand Plateaus: Capitalism and Schizophrenia*. London: Athlone Press.

Dent, M. (2003) Managing doctors and saving a hospital: irony, rhetoric and actor networks. *Organization*, 10(1), 107–27.

Despret, V. (2004) The body we care for: figures of anthropo-zoo-genesis. *Body & Society*, 10(2–3), 111–34.

Despret, V. (2008) The becoming of subjectivity in animal worlds. *Subjectivity*, 23(1), 123–9.

Dicks, B. (2014) Action, experience, communication: three methodological paradigms for researching multimodal and multisensory setting. *Qualitative Research*, 14(6), 656–74.

Doran, L. (1989) Jumping frames: reflexivity and recursion in the sociology of science. *Social Studies of Science*, 19(3), 515–31.

Durepos, G. and Mills, A.J. (2012) Actor-network theory, ANTi-history and critical organizational historiography. *Organization*, 19(6), 703–21.

Elam, M. (1999) Living dangerously with Bruno Latour in a hybrid world. *Theory, Culture & Society*, 16(4), 1–24.

Elam, M. and Bertilsson, M. (2003) Consuming, engaging and confronting science: the emerging dimensions of scientific citizenship. *European Journal of Social Theory*, 6(2), 233–51.

Elias, N. (1978) *What is Sociology?* London: Hutchinson.

Elias, N. (1994/1939) *The Civilizing Process*. Oxford: Blackwell.

Elias, N. (1995) Civilization and technicization. *Theory, Culture & Society*, 12(4–5), 7–42.

Elias, N. (1998) *On Civilization, Power, and Knowledge*. Chicago: The University of Chicago Press.

Englund, H., Gerdin, J. and Burns, J. (2011) 25 years of Giddens in accounting research: achievements, limitations and the future. *Accounting, Organizations and Society*, 36(8), 494–513.

Farias, I. (2011) The politics of urban assemblages. *City*, 15(3–4), 365–74.

Farias, I. and Bender, T. (eds) (2010) *Urban Assemblages: How Actor-Network Theory Changes Urban Studies*. London: Routledge.

Farias, I. and Wilkie, A. (eds) (2016) *Studio Studies: Operations, Topologies and Displacements*. London: Routledge and CRESC.

Felt, U. and Fochler, M. (2010) Machineries for making publics: inscribing and describing publics in public engagement. *Minerva*, 48(3), 219–38.

Fleck, L. (1979) *Genesis and Development of a Scientific Fact*. Chicago: The University of Chicago Press.

Foucault, M. (1979a) Truth and power: interview with A. Fontano and P. Pasquino. In M. Meaghan and P. Patton (eds), *Power, Truth, Strategy*. Sydney: Feral Publications.

Foucault, M. (1979b) *Discipline and Punish*. Harmondsworth: Penguin.

Foucault, M. (1981) *History of Sexuality*, Vol. 1. Harmondsworth: Penguin.

Foucault, M. (1986) Disciplinary power and subjection. In S. Lukes (ed.), *Power* (pp. 229–42). Oxford: Blackwell.

Fox, S. (2000) Communities of practice, Foucault and actor-network theory. *Journal of Management Studies*, 36(6), 853–67.

Fraser, M. (2010) Facts, ethics and event. In C. Bruun Jensen and K. Rödje (eds), *Deleuzian Intersections in Science, Technology and Anthropology* (pp. 57–82). New York: Berghahn Press.

Freeman, L. (2006) *The Development of Social Network Analysis*. Vancouver: Empirical Press.

Friedman, S. (2016) Habitus clivé and the emotional imprint of social mobility. *The Sociological Review*, 64(1), 129–47.

Fukuyama, F. (2002) *Our Posthuman Future*. New York: Profile Books.

Fuller, S. (2005) Is STS truly revolutionary or merely revolting? *Science Studies*, 18(1), 75–83.

Furhman, E.R. and Oehler, K. (1986) Discourse analysis and reflexivity. *Social Studies of Science*, 16(2), 293–307.

Gad, C. and Bruun Jensen, C. (2010) On the consequences of post-ANT. *Science, Technology & Human Values*, 35(1), 55–80.

Garfinkel, H. (1967) *Studies in Ethnomethodology*. Cambridge: Polity Press.

Gaver, W., Boucher, A., Law, A., Pennington, S., Bowers, J., Beaver, J., Humble, J., Kerridge, T., Villar, N. and Wilkie, A. (2008) Threshold devices: looking out from the home. *CHI 2008 Proceedings of the 26th Annual Conference on Human Factors in Computing Systems* (pp. 1429–38). New York: ACM Press.

Gaver, W., Michael, M., Kerridge, T., Wilkie, A., Boucher, A., Ovalle, L. and Plummer-Fernandez, M. (2015) Energy babble: mixing environmentally-oriented internet content to engage community groups. *CHI '15 Proceedings of the 33rd Annual Conference on Human Factors in Computing Systems* (pp. 1115–24). New York: ACM Press.

Geertz, C. (1973) *The Interpretation of Culture*. New York: Basic Books.

Giddens, A. (1984) *The Constitution of Society: Outline of the Theory of Structuration*. Cambridge: Polity.

Giddens, A. (1990) *Consequences of Modernity*. Cambridge: Polity.

Giddens, A. (1991) *Modernity and Self-Identity*. Cambridge: Polity.

Gieryn, T. (1983) Boundary work in professional ideologies of scientists. *American Sociological Review*, 48(6), 781–95.

Gilbert, G.N. and Mulkay, M. (1984) *Opening Pandora's Box: A Sociological Analysis of Scientists' Discourse*. Cambridge: Cambridge University Press.

Gisler, P. and Michael, M. (2011) Companions at a distance: technoscience, blood, and the horseshoe crab. *Society and Animals*, 19(2), 115–36.

Goffman, E. (1959) *The Presentation of Self in Everyday Life*. Harmondsworth: Penguin.

Gomart, E. and Hennion, A. (1998) A sociology of attachment: music lovers, drug addicts. In J. Law and J. Hassard (eds), *Actor Network Theory and After* (pp. 220–47). Oxford and Malden, MA: Blackwell.

Granovetter, M.S. (1973) The strength of weak ties. *American Journal of Sociology*, 78(6), 1360–80.

Granovetter, M.S. (1985) Economic action and social structure: the problem of embeddedness. *American Journal of Sociology*, 91(3), 481–510.

Greenhalgh, T. and Stones, R. (2010) Theorising big IT programmes in health-care: strong structuration meets actor-network theory. *Social Science and Medicine*, 70(9), 1285–94.

Greenhalgh, T., Stones, R. and Swinglehurst, D. (2014) Choose and book: a sociological analysis of 'resistance' to an expert system. *Social Science and Medicine*, 104(3), 210–19.

Greimas, A.J. (1983) *Structural Semantics: An Attempt at a Method*. Lincoln: University of Nebraska Press.

Guggenheim, M. and Potthast, J. (2012) Symmetrical twins: on the relationship between actor-network theory and the sociology of critical capacities. *European Journal of Social Theory*, 15(2), 157–78.

Guthman, J. (2003) Fast food/organic food: reflexive tastes and the making of 'yuppie chow'. *Social & Cultural Geography*, 4(1), 45–58.

Hacking, I. (1986) Making up people. In T.C. Heller, M. Sosna and D.E. Wellberg (eds), *Reconstructing Individualism* (pp. 222–36). Stanford, CA: Stanford University Press.

Halewood, M. (2011) *A Culture of Thought. A.N. Whitehead and Social Theory*. London: Anthem Press.

Halewood, M. and Michael, M. (2008) Being a sociologist and becoming a Whiteheadian: concrescing methodological tactics. *Theory, Culture & Society*, 25(4), 31–56.

Haraway, D. (1991) *Simians, Cyborgs and Nature*. London: Free Association Books.

Haraway, D. (1994) A game of cat's cradle: science studies, feminist theory, cultural studies. *Configurations*, 2(1), 59–71.

Haraway, D. (1997)*Modest_Witness@Second_Millenium.FemaleMan.Meets_ OncoMouse: Feminism and Technoscience*. London: Routledge.

Haraway, D. (2000) *How Like a Leaf*. London: Routledge.

Haraway, D. (2008) *When Species Meet*. Minneapolis: University of Minnesota Press.

Harman, G. (2009) *Prince of Networks: Bruno Latour and Metaphysics*. Melbourne: Re.press.

Hawkins, G. (2011) Packaging water: plastic bottles as market and public devices. *Economy and Society*, 40(4), 534–52.

Hawkins, G., Potter, E. and Race, K. (2015) *Plastic Water*. Cambridge, MA: The MIT Press.

Hekman, S. (2010) *The Material of Knowledge: Feminist Disclosures*. Bloomington: Indiana University Press.

Hennion, A. (2001) Music lovers: taste as performance. *Theory, Culture & Society*, 18(5), 1–22.

Heritage, J. (1984) *Garfinkel and Ethnomethodology*. Cambridge: Polity.

Hess, D. (2011) Bourdieu and science and technology studies: toward a reflexive sociology. *Minerva*, 49(3), 333–48.

Hinchliffe, S. (2007) *Geographies of Nature*. London: Sage.

Hinchliffe, S., Allen, J., Lavau, S., Bingham, N. and Carter, S. (2012) Biosecurity and the topologies of infected life: from borderlines to borderlands. *Transactions of the Institute of British Geographers*, 38(4), 531–43.

Hinchliffe, S., Kearnes, M.B., Degen, M. and Whatmore, S. (2005) Urban wild things: a cosmopolitical experiment. *Environment and Planning D: Society and Space*, 23(5), 643–58.

Hobson-West, P. (2007) Beasts and boundaries: an introduction to animals in sociology, science and society. *Qualitative Sociology Review*, 3(1), 2–41.

Hond, F. den, Boersma, F.K., Heres, L., Kroes, E.H.J. and van Oirschot, E. (2012) Giddens à la carte? Appraising empirical applications of structuration theory in management and organization studies. *Journal of Political Power*, 5(2), 239–64.

Horst, H.A. and Miller, D. (2006) *The Cell Phone: An Anthropology of Communication*. Oxford: Berg.

Horst, M. and Michael, M. (2011) On the shoulders of idiots: rethinking science communication as 'event'. *Science as Culture*, 20(3), 283–306.

Hughes, T.P. (1983) *Networks of Power: Electrification in Western Society, 1880–1930*. Baltimore: Johns Hopkins University Press.

Hull, R. (1999) Actor-network and conduct: the discipline and practice of knowledge management. *Organization*, 6(3), 405–28.

Ingold, T. (2011) *Being Alive: Essays on Movement, Knowledge and Description*. London: Routledge.

Irwin, A. and Michael, M. (2003) *Science, Social Theory and Public Knowledge*. Maidenhead: Open University Press/McGraw-Hill.

Jack, L. and Kholeif, A., (2007) Introducing strong structuration theory for informing qualitative case studies in organization, management and accounting research. *Qualitative Research in Organizations and Management: An International Journal*, 2(3), 208–25.

Jerak-Zuiderent, S. (2015) Keeping open by re-imagining laughter and fear. *The Sociological Review*, 63(4), 897–921.

Kerr, A. and Garforth, L. (2016) Affective practices, care and bioscience: A study of two laboratories. *The Sociological Review*, 64(1), 3–20.

Knorr Cetina, K.D. (1981) *The Manufacture of Knowledge: An Essay on the Constructivist and Contextual Nature of Science*. Oxford: Pergamon.

Knorr Cetina, K. (1988) The micro-social order: towards a reconception. In N.G. Fielding (ed.), *Actions and Structure: Research Methods and Social Theory* (pp. 21–53). London: Sage.

Knorr-Cetina, K. (1999) *Epistemic Cultures: How the Sciences Make Knowledge*. Cambridge, MA: Harvard University Press.

Lash, S. and Lury, C. (2007) *Global Culture Industry: The Mediation of Things*. Cambridge, MA: Polity Press.

Latimer J. (2013) Being alongside: Rethinking relations amongst different kinds. *Theory, Culture and Society*, 30(7–8), 77–104.

Latimer, J. and Miele, M. (2013) Naturecultures? Science, affect and the non-human. *Theory, Culture & Society*, 30(7–8), 5–31.

Latour, B. (1983) Give me a laboratory and I will raise the world. In K. Knorr-Cetina and M. Mulkay (eds), *Science Observed* (pp. 141–70). London and Beverly Hills: Sage.

Latour, B. (1986) The powers of association. In J. Law (ed.), *Power, Action and Belief* (pp. 264–80). London: Routledge and Kegan Paul.

Latour, B. (1987) *Science in Action: How to Follow Engineers in Society*. Milton Keynes: Open University Press.

Latour, B. (1988a) *The Pasteurization of France*. Cambridge, MA: Harvard University Press.

Latour, B. (1988b) The politics of explanation – an alternative. In S. Woolgar (ed.), *Knowledge and Reflexivity: New Frontiers in the Sociology of Knowledge* (pp. 55–177). London: Sage.

Latour, B. (1990) Drawing things together. In M. Lynch and S. Woolgar (eds), *Representations in Scientific Practice* (pp. 19–68). Cambridge, MA: The MIT Press.

Latour, B. (1991) Technology is society made durable. In J. Law (ed.), *A Sociology of Monsters* (pp. 103–31). London: Routledge.

Latour, B. (1992) Where are the missing masses? A sociology of a few mundane artifacts. In W.E. Bijker and J. Law (eds), *Shaping Technology/Building Society* (pp. 225–58). Cambridge, MA: The MIT Press.

Latour, B. (1993a) *We Have Never Been Modern*. Hemel Hempstead: Harvester Wheatsheaf.

Latour, B. (1993b) *On Technical Mediation: The Messenger Lectures on the Evolution of Civilization*. Cornell University, Institute of Economic Research, Working Papers Series.

Latour, B. (1994) Pragmatogonies: a mythical account of how humans and nonhumans swap properties. *American Behavioral Scientist*, 37(6), 791–808.

Latour, B. (1996a) *Aramis, or the Love of Technology*. Cambridge, MA: Harvard University Press.

Latour, B. (1996b) On interobjectivity. *Mind, Culture and Activity*, 3(4), 228–45.

Latour, B. (1999) *Pandora's Hope: Essays on the Reality of Science Studies*. Cambridge, MA: Harvard University Press.

Latour, B. (2002) Gabriel Tarde and the end of the social. In P. Joyce (ed.), *The Social in Question: New Bearings in History and the Social Sciences* (pp. 117–33). London: Routledge.

Latour, B. (2003) Is re-modernization occurring – and if so, how to prove it? A commentary on Ulrich Beck. *Theory, Culture & Society*, 20(2), 35–48.

Latour, B. (2004a) *Politics of Nature*. Cambridge, MA: Harvard University Press.

Latour, B. (2004b) Why has critique run out of steam? From matters of fact to matters of concern. *Critical Inquiry*, 30(2), 225–48.

Latour, B. (2004c) How to talk about the body? The normative dimension of science studies. *Body & Society*, 10(2–3), 205–29.

Latour, B. (2005a) *Reassembling the Social*. Oxford: Oxford University Press.

Latour, B. (2005b) From realpolitik to dingpolitik or how to make things public. In B. Latour and P. Wiebel (eds), *Making Things Public: Atmospheres of Democracy* (pp. 14–43). Cambridge, MA: MIT Press.

Latour, B. (2008) A cautious Prometheus? A few steps toward a philosophy of design (with special attention to Peter Sloterdijk). In F. Hackne, J. Glynne and V. Minto (eds), *Proceedings of the 2008 Annual International Conference of the Design History Society – Falmouth, 3–6 September 2008* (pp. 2–10). e-books, Universal Publishers.

Latour, B. (2010a) Steps toward the writing of a compositionist manifesto. *New Literary History*, 41, 471–90.

Latour, B. (2010b) *On the Modern Cult of the Factish Gods*. Durham, NC: Duke University Press.

Latour, B. (2011) From multiculturalism to multinaturalism: What rules of method for the new socio-scientific experiments? *Nature and Culture*, 6(1), 1–17.

Latour, B. (2012) Biography of an inquiry – about a book on modes of existence. *Social Studies of Science*, 43(2), 287–301.

Latour, B. (2013) *An Inquiry into Modes of Existence: An Anthropology of the Moderns*. Cambridge, MA: Harvard University Press.

Latour, B. and Johnson, J. (1988) Mixing humans with non-humans? Sociology of a few mundane artefacts. *Social Problems*, 35(3), 298–310.

Latour, B. and Strum, S.C. (1986) Human social origins: Oh please, tell us another story. *Journal of Social and Biological Structures*, 9(2), 169–87.

Latour, B. and Weibel, P. (eds) (2002) *Iconoclash: Beyond the Image Wars in Science, Religion and Art*. Cambridge, MA: The MIT Press.

Latour, B. and Woolgar, S. (1979) *Laboratory Life: The Social Construction of Scientific Facts*. London: Sage.

Latour, B., Jensen, P., Venturini, T., Grauwin, S. and Boullier, D. (2012) The whole is always smaller than its parts – a digital test of Gabriel Tarde's monads. *The British Journal of Sociology*, 63(4), 590–615.

Law, J. (1986) On the methods of long distance control: vessels, navigation and the Portuguese route to India. In J. Law (ed.), *Power, Action and Belief: A New Sociology of Knowledge?* (pp. 234–63). London: Routledge and Kegan Paul.

Law, J. (1987) Technology and heterogeneous engineering: the case of Portuguese expansion. In W.E. Bijker, T.P. Hughes and T. Pinch (eds), *Social Construction of Technological Systems* (pp. 111–34). Cambridge, MA: The MIT Press.

Law, J. (1991) Introduction: monsters, machines and sociotechnical relations. In J. Law (ed.), *A Sociology of Monsters* (pp. 1–21). London: Routledge.

Law, J. (1994) *Organizing Modernity*. Oxford: Blackwell.

Law, J. (2002a) Objects and spaces. *Theory, Culture & Society*, 19(5/6), 91–105.

Law, J. (2002b) *Aircraft Stories: Decentring the Object in Technnoscience*. Durham, NC: Duke University Press.

Law, J. (2004a) *After Method: Mess in Social Science Research*. London: Routledge.

Law, J. (2004b) And if the global were small and noncoherent? Method, complexity, and the baroque. *Environment and Planning D: Society and Space*, 22(1), 13–26.

Law, J. (2006) Disaster in agriculture: or foot and mouth mobilities. *Environment and Planning*, 38(2), 227–39.

Law, J. (2009) Actor-network theory and material semiotics. In B.S. Turner (ed.), *The New Blackwell Companion to Social Theory* (3rd edn, pp. 141–58). Oxford: Blackwell.

Law, J. (2011) Collateral realities. In F. Dominguez Rubio and P. Baert (eds), *The Politics of Knowledge* (pp. 156–78). London: Routledge.

Law, J. and Lien, M.E. (2013) Slippery: Field notes in empirical ontology. *Social Studies of Science*, 43(3), 363–78.

Law, J. and Mol, A. (2001) Situating technoscience: an inquiry into spatialities. *Environment and Planning D: Society and Space*, 19(5), 609–21.

Law, J. and Singleton, V. (2000) Performing technology's stories: on social constructivism, performance, and performativity. *Technology and Culture*, 41(4), 765–75.

Law, J. and Singleton, V. (2005) Object lessons. *Organization*, 12(3), 331–55.

Law, J. and Urry, J. (2004) Enacting the social. *Economy and Society*, 33(3), 390–410.

Lee, N. and Brown, S. (1994) Otherness and actor network: the undiscovered continent. *American Behavioral Scientist*, 37(6), 772–90.

Lee, N. and Stenner, P. (1999) Who pays? Can we pay them back? In J. Law and J. Hassard (eds), *Actor Network Theory and After* (pp. 90–112). Oxford: Blackwell and The Sociological Review.

Leeson, P.T. (2013) Vermin trials. *Journal of Law and Economics*, 56(3), Article 8. Available at: http://chicagounbound.uchicago.edu/jle/vol56/iss3/8

Lezaun, J. (2007) A market of opinions: the political epistemology of focus groups. *The Sociological Review*, 55(S2), 130–51.

Lezaun, J. and Soneryd, L. (2007) Consulting citizens: technologies of elicitation and the mobility of publics. *Public Understanding of Science*, 16(3), 279–97.

Lorimer, H. and Lund, K. (2003) Performing facts: finding a way over Scotland's mountains. *The Sociological Review*, 51(S2), 130–44.

Luhmann, N. (2012) *Theory of Society*, Vol. 1. Stanford, CA: Stanford University Press.

Lupton, D. (2015) *Digital Sociology*. London: Routledge.

Lury, C. and Wakeford, N. (eds) (2012) *Inventive Methods: The Happening of the Social*. London: Routledge.

Lynch, M. (1985) *Art and Artifact in Laboratory Science*. London: Routledge and Kegan Paul.

Lynch, M. (1993) *Scientific Practice and Ordinary Action: Ethnomethodology and Social Studies of Science*. Cambridge: Cambridge University Press.

MacKenzie, D., Muniesa, F. and Siu, L. (eds) (2007) *Do Economists Make Markets? On the Performativity of Economics*. Princeton, NJ: Princeton University Press.

McNamara, A. (2012) Six rules for practice-led research. *Text*, Online Issue 14. Available at: www.textjournal.com.au/speciss/issue14/McNamara.pdf (accessed 11 December 2015).

Mann, A.M., Mol, A., Satalkar, P., Savirani, A., Selim, N., Sur, M. and Yates-Doerr, E. (2011) Mixing methods, tasting fingers: notes on an ethnographic experiment. *HAU: Journal of Ethnographic Theory*, 1(1), 221–43.

Marcuse, H. (1964) *One-Dimensional Man*. Boston: Beacon Press.

Marres, N. (2007) The issues deserve more credit: pragmatist contributions to the study of public involvement in controversy. *Social Studies of Science*, 37(5), 759–80.

Marres, N. (2011) The costs of public involvement: Everyday devices of carbon accounting and the materialization of participation. *Economy and Society*, 40(4), 510–33.

Marres, N. (2012) *Material Participation: Technology, the Environment and Everyday Publics*. Basingstoke: Palgrave.

Marres, N. (2015) Why map issues? On controversy analysis as a digital method. *Science, Technology & Human Values*, 40(5), 655–86.

Marres, N. and Lezaun, J. (2011) Materials and devices of the public: an introduction. *Economy and Society*, 40(4), 489–509.

Marston, S.A., Jones, J.P. III and Woodward, K. (2005) Human geography without scale. *Transactions of the Institute of British Geographers*, 30(4), 416–32.

Martin, A., Myers, N. and Viseu, A. (2015) The politics of care in technoscience. *Social Studies of Science*, 45(5), 625–41.

Martin, E. (1989) *The Woman in the Body*. Milton Keynes: Open University Press.

Martin, E. (1994) *Flexible Bodies*. Boston: Beacon Press.

Martin, E. (1998) Anthropology and cultural study of science. *Science, Technology & Human Values*, 23(1), 24–44.

Massey, D. (1991) A global sense of place. *Marxism Today*, 24–29 June.

Massumi, B. (2002) *Parables of the Virtual*. Durham, NC: Duke University Press.

Mennell, S. (1989) *Norbert Elias: Civilization and the Human Self-Image*. Oxford: Blackwell.

Mennell, S. (1995) Comment on technicization and civilization. *Theory, Culture & Society*, 12(3), 1–5.

Merton, R.K. (1973/1942) *The Sociology of Science: Theoretical and Empirical Investigations*. Chicago: The University of Chicago Press.

Michael, M. (2000) *Reconnecting Culture, Technology and Nature: From Society to Heterogeneity*. London: Routledge.

Michael, M. (2001) The invisible car: the cultural purification of road rage. In D. Miller (ed.), *Car Cultures* (pp. 59–80). Oxford: Berg.

Michael, M. (2004) On making data social: heterogeneity in sociological practice. *Qualitative Research*, 4(1), 5–23.

Michael, M. (2006) *Technoscience and Everyday Life*. Maidenhead: Open University Press/McGraw-Hill.

Michael, M. (2009a) Publics performing publics: of PiGs, PiPs and politics. *Public Understanding of Science*, 18(5), 617–31.

Michael, M. (2009b) 'The-cellphone-in-the-countryside': on some ironic spatialities of technonature. In D. White and C. Wilbert (eds), *Technonatures* (pp. 85–104). Waterloo: Wilfrid Laurier University Press.

Michael, M. (2012a) Toward an idiotic methodology: de-signing the object of sociology. *The Sociological Review*, 60(S1), 166–83.

Michael, M. (2012b) 'What are we busy doing?': Engaging the idiot. *Science, Technology & Human Values*, 37(5), 528–54.

Michael, M. and Gaver, W. (2009) Home beyond home: Dwelling with threshold devices. *Space and Culture*, 12(3), 359–70.

Michael, M. and Lupton, D. (2016) Toward a manifesto for the public understanding of big data. *Public Understanding of Science*, 25(1), 104–16.

Michael, M. and Rosengarten, M. (2012a) HIV, globalization and topology: of prepositions and propositions. *Theory, Culture & Society*, 29(4–5), 93–115.

Michael, M. and Rosengarten, M. (2012b) Medicine: experimentation, politics, emergent bodies. *Body and Society*, 18(3–4), 1–17.

Michael, M., Costello, B., Kerridge, I. and Mooney-Somers, J. (2015) Manifesto on art, design and social science – method as speculative event. *Leonardo*, 48(2), 190–1.

Miller, D.(2002) Turning Callon the right way up. *Economy and Society*, 31(2), 218–33.

Mitroff, I.I. (1974) Norms and counter-norms in a select group of the Apollo moon scientists: a case study of the ambivalence of scientists. *American Sociological Review*, 39(4), 579–95.

Mol, A. (1999) Ontological politics: a word and some questions. In J. Law and J. Hassard (eds), *Actor-Network Theory and After* (pp. 74–89). Oxford and Keele: Blackwell and The Sociological Review.

Mol, A. (2002) *The Body Multiple: Ontology in Medical Practice*. Durham, NC: Duke University Press.

Mol, A. (2008a) I eat an apple: on theorizing subjectivities. *Subjectivity*, 22(1), 28–37.

Mol, A. (2008b) *The Logic of Care: Health and the Problem of Patient Choice*. Abingdon: Routledge.

Mol, A. (2010) Actor-network theory: sensitive terms and enduring tensions. *Kölner Zeitschrift für Soziologie und Sozialpsychologie*, Sonderheft, 50(1), 253–69.

Mol, A. and Law, J. (1994) Regions, networks and fluids: anaemia and social topology. *Social Studies of Science*, 24(4), 641–71.

Mol, A. and Law, J. (2004) Embodied action, enacted bodies: the example of hypoglycaemia. *Body and Society*, 10(2–3), 43–62.

Mol, A., Moser, I. and Pols, J. (eds) (2010) *Care in Practice: On Tinkering in Clinics, Homes and Farms*. Bielefeld: Verlag.

Mol, A., Moser, I., Piras, E.M., Turrin, M., Pols, J. and Zanutto, A. (2011) Care in practice: on normativity, concepts, and boundaries. *Technoscienza*, 2(1), 73–86.

More, R. (2012) Capital. In M. Grenfell (ed.), *Pierre Bourdieu – Key Concepts* (pp. 98–113). Durham, NC: Acumen.

Mulkay, M. (1979) *Science and the Sociology of Knowledge*. London: Allen and Unwin.

Mulkay, M. (1985) *The Word and the World*. London: Allen and Unwin.

Muniesa, F., Millo, Y. and Callon, M. (2007) An introduction to market devices. In M. Callon, Y. Millo and F. Muniesa (eds), *Market Devices* (pp. 1–12). Oxford: Blackwell.

Murdoch, J. (1997a) Towards a geography of heterogeneous association. *Progress in Human Geography*, 21(3), 321–37.

Murdoch, J. (1997b) Inhuman/nonhuman: actor-network theory and the prospects of a nondualistic and symmetrical perspective on nature and society. *Environment and Planning D: Society and Space*, 15(4), 731–56.

Murdoch, J. (1998) The spaces of actor-network theory. *Geoforum*, 29(4), 357–74.

Mutch, A. (2002) Actors and networks or agents and structures: towards a realist view of Information systems. *Organization*, 9(3), 477–96.

Myers, G. (1990) *Writing Biology: Texts in the Social Construction of Scientific Knowledge*. Madison: Wisconsin University Press.

Newton, T. (2001) Organization: the relevance and limitations of Elias. *Organization*, 8(3), 467–95.

Newton, T.J. (2002) Creating the new ecological order? Elias and actor-network theory. *The Academy of Management Review*, 27(4), 523–40.

Neyland, D. (2015) On organizing algorithms. *Theory, Culture & Society*, 32(1), 119–32.

Nimmo, R. (2010) *Milk, Modernity and the Making of the Human: Purifying the Social*. Abingdon: Routledge.

Nimmo, R. (2011) Actor-network theory and methodology: social research in a more-than-human world. *Methodological Innovations*, 6(3), 108–19.

Osborne, T. and Rose, N. (1999) Do the social sciences create phenomena: the case of public opinion research. *British Journal of Sociology*, 50(3), 367–96.

Parisi, L. (2012) Speculation. In C. Lury and N. Wakeford (eds), *Inventive Methods: The Happening of the Social* (pp. 232–44). London: Routledge.

Passoth, J., Peuker, B. and Schillmeier, M. (eds) (2012) *Agency Without Actors? New Approaches to Collective Action*. London: Routledge.

Pegg, K. (2009) A hostile world for nonhuman animals: human identification and the oppression of nonhuman animals for human good. *Sociology*, 43(1), 85–102.

Pellizzoni, L. (2015) *Ontological Politics in a Disposable World: The New Mastery of Nature*. Farnham: Ashgate.

Pfaffenberger, B. (1992) Technological dramas. *Science, Technology & Human Values*, 17(3), 282–312.

Pickering, A. (1995) *The Mangle of Practice: Time, Agency and Science*. Chicago: The University of Chicago Press.

Pinch, T.J. and Bijker, W.E. (1984) The social construction of facts and artefacts: or how the sociology of science and the sociology of technology might benefit each other. *Social Studies of Science*, 14(3), 399–441.

Pink, S. (2012) *Situating Everyday Life: Practices and Places*. London: Sage.

Pippan, T. and Czarniawska, B. (2010) How to construct an actor-network: management accounting from idea to practice. *Critical Perspectives on Accounting*, 21(3), 243–51.

Ponzoni, E. and Boersma, K. (2011) Writing history for business: the development of business history between 'old' and 'new' production of knowledge. *Management and Organizational History*, 6(2), 123–43.

Power, M. (1999) *The Audit Society*. Oxford: Oxford University Press.

Prior, N. (2008) Putting a glitch in the field: Bourdieu, actor network theory and contemporary music. *Cultural Sociology*, 2(3), 301–19.

Puig de la Bellacasa, M. (2011) Matters of care in technoscience: assembling neglected things. *Social Studies of Science*, 41(1), 85–106.

Puig de la Bellacasa, M. (2012) 'Nothing comes without its world': Thinking with care. *The Sociological Review*, 60(2), 197–216.

Puig de la Bellacasa, M. (2015) Making time for soil: technoscientific futurity and the pace of care. *Social Studies of Science*, 45(5), 691–716.

Richards, E. and Ashmore, M. (1996) More sauce please! The politics of SSK: neutrality, commitment and beyond. *Social Studies of Science*, 26(2), 219–28.

Rodríguez-Giralt, I., Tirado, T. and Tironi, M. (2014) Disasters as meshworks: migratory birds and the enlivening of Doñana's toxic spill. *The Sociological Review*, 62(S1), 38–60.

Rose, N. (1996) *Inventing Our Selves*. New York: Cambridge University Press.

Rose, N., O'Malley, P. and Valverde, M. (2006) Governmentality. *Annual Review of Law and Society* 2, 83–104.

Ruming, K. (2009) Following the actor: mobilising an actor-network theory methodology in geography. *Australian Geographer*, 40(4), 451–69.

Ruppert, E., Law, J. and Savage, M. (2013) Reassembling social science methods: the challenge of digital devices. *Theory, Culture & Society*, 30(4), 22–46.

Saito, H. (2015) Cosmopolitics: towards a new articulation of politics, science and critique. *The British Journal of Sociology*, 66(3), 441–59.

Savage, M. and Burrows, R. (2007) The coming crisis of empirical sociology. *Sociology*, 41(5), 885–99.

Sayes, E. (2014) Actor-network theory and methodology: just what does it mean to say that nonhumans have agency? *Social Studies of Science*, 44(1), 134–49.

Schatzki, T., Knorr Cetina, K. and von Savigny, E. (eds) (2001) *The Practice Turn in Contemporary Theory*. London: Routledge.

Schillmeier, M. (2014) *Eventful Bodies: The Cosmopolitics of Illness*. Farnham: Ashgate.

Schinkel, W. (2007) Sociological discourse of the relational: the cases of Bourdieu and Latour. *The Sociological Review*, 55(4), 707–29.

Scott, P., Richards, E. and Martin, B. (1990) Captives of controversy: the myth of the neutral science researcher in contemporary scientific controversies. *Science, Technology & Human Values*, 15(4), 474–94.

Serres, M. (1982a) *Hermes: Literature, Science, Philosophy*. Baltimore: Johns Hopkins University Press.

Serres, M. (1982b) *The Parasite*. Baltimore: Johns Hopkins University Press.

Serres, M. (1991) *Rome: The Book of Foundations*. Stanford, CA: Stanford University Press.

Serres, M. (1995a) *Angels: A Modern Myth*. Paris: Flammarion.

Serres, M. (1995b) *Genesis*. Ann Arbor: Michigan University Press.

Serres, M. and Latour, B. (1995) *Conversations on Science, Culture and Time*. Ann Arbor: Michigan University Press.

Shapin, S. and Schaffer, S. (1985) *Leviathan and the Air-Pump: Hobbes, Boyle, and the Experimental Life*. Princeton, NJ: Princeton University Press.

Shove, E. (2003) *Comfort, Cleanliness and Convenience*. Oxford: Berg.

Shove, E., Pantzar, M. and Watson, M. (2012) *The Dynamics of Social Practice*. London: Sage.

Singleton, V. (1993) Science, women and ambivalence: an actor network analysis of the cervical screening programme. Unpublished PhD thesis, Lancaster University.

Singleton, V. (1996) Feminism, sociology of scientific knowledge and postmodernism: politics, theory and me. *Social Studies of Science*, 26(2), 445–68.

Singleton, V. and Michael, M. (1993) Actor-networks and ambivalence: general practitioners and the cervical smear test. *Social Studies of Science*, 23(2), 227–64.

Sismondo, S. (2015) Ontological turns, turnoffs and roundabouts. *Social Studies of Science*, 45(3), 441–8.

Spierenberg, P. (1984) *The Spectacle of Suffering*. Cambridge: Cambridge University Press.

Star, S.L. (1991) Power, technologies and the phenomenology of conventions: on being allergic to onions. In J. Law (ed.), *A Sociology of Monsters* (pp. 26–56). London: Routledge.

Star, S.L. (2010) This is not a boundary object: reflections on the origin of a concept. *Science, Technology & Human Values*, 35(5), 601–17.

Star, S. and Griesemer, J. (1989) Institutional ecology, 'translations' and boundary objects: amateurs and professionals in Berkeley's museum of vertebrate zoology, 1907–39. *Social Studies of Science*, 19(3), 387–430.

Stengers, I. (2005a) The cosmopolitical proposal. In B. Latour and P. Webel (eds), *Making Things Public* (pp. 994–1003). Cambridge, MA: The MIT Press.

Stengers, I. (2005b) Introductory notes on an ecology of practices. *Cultural Studies Review*, 11(1), 183–96.

Stengers, I. (2010a) *Cosmopolitics I*. Minneapolis: University of Minnesota Press.

Stengers, I. (2010b) Including nonhumans in political theory: opening Pandora's box? In B. Braum and S.J. Whatmore (eds), *Political Matter: Technoscience, Democracy and Public Life* (pp. 3–33). Minneapolis: University of Minnesota Press.

Stengers, I. and Bordeleau, E. (2011) The care of the possible: Isabelle Stengers interviewed by Erik Bordeleau. *Scapegoat*, Summer Issue 1. Available at:

www.scapegoatjournal.org/docs/01/01_Stengers_Bordeleau_CareOfThe Possible.pdf (accessed 30 October 2015).

Stones, R. (2005) *Structuration Theory*. Basingstoke: Palgrave Macmillan.

Storni, C., Binder, T., Linde, P. and Stuedahl, D. (2015) Designing things together: intersections of co-design and actor-network theory. *Co-Design*, 11(3–4), 149–51.

Strathern, M. (1996) Cutting the network. *Journal of Royal Anthropological Institute* (N.S.), 2(3), 517–35.

Strathern, M. (1999) What is intellectual property after? In J. Law and J. Hassard (eds), *Actor Network Theory and After* (pp. 156–80). Oxford: Blackwell.

Strum, S.S. and Latour, B. (1988) Redefining the social link: from baboons to humans. *Social Science Information*, 26(4), 783–802.

Symons, G.L. (2009) Choreographing identities and emotions in organizations: doing 'huminality' on a geriatric ward. *Society & Animals*, 17(2), 115–35.

Thompson, P. (2012) Field. In M. Grenfell (ed.), *Pierre Bourdieu – Key Concepts* (pp. 65–80). Durham, NC: Acumen.

Thrift, N. (1996) *Spatial Formation*. London: Sage.

Thrift, N. (2005) *Knowing Capitalism*. London: Sage.

Thrift, N. (2008) *Non-Representational Theory*. London: Routledge.

Toennesen, C., Molloy, E. and Jacobs, C. (2006) Lost in translation? Actor network theory and organization studies. EGOS, 6–8 July 2006, Bergen, Norway. Available at: http://burn.dk/talk/wp-content/ct_ant.pdf (accessed 27 May 2015).

Turner, B. (2007) Culture, technologies and bodies: the technological Utopia of living forever. *Sociological Review*, 55(S1), 19–36.

Turner, J.H. (1986) The theory of structuration. *American Journal of Sociology*, 91(4), 969–77.

Urry, J. (2000) *Sociology Beyond Societies: Mobilities in the Twenty-First Century*. London: Routledge.

Urry, J. (2003) *Global Complexity*. Cambridge: Polity.

Urry, J. (2004) The 'system' of automobility. *Theory, Culture & Society*, 21(4–5), 25–39.

Urry, J. (2007) *Mobilities*. Cambridge: Polity.

Van Krieken, R. (1998) *Norbert Elias*. London: Sage.

Van Krieken, R. (2001) Norbert Elias and process sociology. In G. Ritzer and B. Smart (eds), *Handbook of Social Theory* (pp. 353–67). Thousand Oaks, CA: Sage.

Van Krieken, R. (2002) The paradox of the 'two sociologies': Hobbes, Latour and the constitution of modern social theory. *Journal of Sociology*, 38(3), 255–73.

Wacquant, L. (1989) Towards a reflexive sociology: a workshop with Pierre Bourdieu. *Sociological Theory*, 7(1), 26–63.

Wacquant, L. (1997) Foreword. *The State Nobility*. Cambridge: Polity Press.

Waldby, C. (2000) *The Visible Human Project: Informatic Bodies and Posthuman Medicine*. London: Routledge.

Weininger, E.B. (2005) Foundations of Pierre Bourdieu's class analysis. In E.O. Wright (ed.) *Approaches to Class Analysis* (pp. 92–118). Cambridge: Cambridge University Press.

Welsh, I. and Wynne, B. (2013) Science, scientism and imaginaries of publics in the UK: passive objects, incipient threats. *Science as Culture*, 22(4), 540–66.

Wenger, E. (1998) *Communities of Practice: Learning, Meaning and Identity*. Cambridge: Cambridge University Press.

Wetherell, M. (2012) *Affect and Emotion: A New Social Science Understanding*. London: Sage.

Whatmore, S. (2002) *Hybrid Geographies*. London: Sage.

Whatmore, S. (2013) Earthly powers and affective environments: an ontological politics of flood risk. *Theory, Culture & Society*, 30(7–8), 33–50.

Whatmore, S. and Thorne, L. (2000) Elephants on the move: spatial formations of wildlife exchange. *Environment and Planning D: Society and Space*, 18(2), 185–203.

Whitehead, A.N. (1926) *Science and the Modern World*. Cambridge: Cambridge University Press.

Whitehead, A.N. (1964/1920) *The Concept of Nature*. Cambridge: Cambridge University Press.

Whitehead, A.N. (1967/1933) *Adventures of Ideas*. New York: Free Press.

Whitehead, A.N. (1978/1929) *Process and Reality: An Essay in Cosmology* (Gifford Lectures of 1927–8). New York: The Free Press.

Whitley, R. (2000) *The Intellectual and Social Organization of the Sciences*, 2nd edn. Oxford: Oxford University Press.

Whittle, A. and Spicer, A. (2008) Is actor-network theory critique? *Organization Studies*, 29(4), 611–29.

Wilkie, A., Michael, M. and Plummer-Fernandez, M. (2015) Speculative method and twitter: bots, energy and three conceptual characters. *The Sociological Review*, 63(1), 79–101.

Williams, C., Wainwright, S., Ehrich, K. and Michael, M. (2008) Human embryos as boundary objects? Some reflections on the biomedical worlds of embryonic stem cells and preimplantation genetic diagnosis. *New Genetics and Society*, 27(1), 7–18.

Winner, L. (1985) Do artifacts have politics? *Daedelus*, 109, 121–36.

Woolgar, S. (1981) Interests and explanation in the social study of science. *Social Studies of Science*, 11(3), 365–94.

Woolgar, S. (ed.) (1988) *Knowledge and Reflexivity*. London: Sage.

Woolgar, S. and Neyland, D. (2013) *Mundane Governance: Ontology and Accountability*. Oxford: Oxford University Press.

Yaneva, A. (2009) Making the social hold: towards an actor-network theory of design. *Design and Culture*, 1(3), 273–88.

INDEX

Note: Page numbers in *italic* refer to the glossary.